False-Memory Creation in Children and Adults

Theory, Research, and Implications

False-Memory Creation
in Children and Adults

Theory, Research, and Implications

Edited by

David F. Bjorklund
Florida Atlantic University

LAWRENCE ERLBAUM ASSOCIATES, PUBLISHERS

2000   Mahwah, New Jersey   London

Lawrence Erlbaum Associates, Inc., Publishers
10 Industrial Avenue
Mahwah, NJ 07430

Cover design by Kathryn Houghtaling Lacey

Library of Congress Cataloging-in-Publication Data

False-memory creation in children and adults : theory, research, and implications / edited by David F. Bjorklund.
p. cm.
Includes bibliographical references and index.
ISBN 0-8058-3169-X (cloth : alk. paper)
1. False memory syndrome. I. Bjorklund, David F., 1949-
RC455.2.F35 F34 2000
616.85'8369—dc21   99-055909
                                                        CIP

Books published by Lawrence Erlbaum Associates are
printed on acid-free paper, and their bindings are chosen for
strength and durability.

Printed in the United States of America
10 9 8 7 6 5 4 3 2 1

Contents

Preface

Memory has always been of interest to psychologists, going back to the days of Ebbinghaus. Research in memory usually followed the prevailing theoretical winds that influenced academic psychology, being conceived in terms of associative stimulus–response connections, the differential accessibility and availability of information in a computer-like system, or a highly constructive process based as much on the previously organized knowledge possessed by the rememberer as on the retrieval of the representation of a specific experience. Because memory is central to all other forms of complex cognition, theorists investigating other aspects of human psychological functioning could not ignore what memory researchers had to say, and they in turn contributed to our understanding of the complexities of human memory.

It is this interface between basic research in memory and how people use memory to solve other types of "problems" that is the focus of this book. Specifically, to what extent can and do children and adults form *false memories*, particularly when in the context of recalling important personal, and sometimes forensically significant, information? This question became particularly important when, during the latter part of the 1980s through the middle of the 1990s, substantial numbers of adults, usually during the course of psychotherapy, recalled events of sexual abuse from their childhoods. Also at this same time, preschool children, usually during extensive interviews with law enforcement officers or therapists, told of sexual abuse at the hands of day-care providers. These were shocking tales, but initially quite believable, given the details of what people recalled and, in the cases of the preschoolers, the number of children who told similar, horrific stories. But soon many of these claims of childhood abuse began to be questioned. There was rarely corroborating physical evidence, and the extent of the abuse that occurred in the preschools was amazing, given that it happened unnoticed by other care givers and parents. But the adults and children claiming abuse were sincere. If these things actually did happen, why and how were they buried away for so many years? And if they did not really happen, how could people be so convinced that something as traumatic as sexual abuse occurred?

The question involved the nature of memory. Were these adults actually retrieving repressed memories under the careful direction of therapists and fellow victims during group therapy, or were these memories being "created" by repeated suggestion? Evidence for both claims existed in the psychological literature. And were children telling the investigators about events that actually happened to them, or were the interviewing techniques used to get at children's unpleasant experiences serving to implant false memories that eventually became their own?

Most issues investigated by psychologists doing basic research in cognition, cognitive development, and psychotherapy do not have the potential for social impact that these issues have. Depending on where the truth lay, at stake were the lives of innocent victims of sexual abuse and their abusers, or the lives of falsely accused family members and child-care workers and their duped accusers. People were going to jail and families were being destroyed. If the memories were true, few of us would disagree that the abusers should be punished and put away so that they cannot practice their evil on other unsuspecting children; but if the memories were false, the lives of innocent people, both the alleged victims and the alleged abusers, were being ruined.

Memory researchers responded, and studies of memory for traumatic events, suggestibility, and false-memory creation in children and adults boomed in the late 1980s and continued through the next decade. The American Psychological Association, recognizing the explosive nature of this problem, asked three clinical psychologists and three memory researchers to explore the issue, hoping to arrive at a consensus. When the report was completed, a consensus had not been reached (Alpert et al., 1997). All could agree that both repression and false-memory creation were possible, but the clinical psychologists and the memory researchers generally disagreed on the extent to which such phenomena occurred in clinical practice and forensic interviews. By then, however, the tide had turned, and the number of new abuse cases based on "recovered memories" and the number of new preschool abuse cases diminished. It seems that many of the cases over the previous decade were indeed the product of false-memory creation.

In February 1998, Florida Atlantic University hosted a symposium titled "False Memory Creation: Theory, Research, and Clinical and Legal Implications," sponsored by The Eleanor and Elliot Goldstein Foundation. The three memory researchers who contributed to the APA's *Working Group on Investigation of Memories of Childhood Abuse*—Stephen Ceci, Elizabeth Loftus, and Peter Ornstein—were invited to present their research. Also invited was Daniel Schacter, whose research on the neurological basis of memories, both true and false, added a new dimension to the debate. Each of these scientists contributed a chapter to this volume, and are joined by other prominent memory researchers who have taken seriously the charge to investigate the "recovered memory–false-memory creation" problem.

The first chapter, by Rhonda Douglas Brown, Eleanor Goldstein, and David Bjorklund, sets the stage for the chapters that follow by providing a brief history of both the science and sociology of the "repressed memory–false memory" debate. In the second chapter, Amy Tsai, Elizabeth Loftus, and Danielle Polage review evidence of interview techniques that serve to create false memories, including repeated suggestion by authoritative and credible figures. They review new research from their laboratory demonstrating that *imagination inflation* can produce false memories even in the analysis of dreams and when participants keep diaries of events they are questioned about. In chapter 3, Mark Oakes and Ira Hyman, Jr. review research and present a theory of how adults create false memories of childhood events, and thus a false self. They propose that three processes are involved in the creation of false childhood memories: plausibility judgments, memory construction, and source-monitoring errors. In chapter 4, Kathy Pezdek and Jennifer Taylor evaluate different methods that have been used to differentiate between true and false memories. They synthesize the extant literature and conclude that, although there is no fail-safe technique for determining the truth of a statement, memories for true events have greater clarity, are held more confidently, and are described with more words than memories for false events. Charles Brainerd, Valerie Reyna, and Debra Poole argue in chapter 5 that the development of better theories to explain false-memory creation is important not just for scientists, but also for the legal profession. They then review research and generate a theory, based on fuzzy-trace theory, to account for both the spontaneous and implanted memories in children and adults. In chapter 6, Daniel Schacter, Kenneth Norman, and Wilma Koutstaal present a somewhat different approach to false memories compared to the other contributors of this volume, focusing on the neuropsychology of constructive memory. They present a constructive memory framework (CMF) that examines aspects of encoding, decision making, and retrieval from a neuropsychological perspective to account for false-memory creation. In chapter 7, Stephen Ceci, Maggie Bruck, and David Battin explore the factors, both in the laboratory and in forensic interviews, that contribute to the suggestibility of young children. They focus on the effects of leading questions, stereotype induction, and other types of interviewer biases, as well as specific techniques that are aimed at enhancing memory, such as visualization and the use of anatomically correct dolls. In the final chapter, Peter Ornstein and Andrea Follmer Greenhoot argue that researchers and practitioners must take seriously, and from a developmental perspective, four themes of memory: (a) not everything gets into memory; (b) what gets in memory varies in strength; (c) the status of information in memory changes over time; and (d) retrieval is not perfect. They then use findings from their research program on children's recollections of medical procedures to evaluate the third and most important theme with respect to false-memory creation, the changing nature of information in memory over time.

The contributors to this volume not only review the seminal work from their own laboratories pertinent to false-memory creation in experimental and legal settings, but also provide critical evaluation of the research. They also present much needed theory about the nature of false memories and how theory can be translated into practice.

ACKNOWLEDGMENTS

I would like to thank Eleanor and Elliot Goldstein for sponsoring the symposium that gave rise to this book. The idea for the conference originated with Eleanor, and she remained the guiding force behind this project. I would also like to thank John Wiesenfeld, Dean of the Charles E. Schmidt College of Science at Florida Atlantic University, for playing the role of catalyst and introducing me to Eleanor Goldstein. I am also indebted to Kathy Piercy and Joan Gove for their efforts in coordinating the conference, and to my students Rhonda Douglas Brown, Cynthia Park, and Kristina Rosenblum for their help during all phases of this project.

—*David F. Bjorklund*

REFERENCE

Alpert, J. L., Brown, L. S.., Ceci, S. J., Courtois, C. A., Loftus, E. F., & Ornstein, P. A. (1997). *Working group on investigation of memories of childhood abuse: Final report.* Washington, DC: American Psychological Association.

CHAPTER ONE

The History and Zeitgeist of the Repressed–False-Memory Debate

Scientific and Sociological Perspectives on Suggestibility and Childhood Memory

RHONDA DOUGLAS BROWN
Texas Tech University

ELEANOR GOLDSTEIN
Social Issues Resources Series, Inc.

DAVID F. BJORKLUND
Florida Atlantic University

The history of the interface between the psychology of childhood memories and legal cases is a notorious one. Perhaps the phenomena that left the deepest historical scar regarding this issue are the 17th-century witch trials that took place in Europe and America (see Ceci & Bruck, 1993, 1998, for reviews). In Sweden between 1668 and 1676, as a result of children's statements elicited by village priests concerning the alleged sorcery of community members, more than 40 adults were either burned at the stake or beheaded (Ceci & Bruck, 1995). Most notable in U.S. history were the Salem witch trials, in which a group of children called the "circle girls" testified to witnessing community members flying on broomsticks and commanding insects to fly into their mouths to drop bent nails and pins into their stomachs. As a result, 20 defendants were convicted of witchcraft and executed. In the wake of the executions, some of the children publicly recanted their statements, admitting that they had produced false testimonies.

More recently, a less extreme but eerily similar case emerged in Wenatchee, Washington. In 1996, 28 adults from this small town were charged with rape and molestation, and more than 40 children were removed from their homes because of investigators' claims of a widespread child-sex ring. Of those charged, 19 adults were sentenced to prison (14 pleaded guilty and 5 were convicted), and the remainder were either acquitted or their cases were dismissed. As in the 17th-century witch trials, two young sisters, called M. E. and D. E., provided the substantial testimony in these cases, which included allegations against their own parents. Despite the fact that M. E., D. E., and their brother each originally denied any parental sexual abuse, their mother, who was classified as mentally re-tarded, was sentenced to 4 years in prison after agreeing to testify against their father, who was sentenced to 23 years in prison. M. E. later recanted her testimony, claiming that she fabricated her reports of ritualistic abuse under pressure from the girls' foster father, Wenatchee Police Detective Robert Perez, who led the investigation. Civil suits totaling at least $100 million were filed by residents of Wenatchee for wrongful prosecution (Tizon, 1996).

Ceci and Bruck (1995) reviewed a number of related cases involving child witnesses that occurred during the mid-1980s to early 1990s, such as the Country Walk day care case. The rapid emergence of such cases in recent history has led groups such as Concerned Citizens for Legal Accountability to request that U.S. Attorney General Janet Reno open an investigation into matters of wrongful prosecution. Reno, who inciden-tally was involved as a prosecutor in the Country Walk case, denied the group's appeal.

These cases were primarily concerned with the effects of suggestibility on children's reliability as witnesses. Yet, during this same period, a differ-ent but related breed of cases emerged in which the reliability of adults' memories of their childhood experiences was questioned. First, there was a rapid increase in cases in which adults were suing their parents, relatives, or religious leaders for sexual abuse that allegedly occurred during child-hood. The prosecution was based on the notion that the memories for abuse were "repressed" before adulthood or therapeutic treatment. Sec-ond, as a result of increased public awareness of suggestive therapeutic techniques and the mechanisms of childhood memories, the number of repressed memory cases declined, and reactionary cases, in which clients sued their therapists for false-memory implantation, increased. For example, Patricia Burgus alleged that two psychiatrists at Rush-Presbyterian-St. Luke's hospital in Chicago persuaded her, through the use of hypnosis and other therapeutic techniques, to believe that she was a member of a satanic cult, that she was sexually abused by multiple men, and that she engaged in cannibalism and abused her own children. In 1997, Ms. Burgus reached the largest settlement to that date in a false-memory lawsuit—$10.6 million, although the defendants failed to admit wrongdoing (Belluck, 1997).

In this chapter, we reflect on the zeitgeist or spirit of the times in which the cases just described emerged, climaxed, and waned. First, we examine the impact of early research on current investigations relevant to the cases concerning children's reliability as witnesses. We also examine theoretical and empirical considerations of mechanisms of memory important to the repressed–false-memory debate that surrounds the cases involving accusations based on "recovered" memories of childhood sexual abuse, which usually emerge during the course of therapy. Finally, we delineate how various social movements and changes in the legal system have led to the upsurge in childhood memory cases during the past two decades, and we present the current state of the childhood memory debate.

RESEARCH ON CHILDHOOD MEMORY

The Salem witch trials had a dramatic impact on the U.S. legal system and on psychologists' willingness, or lack thereof, to investigate suggestibility and childhood memory. There was little need for such studies because children did not typically testify during the period after the witch trials. However, early in the 20th century, several European psychologists conducted research investigating children's suggestibility (see Ceci & Bruck, 1993, 1995, 1998, for reviews), and Freud considered the nature of traumatic childhood memories. After these early investigations, however, the topic was not examined in any depth again until the late 1970s, when changes in the legal system and social movements led to a resurgence of interest. Here, we examine the roots of early research on suggestibility and childhood memory to provide a historical context for current views of these issues.

Children as Eyewitnesses

Perhaps the earliest and most influential research on children's suggestibility and memory was conducted by Alfred Binet, a French developmental psychologist and father of the IQ test, along with Simon. Binet (1900) outlined two major sources of suggestibility: (a) *autosuggestion,* which arises from a child's internal sources; and (b) *external suggestibility,* which arises from others influencing the child's recollections.

In one demonstration of autosuggestibility, Binet showed children five lines of increasing length and then a series of "target" lines that were the same length as the longest line of the original series, which he asked the children to draw on paper. Binet found that children's drawings of the target line were systematically too long, leading him to conclude that internal suggestions influenced children to deduce that each target line was longer than the line that had come before it.

Reyna (1994) investigated autosuggestibility more directly and attributes developmental differences in internal suggestions to interference effects, with younger children showing more interference sensitivity than older children. Other researchers describe young children's event memory as relying heavily on generalized knowledge of typical events, or *scripts,* which are used as a context for interpreting novel information (Nelson, 1996). This general knowledge may interfere with young children's ability to reconstruct what they witnessed in a specific event to a greater extent than it does for older children (Ceci & Bruck, 1993). In Binet's study, children's prior knowledge of the line series clearly influenced their reconstruction of the target lines.

Although current research has invoked Binet's concept of autosuggestibility, his greatest contribution to the childhood memory literature resulted from his investigations of external suggestibility. In one experiment, Binet examined the effects of an interviewer's suggestions on children's responses by asking them to study five objects (e.g., a button glued onto a poster board) for 10 seconds. He then assessed memory using free recall, direct questions (e.g., "How is the button attached to the board?"), leading questions (e.g., "Wasn't the button attached by a thread?"), or misleading questions (e.g., "What was the color of the thread that attached the button to the board?"). Binet's findings were highly similar to those of current research: (a) Free recall yielded the highest levels of accuracy, whereas misleading questions produced the most inaccurate statements; and (b) children expressed confidence in their responses, regardless of accuracy. Binet concluded that children responded inaccurately because they did not remember the information but felt pressured to answer the questions posed by the interviewer. On the basis of his finding that children rarely corrected inaccurate answers to misleading questions, Binet suggested that the inaccurate information becomes incorporated into memory. He also studied these effects at the group level by asking children in groups of three to respond to misleading questions as quickly as possible.

He found that children who responded later were more likely to provide the same answer as the first respondent, even when the response was incorrect—a classic demonstration of small-group conformity.

Binet's study that compared the responses of children ages 7 through 14 to free recall and types of leading questions anticipated modern suggestibility research. For example, Cassel and Bjorklund (1995) examined children's responses to free recall, unbiased questions (similar to Binet's direct questions), positive-leading questions (suggesting a correct answer), and misleading questions (suggesting an incorrect answer) about a witnessed event. Their findings were consistent with Binet's concerning the effects of question type on memory accuracy: near zero levels of incorrect responses to free recall in contrast to the more directive and suggestive questions (unbiased: 17% incorrect; positive leading: 16% incorrect; and misleading: 60% incorrect). Similar to Binet, Cassel and Bjorklund noted that although the amount of information young children produce in free recall is typically low, it is highly accurate (Goodman, Aman, & Hirschman, 1987; Poole & White, 1995). Furthermore, even unbiased questions, despite yielding more information, led to the production of inaccurate information (e.g., Bjorklund, Bjorklund, Brown, & Cassel, 1998; Cassel, Roebers, & Bjorklund, 1996).

In addition to providing empirical evidence of suggestibility effects, Binet's conclusion that misinformation becomes incorporated into children's memories foreshadowed a major theoretical and empirical question: When children assent to leading questions, are they just agreeing with an authoritative interviewer or do they actually come to believe that the misinformation is the truth? Some researchers have explained children's responses to leading questions as acquiescence effects or products of the social demand characteristics present in the forensic interviewing context that do not necessarily lead to changes in memory representations (e.g., Zaragoza, 1991). Other researchers have suggested, like Binet, that misinformation becomes incorporated into memory either through an "overwriting" process, in which misinformation replaces original information, or through integration, in which old information is combined with suggested information (e.g., Hyman, Husband, & Billings, 1995; Loftus, 1979). The current consensus acknowledges that suggestibility effects are complex phenomena that cannot be explained by a single mechanism. Thus, it is likely that acquiescence and changes in memory representation interact to produce the phenomena. For example, a child may initially comply with misinformation, and in reconstructing the event, he or she may begin to question the experience, which may lead to changes in memory representation.

Although Binet provided evidence that misleading questions lead to memory inaccuracy, German psychologist William Stern (1910) offered more applied and ecologically valid demonstrations of suggestibility effects, developing two paradigms that are used in current research. In the first paradigm, participants viewed a picture and were asked to study it for a short period of time, after which free recall was assessed. Then, participants answered questions requesting information that was actually represented in the picture as well as misleading questions that requested information that was not represented in the picture. In one study that tested 7- to 18-year-olds, free recall produced the fewest errors, whereas misleading questions produced the most errors (Stern, 1910). Consistent with modern findings, Stern's results revealed developmental differences, with the youngest children showing the highest levels of susceptibility to misleading questions.

Stern's second paradigm, called the *reality experiment,* in which unsuspecting participants observed staged events, established a more ecologically valid design for investigating the effects of suggestive questioning on eyewitness memory. For example, in one typical experiment, unsuspecting university students observed as an argument broke out between two students in a classroom that escalated to the point of one student drawing a gun on the other. The students in the class who witnessed the incident were questioned afterwards. In drawing conclusions from such reality experiments, Stern cautioned against repeatedly questioning witnesses about the same event because participants may remember their answers to the questions (which may be erroneous) better than the actual event that they witnessed. He also suggested that children might interpret suggestive misleading questions delivered firmly by an authority figure as imperatives; therefore, Stern pinned responsibility for unreliable testimony on the interviewer who poses questions in this manner.

Although technology has somewhat changed the reality experiment from live staged scenes to video presentations of events, it is alive and well in research today. For example, Bjorklund et al. (1998) showed 5- and 7-year-olds a brief video depicting a theft and interviewed them over a 6-week period using free recall, unbiased or misleading questions, and recognition memory assessments. They found that correct free recall and recognition memory declined significantly across the 6-week period, confirming Stern's cautions against repeatedly questioning witnesses about the same event. The results from this study suggest that multiple interviews with suggestive questions lead children, especially 5-year-olds, to not only change their answers but also their memories.

Stern's conclusions imply that results such as these may occur because children remember their answers to questions during an interview better than the actual witnessed event. Modern theorists have provided support for this hypothesis. For example, according to fuzzy-trace theory, information can be represented by verbatim traces, which are more susceptible to forgetting, or gistlike traces, which preserve meaning over details (Reyna & Brainerd, 1995). Brainerd, Reyna, and their colleagues provided evidence illustrating that memory for distractors or misinformation can be more persistent than memory for target or witnessed information depending on whether memories are supported by verbatim or gist traces (Brainerd & Poole, 1997; Brainerd & Reyna, 1998; Brainerd, Reyna, & Brandse, 1995; Brainerd, Reyna, & Poole, chap. 5, this volume).

As indicated by the modern research just discussed, explanations of suggestibility effects have progressed significantly in proposing possible cognitive mechanisms responsible for the false-memory phenomenon. Historically, it was German psychologist Lipmann (1911) who emphasized how children's cognitive abilities impact their effectiveness as eyewitnesses. He hypothesized that attentional factors influence developmental differences in children's eyewitness memories. More specifically, Lipmann reasoned that children attend to and encode different characteristics of stimuli than adults, making their memories qualitatively different. Typically in interrogative contexts, the questions posed to children focus on attributes of a crime relevant to proving a case; however, children do not necessarily attend to these adult-defined attributes. Lipmann proposed that when children are confronted with questions posed by authoritative adults, they report any information that readily comes to mind, fact or fiction, in order to provide a response, which in turn leads to reconstruction of memories to maintain consistency.

Ultimately, Lipmann's contribution was in emphasizing how children's attentional characteristics and their inability to distinguish fantasy from reality influence their reliability as witnesses, issues that have also been addressed by modern researchers. For example, modern researchers have provided evidence that young children have difficulty in reality monitoring, in other words, separating information that is imagined from information that is actually perceived (e.g., Foley, Santini, & Sopasakis, 1989; Johnson, Hashtroudi, & Lindsay, 1993). Moreover, many of the memory errors children make may be attributed to their difficulty in attributing the source of their knowledge (e.g., Mazzoni, 1998). Contemporary researchers have investigated a host of other cognitive and social factors that influence children's increased susceptibility to suggestion. These factors include a limited knowledge of the event they experienced or witnessed (e.g., Goodman, Quas, Batterman-Faunce, Riddlesberger, & Kuhn, 1997;

Ornstein, Shapiro, Clubb, Follmer, & Baker-Ward, 1997), the parent–child relationship (Goodman, Quas, Batterman-Faunce, Riddlesberger, & Kuhn, 1994; Goodman et al., 1997), their beliefs that their memory is invulnerable to suggestion (O'Sullivan, Howe, & Marche, 1996), age differences in the representation of experiences (e.g., Brainerd & Poole, 1997; Reyna & Brainerd, 1995), responsivity to social-demand characteristics (e.g., Cassel & Bjorklund, 1995; McCloskey & Zaragoza, 1985), and how the interview is conducted (see Ceci & Bruck 1995; Qin, Quas, Redlich, & Goodman, 1997), among others. The general conclusion from over a decade of contemporary research often echoes the interpretation of researchers from the beginning of the 20th century: For a host of cognitive and social reasons, young children's memory is more susceptible to the influences of suggestion than the memories of older children and adults, and care and caution must be taken when interviewing children about important events they have witnessed or experienced, lest the interpretation of the interviewer become the "memory" (or memory report) of the child.

Adult's Memories of Childhood Experiences

The history that is most relevant to the repressed–false-memory cases reviewed earlier concerns two interrelated concepts of Sigmund Freud's (1915/1957) psychoanalytic theory. First, through his clinical interviews with neurotic patients, Freud came to the conclusion that many of his female patients were sexually abused as young children, an idea that is referred to as his *seduction theory*. Second, Freud also theorized that these memories of childhood sexual abuse were repressed, or forced out of the conscious level of awareness, to protect the ego from the traumatic information. However, repression was viewed as incompletely dominating traumatic memories, in that indicators of childhood sexual abuse may seep into consciousness indirectly through dreams, behaviors, neuroses, and other psychological maladies. According to Freud (1940/1963),

> Analytic experience has convinced us of the complete truth of the assertion so often to be heard that the child is psychologically father to the adult and the events of his first years are of paramount importance for his later life. It will thus be of special interest to us if there is something that may be described as the central experience of this period of childhood. Our attention is first attracted by the effects of certain influences which do not apply to all children though they are common enough—such as the sexual abuse of children by adults, their seduction by other children slightly their senior, and what we should not expect, their being deeply stirred by seeing or hearing at first hand sexual behavior between adults (their parents) mostly

at a time at which one would not have thought they could either be interested in or understand any such impressions, or be capable of remembering them later. Since these impressions are subjected to repression either at once or as soon as they seek to return as memories, they constitute the determinant for the neurotic compulsion which will subsequently make it impossible for the ego to control the sexual function and will probably cause it to turn away from that function permanently. (pp. 68–69)

In these statements, Freud set forth several defining features of his psychoanalytic theory that would later influence public perceptions of childhood sexual abuse (see later discussion on feminist perspectives): (a) early childhood experiences determine adult personality; (b) childhood sexual abuse by relatives is fairly common; (c) memories of childhood abuse are repressed; and (d) neuroses serve as indicators of repressed abuse memories. (Freud later recanted his seduction theory, realizing that his patients' stories of childhood sexual abuse were all similar because of the suggestive methods, including hypnosis, dream analysis, and trance induction, he used to retrieve memories that were supposedly buried in the unconscious mind.[1])

Despite Freud's rejection of his own seduction theory, his conceptualizations of the relationship between stress and memory have prevailed. In describing the defense mechanism of repression, Freud held that traumatic stress has qualitatively different effects on memory than moderate levels of stress (see also van der Kolk & Fisler, 1995). His defense mechanism inherently predicted a negative relationship between stress and memory, with traumatic events being accessible to memory only within highly supportive contexts, such as the therapeutic atmosphere.

Ethical concerns obviously limit experimental investigations of the relationship between trauma and memory. Consequently, such research has led to conflicting results and constraints on generalizability. Some research has demonstrated a negative relationship between trauma and memory,

---

[1]Later in his career, Freud wrote,

Under the influence of the technical procedure which I used at that time, the majority of my patients reproduced from their childhood scenes in which they were sexually seduced by some grown-up persons. With female patients the part of seducer was almost always assigned to their father. I believed these stories, and consequently supposed that I had discovered the roots of the subsequent neurosis in these experiences of sexual seduction in childhood. . . . If the reader feels inclined to shake his head at my credulity, I cannot altogether blame him. When, however, I was at last obliged to recognize that these scenes of seduction had never taken place, and that they were only phantasies which my patients had made up or which I myself had perhaps forced on them, I was for sometime completely at a loss. (as cited in Masson, 1992, p. 198)

consistent with Freud's general view (e.g., Bugental, Blue, Cortez, Fleck, & Rodriguez, 1992; Merritt, Ornstein, & Spicker, 1994; Peters, 1991); other research has revealed positive effects, supporting the idea that representations of highly charged emotional events exhibit a photographic quality, preserving vivid, detailed information in long-term memory over substantial delays (e.g., Goodman, Hirschman, Hepps, & Rudy, 1991, Experiment 3; Loftus, Polonsky, & Fullilove, 1994; Oates & Shrimpton, 1991); and still other studies have found no significant effects of stress on memory (e.g., Eisen, Goodman, & Qin, 1995; Goodman et al., 1991, Experiment 1; Howe, Courage, & Peterson, 1995; Steward, 1989).

Concerning the recovery of memories, evidence is even more scant. Most studies have involved short-term amnesia recovery from traumatic episodes, thus limiting generalizability (Christianson & Nilsson, 1989). Indeed, memory experts have recently expressed concern regarding claims that memories recovered during the course of therapy were previously repressed and suggest that these memories may be false, products of suggestive techniques as indicated by Freud's rejection of his seduction theory (e.g., Lindsay & Read, 1994; Loftus, 1993; Ofshe & Watters, 1994). Several researchers have attempted to demonstrate that children and adults can create memories of entire events. In the typical false-memory paradigm, participants are asked to remember both true and false events presented in the same manner across multiple interviews. Descriptions of true events are developed from information provided by family members, and experimenters create false events. The false-memory paradigm is designed to assess whether participants will create a personal memory based on a description of a fictitious event.

Research using the false-memory paradigm reveals that children and adults can create false memories of complete, emotional, and self-involving events. In a series of studies, Ceci and his colleagues tested the hypothesis that asking preschoolers to repeatedly think about and create mental images of fictitious events would result in source misattributions and the creation of false memories. In an initial experiment (Ceci, Crotteau-Huffman, Smith, & Loftus, 1994), 58% of preschoolers generated elaborate descriptions, including contextual and affective information, of at least one of the fictitious events (e.g., getting his or her finger caught in a mousetrap and going to the emergency room to have it removed), and 25% generated descriptions for the majority of the fictitious events. A second study (Ceci, Loftus, Leichtman, & Bruck, 1994) investigated whether children really create memories of the fictitious events or whether they merely comply with an authoritative interviewer. After 11 consecutive weekly interviews, a different interviewer informed each preschooler that the previous interviewer had made mistakes by telling him or her things had happened that did not really happen. Then, the experimenter asked each child which events had really happened. It was predicted that if the children were responding to social demands in previous interviews, then the different interviewer would provide them with the opportunity to correctly reject the false events, demonstrating acquiescence effects. Conversely, if the preschoolers actually believed that the fictitious events happened to them, then they would continue to incorrectly accept the occurrence of fictitious events. Results revealed that most of the children who agreed to the occurrence of fictitious events in previous interviews continued to do so with a different interviewer, providing evidence for memory effects.

The creation of false memories is a phenomenon that is not unique to childhood. Several researchers have shown that even adults demonstrate susceptibility to suggestion. For example, Loftus and Pickrell (1995) demonstrated that 25% of adults provided full or partial accounts of getting lost in a shopping mall during childhood. Similarly, Hyman et al. (1995) found the same percentage of adults reporting false memories using a variety of events (e.g., spilling punch at a wedding reception). Pezdek and Hodge (1999) also replicated Loftus and Pickrell's (1995) findings for getting lost in a mall but provided evidence that it is difficult to implant memories in children for an event that more closely approximates sexual abuse (e.g., a childhood enema). Nevertheless, this line of research clearly indicates that suggestive techniques can lead to a variety of memory distortions. Hyman et al. (1995) observed that their susceptible adults incorporated false information into their autobiographical memories by relying on their stored knowledge of true events. Thus, as Goodman, Emery, and Haugaard (1998) pointed out, some false memories may be based in reality; that is, true memories with false details and false memories with true details may be products of suggestive techniques.

How Are Early Memories Represented?

A major issue relevant to adults' memory of childhood involves the nature of such representations. The primary question concerns whether adults can remember early childhood experiences. Despite research, such as that of Rovee-Collier using conditioning techniques (see Rovee-Collier, 1995; Rovee-Collier & Gerhardstein, 1997, for reviews) and research showing deferred imitation of novel behaviors (see Bauer, 1996; Meltzoff, 1995, for reviews) demonstrating that infants can remember over long delays, the modern consensus maintains that such representations are not likely accessible in later childhood and adulthood; that is, early infancy and childhood memories do not show remarkable stability. Freud referred to the inability to recall early infancy and childhood experiences as *infantile amnesia*. In their review, Pillemer and White (1989) provided support for Freud's insights, reporting that memories of experiences before age 3 are not available to adult consciousness (average age of earliest memory was 3 years) and that memories of experiences between ages 3 and 6 show highly limited accessibility (see Nelson, 1996).

Freud's conception of infantile amnesia was linked to his seduction theory and to repression as a defense mechanism, in that he theorized that adults' memories for early childhood experiences are repressed because of the traumatic nature of sexual overtones present in early infant–parent interactions. Modern explanations of infantile amnesia rely on considerations of the nature of representation, the development of self-concept, information-processing abilities, and language, rather than on universal experiences of infant sexuality (see Bjorklund, 2000). For example, several authors have suggested that for long-term autobiographical memories to be accessible, the "auto" or "self," which develops gradually over early childhood, must be present to provide an anchor for representations of events (Fivush, 1988; Howe & Courage, 1993; Welch-Ross, 1995). Alternatively, Leichtman and Ceci (1993) used fuzzy-trace theory (Brainerd & Reyna, 1990; see earlier discussion on persistence of misinformation) to explain how developmental shifts in information processing (from reliance on verbatim traces to gistlike traces) affect children's event representations. From this perspective, memories from infancy and early childhood are most susceptible to forgetting because they are encoded primarily in the form of verbatim traces; memories from later childhood are increasingly encoded in the form of fuzzy traces, which are less susceptible to forgetting. Leichtman and Ceci also acknowledge the role of increasing language abilities in contributing to children's representational systems.

What do these modern theories of infantile amnesia lend to the understanding of adults' memories for childhood experiences? They lead to a cautious approach to interpreting reported memories of very early childhood sexual abuse, such as U.S. actress Rosanne's claim that she was molested by her mother at 6 months of age. Research reveals that social-demand characteristics can lead up to 30% of adults to report memories from the first year of life, with some adults reporting memories from the first week of life (Malinoski et al., 1995). Considering what scientists know about transitions between early and later representational systems, it is unlikely that these reports represent veridical autobiographical memories.

The historical perspective offered above established major theoretical and empirical considerations of behavioral science research relevant to children's reliability as witnesses and the nature of adults' memories for childhood experiences. Overall, we can conclude from this research that young children and even adults are susceptible to misleading questions, that the effects of trauma on memory are unclear, and that it is quite difficult for adults to remember very early childhood experiences. Granted that many of the milestones within this area of research have occurred in reaction to the upsurge in childhood memory cases, this historical perspective still allows us to pose the question: Given what has been and is currently known scientifically about memory and considering even the contradictions within the literature, why have countless cases emerged in which children were subjected to misleading questions (as in the Wenatchee, Washington situation) and adults' memories were distorted through suggestive therapeutic techniques (as in the Burgus case)? Next we present a sociological analysis of the zeitgeist that led to the crescendo of such cases during the past two decades.

A SOCIOLOGICAL PERSPECTIVE

Salem's Legacy

Returning to the 17th-century witch-hunt that occurred in Salem, it is clear that the cultural atmosphere permitted the phenomenon. Ceci, Toglia, and Ross (1990) argued that the social and cultural forces that influenced Salem's children are present to some degree in the current times. The zeitgeist that led to the witch trials in Salem can be described as an emotionally laden hysteria concerning the practice of witchcraft. The community's shared belief in witchcraft led adults to seek out "evidence" from children, who they believed would always tell the truth, by posing leading questions and encouraging statements confirming their beliefs (Ceci & Bruck, 1993).

From the mid-1980s through the mid-1990s, Americans have witnessed a modern witch-hunt of sorts, with childhood sexual abuse as the target crime rather than witchcraft, as evidenced by the virtual floodgate of sensationalized stories reporting cases of children testifying to widespread sexual abuse in day-care centers and adults suing their parents, relatives, and religious leaders for sexual abuse that allegedly occurred during childhood. In this section, we reflect on this decade and consider the spirit of the times and shared belief systems that provided the social milieu for such cases to flourish. Here, we summarize and expand on arguments made by Goldstein concerning the social movements that preceded and led to a climax of childhood-memory cases during the past two decades (Goldstein, 1997; Goldstein & Farmer, 1993). More specifically, we outline how the radical feminist and recovery movements collaborated in voicing the following shared beliefs concerning childhood sexual abuse:

1. The prevalence of childhood sexual abuse greatly surpasses society's imagination.
2. What constitutes abuse is defined by the victim and can include any inappropriate behavior.
3. Memories for childhood sexual abuse are often repressed or dissociated.
4. Indicators of childhood sexual abuse include numerous physical and emotional maladies, such as headaches, eating disorders, and low self-esteem.
5. Psychotherapy, and group therapy more specifically, are recommended as treatment for recovery from the emotional trauma of childhood sexual abuse (see Forward & Buck, 1978).

We also discuss how the New Age movement influenced individuals' willingness to subject themselves to suggestive techniques and how this movement may have exacerbated the possibility of false-memory creation by addressing doubts with a reliance on antiscientific attitudes.

Radical Feminism and the Recovery Movement

How can one reconcile the glaring lack of evidence for repressed memories and organized satanic cult activity with the public's beliefs that these phenomena are pervasive in our society? Dawes (1992) explained that beliefs that contradict evidence are developed and sustained by the presence of a group of "authorities" who establish a social consensus to support their beliefs. In the case of repressed memories, representatives from two major social movements, the feminist and recovery movements, comprised the group of "authorities" who carried broad ranges of credentials, from self-proclaimed experts to psychiatrists. These "authorities" actively promoted the theory that women who seek therapy and exhibit fairly general symptoms were repressing memories of childhood sexual abuse. Although we credit the feminist movement for their positive contribution of raising the public's awareness of childhood sexual abuse and the recovery movement for making support accessible to virtually anyone, we believe that these movements contributed to the hysteria that underlies recent cases. Here, we address more specifically how these two movements developed a social consensus that childhood sexual abuse is common and that memories for such abuse are repressed.

How Frequent Is Childhood Sexual Abuse?   One goal of the feminist and recovery movements was to establish that the frequency of sexual abuse in society greatly surpassed the public's awareness. Representing the feminist perspective, Forward and Buck (1978) claimed, without referencing the source of their information, that between 10 and 20 million Americans are victims of abuse. Radical feminist social worker Florence Rush (1980) stated that childhood sexual abuse is not "an occasional deviant act, but a devastating commonplace fact of everyday life" (p. xii).

To bolster the impression that childhood sexual abuse is rampant, feminist authors labeled society as "patriarchal" and argued that incest has been used systematically, historically, and universally, as a means of female oppression perpetrated by adult males, and furthermore, that anyone could be guilty of such acts. Rush (1980) attempted to establish a social history of universal acceptance of childhood sexual abuse by men, citing references such as the Talmud, the Bible, ancient Greek writings, traditional fairy tales, and modern films. Herman (1981) attributed society's increased awareness of childhood sexual abuse to the women's liberation movement, proclaimed that the feminist perspective offered the best explanation of the data, and articulated this perspective by stating, "Female children are regularly subjected to sexual assaults by adult males who are part of their intimate social world. The aggressors are not outcasts and strangers; they are neighbors, family friends, uncles, cousins, stepfathers, and fathers" (p. 7).

Thus, the major result of the feminist interpretation of childhood sexual abuse during the 1970s was to establish, by reiteration rather than by evidence, that incest is commonplace in American families. Indeed, Masson (1992) credited the feminist literature of the 1970s with breaking the silence concerning the prevalence of incest. Yet, the National Committee for the Prevention of Child Abuse (1996) reported the following:

> While many estimates have been made, the national incidence rate of sexual abuse remains unknown. The estimate that one in four girls and one in ten boys are abused prior to age 18 became widely known statistically simply from being repeated. Retrospective surveys reveal great variation with 6% to 62%. (p. 1)

Defining Abuse.   Another factor that contributed to bolstering the public's impression of the high prevalence of childhood sexual abuse was the expansion of the definition of what constitutes abuse. Herman (1981) effectively expanded the pool of possible incest victims by conceptualizing abuse as occurring along a continuum from the most extreme exaggeration of patriarchal norms, overt incest, to *covert incest,* the term that she used to describe women who had seductive but not incestuous fathers. According to Herman, victims of covert incest were larger in number and experienced similar consequences as victims of overt incest. Forward (1989) continued this loosening of the term *incest* by stating, "Victims of psychological incest may not have been actually touched or assaulted sexually, but they have experienced an invasion of their sense of privacy or safety" (p. 139).

The recovery movement exaggerated society's perception of victimization by promoting the notion that most of us grew up in or live within the context of a dysfunctional family. On his public television "infomercials" and in his various books, John Bradshaw has claimed that 100% of families are dysfunctional, which implies that everyone needs to recover from something. Bradshaw used the term *emotional incest* as the recovery movement's parallel to Herman's concept of covert incest. Blume (1990) described this emotional incest more explicitly by claiming the following:

> It can be the way a father stares at his daughter's developing body, and the comments he makes. . . . It can be forced exposure to the sounds or sights of one or both parents' sexual acts . . . or it can be a father's jealous possessiveness and suspicion of the boys his daughter associates with, his inquisitorial insistence on knowing the details of her sexual encounters. . . . Horribly, increasingly, it can occur as part of a cult ritual activity engaged in by a network of adults and involving many children—violence and abuse of animals as well." (pp. 8–9)

In response to these claims, Kaminer (1992) stated, "If child abuse is every form of inadequate nurturance, then being raped by your father is in the same class as being ignored or not getting help with your homework. When everything is child abuse, nothing is" (p. 27). Thus, these perpetual reconceptualizations of abuse had the effect of making child abuse seem even more prevalent, increasing the numbers of the incest survivor movement.

Repression of Abuse Memories: Freud's Seduction Theory Revisited. As noted previously, because several of his female patients shared similar stories of early sexual experiences, Freud speculated that many of the psychological maladies exhibited by these patients originated from and served as indicators of repressed memories of childhood sexual abuse. Despite Freud's own rejection of this seduction theory, feminist authors, such as

Herman and Forward, resurrected and steadfastly maintained Freud's original ideas. Herman asserted that Freud rejected his seduction theory as a means of protecting patriarchy and that psychiatrists have conspired to represent women's reports of sexual abuse as fantasies. In the conclusion to one of her studies, she claimed that her findings validate the theory. In 1987, Herman and Schatzow wrote,

> The presumption that most patients' reports of childhood sexual abuse can be ascribed to fantasy no longer appears tenable. . . . No positive evidence was adduced that would indicate that any of the patients' reports of sexual abuse were fantasies. In the light of these findings, it would seem warranted to return to the insights offered by Freud's original statement of the etiology of hysteria, and to resume a line of investigation that mental health professionals prematurely abandoned 90 years ago. (p. 11)

Without delineating the mechanisms of memory repression and recovery, Masson (1992), a psychoanalyst and former director of the Freud Archives, supported the feminist perspective's adoption of Freud's seduction theory. Masson referred to Freud's rejection of his seduction theory as a personal failure of courage and abandonment of truth, and believes, as Freud initially did, that adult neuroses are indicators of traumatic memories of sexual abuse that are buried in the unconscious mind.

Representing the recovery movement, Blume (1990) claimed, "Indeed, so few incest survivors in my experience have identified themselves as abused in the beginning of therapy that I have concluded that perhaps half of all incest survivors do not remember that the abuse occurred" (p. 81). She developed The Incest Survivors' Aftereffects Checklist to aid readers in considering whether they have repressed memories of abuse. Some of Blume's symptoms of child abuse from this list of approximately 100 items include nightmares, gastrointestinal problems, arthritis, wearing baby clothes, eating disorders, drug or alcohol abuse, depression, constant anger, high risk-taking, low risk-taking, fear of losing control, low self-esteem, high appreciation of small favors, feeling crazy, feeling different, being compulsively seductive or asexual, avoidance of mirrors, and wanting to change one's name. Blume states, "Among women who had not been aware of childhood sexual abuse but who recognize characteristics in themselves on the checklist, a surprising number began to uncover previously repressed incest" (p. xxiv; for a similar interpretation, see Fredrickson, 1992). This inclusion of individuals who do not remember abuse or exhibit "indicators" elevated the prevalence of childhood sexual abuse once again.

Psychotherapy Unburies Repressed Memories. The majority of feminist authors sanctioned psychotherapy for the recovery of lost memories of abuse and extended advice to therapists concerning inquiries of abuse. Herman (1981) recommended that every patient be questioned about the possibility of childhood sexual abuse:

> Questions about sexual abuse should be incorporated into any clinician's ordinary history-taking. The prevalence of child sexual abuse even in the general population is great enough to warrant routine questioning. . . . The burden of responsibility for obtaining a history of incest should lie with the therapist. (p. vii)

Furthermore, she asserted that recovery of repressed memories can alleviate the symptoms discussed previously as indicators of childhood sexual abuse (Herman & Schatzow, 1987). Forward (1989) supported Herman's opinion by stating "many victims still won't mention the incest without prodding from the therapist" (p. 152).

This position was adopted by many psychotherapists. Courtois (1992) expressed her belief that patients should be "educated" (or indoctrinated) by therapists about posttraumatic stress disorder and therapeutic and memorial processes. She stated,

> Education precedes formal recall strategies to insure the survivor a cognitive framework within which to process emotions which accompany recall. . . . At times, it may be necessary for the therapist to put the pieces together and speculate about the emerging picture and its significance. (pp. 25–26)

Courtois recommended group therapy as a memory retrieval cue. She claimed, "Groups are very powerful in eliciting memories since survivors associate or 'chain' to each others' recollections and feelings" (pp. 28–29).

Given what the research literature informs us about people's susceptibility to suggestion from authority figures, one would not be surprised if many of the memories recovered under such interviewing techniques were false. These arguments apply to the group-therapy context as well. The process of "chaining" to other group members' recollections described by Courtois appears dangerously close to Binet's findings of suggestibility at the group level. Current conceptualizations of source monitoring suggest that clients in group settings may misattribute others' memories as their own (e.g., Johnson et al., 1993).

In concluding our discussion of the impact of feminist and recovery movement "authorities" in forming a social consensus that childhood sexual abuse is rampant and that memories for such abuse are repressed, we cite a clear example of how politics often overrides science on this issue. In her book, *Revolution From Within: A Book of Self-Esteem* (1992), Gloria Steinem addressed the prevalence of childhood sexual abuse and its indicators and advocated theories of repression and dissociation of sexual abuse memories by making this statement:

> Perhaps, the memory has been pushed out of our consciousness completely. But those images and feelings remain alive in our unconscious— and they can be uncovered. Even abuse so long-term and severe that a child survived only by dissociating from it while it was happening still leaves markers above its burial ground. (p. 72)

Later in the same book, she asserted the following:

> There are telltale signs of such buried trauma . . . fear of expressing anger at all; substantial childhood periods of which you have no memory of emotions or events . . . depression . . . severe eating disorders. . . . Trust these clues—there is statistical as well as personal evidence that the conditions they point to are widespread. Perhaps a third of the children in the United States have been subjected to sexual and other kinds of severe abuse or neglect. . . . Frequently, such memories are so painful that they don't surface fully until years after the events occurred. The more extreme and erratic these events, the younger we were when we experienced them, and the more dependent we were on the people who inflicted them, the more repressed they are likely to be. (pp. 162–163)

Go Where Your Mind Takes You: The New Age Movement, Suggestive Therapeutic Techniques, and Antiscience

The impact of the New Age movement on society's thinking has been underestimated, yet a venture into many bookstores reveals numerous books on past-life channeling and fortune-telling that often outnumber books in the science section. Society has embraced the notion of exploring mind-altering techniques, which obviously have some benefits that contribute to the movement's popularity. For example, relaxation techniques, such as meditation, yoga, and visualization, can yield healing and health maintenance effects. However, such mind-altering techniques can also render unexpected deleterious effects. Here, we discuss the role such techniques have played in contributing to false-memory cases, such as Patricia Burgus', and how the New Age movement has promoted antiscientific attitudes.

The reach of New Age techniques has extended beyond bookstores and into therapeutic practices. As noted previously, representatives of the feminist and recovery movements offered psychotherapy as the prescription for retrieving lost memories of abuse. Coincidentally (or perhaps not), many of the prominent players in the feminist and recovery movements have offered weekend seminars training therapists in the use of

New Age techniques to retrieve memories. Courtois (1992), a clinical psychologist, endorsed a host of "experiential/expressive-cathartic techniques" to aid in the retrieval of lost memories, including hypnosis, imagery, guided movement, body work, and psychodrama. Considering the adverse effects of one such technique, hypnosis, research clearly demonstrates that although hypnosis increases how much a person remembers, much of the information gained is erroneous (e.g., Lynn, Lock, Myers, & Payne, 1997); furthermore, hypnosis increases an individual's confidence in correct and incorrect information. The general consensus among memory researchers concerning the accuracy of information produced by such New Age techniques is that less is more in these cases (Ornstein, Ceci, & Loftus, 1996).

Perhaps the most disturbing product of the New Age movement is the penetration of antiscientific attitudes into public consciousness. New Age abandons science by relying on intuition rather than evidence. Kaminer (1992) expressed her concern with this rejection of scientific findings by stating,

> New Age is an attitude. To demand precision and specificity (what some would call meaning) in a discussion of consciousness paradigms or transpersonal energy vibrations is to reveal yourself as only 'half-minded,' a sorry left-brained creature trapped in rationalism, foolishly focused on the external world. It is to absent yourself from the postbiological, postverbal phase of human evolution and to dwell spiritually in nonlivingness. New Age is aggressively anti-intellectual, proudly nonrational. It's not supposed to make sense. (p. 102)

Representatives of the recovery movement are particularly guilty of disseminating antiscientific attitudes into the public domain. Although Bass and Davis noted in the preface of their book *The Courage to Heal* (1988) that "none of what is presented here is based on psychological theories" (p. 14), they made assertive statements that may sound like scientific fact to readers, such as the following: "Forgetting is one of the most common and effective ways children deal with sexual abuse. . . . The human mind has tremendous powers of repression" (p. 42). They also posited, "There are many women who show signs of having been abused without having any memories" (p. 71). Furthermore, Bass and Davis (1988) encouraged intuition over evidence by stating, "If you think you were abused and your life shows the symptoms, then you were. . . . To say 'I was abused,' you don't need the kind of recall that would stand up in a court of law" (p. 22). Davis (1991) further promoted the antiscientific notion that memory is not required in realizations of abuse by instructing potential victims to tell themselves, "I'm going to accept the fact that I was abused and make a commitment to heal, even if I never remember the specifics" (p. 118).

In general, the New Age belief in intuitive, nonrational explanations and the disdain for conventional scientific, evidence-based explanations influenced some therapists' practices, particularly when it came to the recovery of repressed childhood memories. The result was an environment that encouraged recollections of events that may never have happened but that were consistent with the prevailing theory of a patient's therapist or of the recollections of one's group members.

The discussion to this point has focused on the role of "authorities" in developing a social consensus that perpetuated false beliefs concerning the nature of childhood memory and how social movements have created a climate that made false-memory cases possible. Next, we address how changes in the judicial system itself have increased the frequency of such cases.

Changes in the Legal System

Although Ceci and Bruck (1993) outlined a number of changes in the legal system since the Salem witch trials, here we focus on two primary issues: (a) changes related to children's testimony and (b) changes in the statute of limitations for crimes that allegedly occurred during childhood.

In response to an increased awareness of childhood sexual abuse, which can partly be attributed to the feminist movement's concerted effort to expose such abuse, the legal system changed their procedures for handling child witnesses. Most jurisdictions abandoned the requirement for corroboration in sexual abuse cases, and many states, after centuries of skepticism, began to permit child testimony, allowing the jury to determine the credibility of children's assertions. Eventually, this loosening of rules resulted in hearsay exceptions, which allowed the admissibility of statements by therapists, pediatricians, and others concerning statements made by children. These changes in the legal system were adopted with the intent of increasing accurate testimony (Harvard Law Review Notes, 1985; Montoya, 1992); however, given the research reviewed at the outset of this chapter, children's ability to accurately testify depends on a number of factors, including their age and the type of questions used for interrogation.

Some researchers have doubted the applicability of current findings to cases of childhood sexual abuse. For example, Goodman and Clarke-Stewart (1991) pointed out that most research investigating children as eyewitnesses tests situations that are qualitatively different from personally experienced sexual abuse. However, although ethical limitations prohibit specific tests of children's eyewitness memory for sexual abuse, research indicates that children are suggestible and can even be persuaded to report that a complete, emotionally laden event involving physical contact happened to them when it really did not as demonstrated in the case that took place in Wenatchee, Washington.

Cases in which adults are suing others for abuse that occurred in childhood have been more drastically influenced by politics. The National Organization for Women (NOW) published a Legal Resource Kit on Incest and Child Sexual Abuse (NOW Legal Defense and Education Fund, 1992) that advocated the view that victims of childhood sexual abuse repress their memories of the trauma and that such memories may be uncovered through therapeutic processes. Furthermore, they argued that women who are victims of such abuse but who do not uncover their lost memories of abuse until later in life experience a violation of rights because they cannot sue the perpetrator because of statute of limitations restrictions. To remedy this situation, the NOW Legal Defense and Education Fund proclaimed,

> We have developed a sophisticated legal argument that proves that the statute of limitations for civil incest cases should begin to run not when acts of incest end, and not at the age of majority, but rather when the victim discovers the injuries she has suffered and their cause. (p. 2)

NOW filed amicus curiae (friend of the court) briefs on this issue and successfully lobbied 20 state legislatures to increase the statute of limitations in cases that involve memories of childhood sexual abuse recovered in therapy. The result of these politically motivated changes in the legal system is that nonabusers (often parents) may be convicted of or pay civil fines for crimes they may not have committed because the judicial system itself, however indirectly, is advocating a theory for which there is little evidence.

CHANGES IN THE TIDE

False accusations by children (usually groups of children in a single daycare center) of sexual abuse by their caretakers (usually uncovered by persistent questioning by therapists or police officers) and court cases of recovered childhood sexual abuse brought mostly by adult women against a relative or former family friend (again, usually recovered in therapy) peaked by the mid-1990s and are now in decline. Figure 1.1 presents the

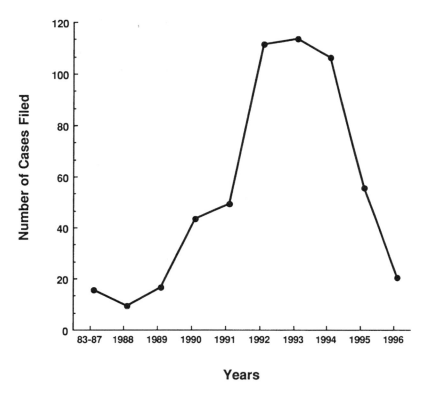

FIG. 1.1. Number of recovered memory suits filed between 1983 and 1996 (from letter by P. Freyd, 1997, *False Memory Syndrome Foundation Newsletter*, 6[2], 1. Copyright © 1997 by The FMS Foundation. Adapted with permission).

number of court cases filed alleging childhood sexual abuse that were recovered only in adulthood. By the late 1990s, there were as many or more cases of women suing their therapists for misguided therapy, purporting that memories of abuse were planted by the therapist when in fact no abuse had occurred. What was responsible for this change?

The movements that supported the suggestive interviewing of children and the belief in the recovery of repressed memory did not just run out of steam. Rather, the scientific research that was generated in large part by the social phenomena under discussion here revealed problems that were not easy to ignore. Children are highly suggestible and, although repression may in fact occur, there was no scientific evidence that it occurred to the extent proposed by practitioners of the recovery movement, and memories of abuse from infancy were highly unlikely if not impossible.

But papers published in scientific journals rarely influence potent social movements or belief systems. What turned the tide was scientists becoming involved in the social discussion. They served as expert witnesses in many court cases, and filed amicus curiae statements in appeals of several prominent abuse cases, which resulted in convictions being overturned and wrongly accused people freed. For example, Maggie Bruck and Stephen Ceci (1995) led a group of social scientists in filing an amicus brief in the Kelly Michaels case. Kelly Michaels was a nursery school teacher in Maplewood, New Jersey, who was accused of multiple charges of sexual abuse of the children in her care. Despite the lack of physical evidence, the often bizarre statements made by the children (e.g., she licked peanut butter off children's genitals, played the piano in the nude), and the highly suggestive questioning of the children, Kelly Michaels was convicted and sentenced to 47 years in prison. On the grounds of faulty interview techniques, the Appeals Court of New Jersey reversed her conviction in 1993. Following is a paragraph from the amicus brief authored by Bruck and Ceci and signed by 45 social scientists. It turned the tables on those prosecuting sexual child abuse, and made it clear that it is not a issue of "child advocates" versus "cold-hearted scientists":

> The authors of this brief also wish to convey their deep concern over the children in this case. Our concern is that if there were incidents of sexual abuse, the faulty interviewing procedures make it impossible to ever know who the perpetrators were and how the abuse occurred. Thus, poor interviewing procedures make it difficult to detect real abuse. But we have further concerns. And these involve the interviewing techniques which we view as abusive in themselves. After reading a number of these interviews, it is difficult to believe that adults charged with the care and protection of young children would be allowed to use the vocabulary that they used in these interviews, that they would be allowed to interact with children in such sexually explicit ways, or that they would be allowed to bully and frighten their child witnesses in such a shocking manner. No amount of evidence that sexual abuse had actually occurred could ever justify the use of these techniques especially with three- and four-year-old children. Above and beyond the great stress, intimidation, and embarrassment that many of the children obviously suffered during the interviews, we are deeply concerned about the long-lasting harmful effects of persuading children that they have been horribly sexually and physically abused when in fact there may have been no abuse until the interviews began. The authors of this brief will be permanently disturbed that children were interviewed in such abusive circumstances regardless of the ultimate innocence or guilt of the accused. (cited in Ceci & Bruck, 1995, pp. 292–293)

The reversals of this and other high-profile cases, supported by research scientists, made the evening news and brought another perspective on these and related cases to the public. Prominent scientists such as Elizabeth Loftus and Stephen Ceci appeared on national television news programs, presented their research, and discussed the undesired consequences of some of the interviewing techniques used both with children and adults in recovering memories of abuse. And although books on New Age and the recovery movement still outnumber books based on scientific evidence on the bookshelves of major book retailers, popular books began to appear written by scientists on the issues of recovered memories (e.g., Loftus & Ketchum, 1994, *The Myth of Repressed Memory;* Ofshe & Watters, 1994, *Making Monsters: False Memories, Psychotherapy, and Sexual Hysteria*) and the credibility of children's testimony following extensive and suggestive interviewing (Ceci & Bruck, 1995, *Jeopardy in the Courtroom: A Scientific Analysis of Children's Testimony*). Gradually, the weight of science, along with the energies of attorneys representing accused parents, began to chip away at claims made by advocates of the recovery movement. The result today, we believe, is a climate in which the horrors of child abuse are not overlooked or minimized but in which society no longer believes that every adult emotional malady is a result of long-forgotten abuse.

CONCLUSION

"'It was the best of times, it was the worst of times. . . .' With apologies to Charles Dickens, we find it likely that future historians of our discipline will characterize current research on the development of memory and cognition in this bipolar manner" (Baker-Ward, Ornstein, & Gordon, 1993, p. 13).

Although Baker-Ward et al. (1993) used this quotation to refer to the distinction between basic and applied research, the sentiment is appropriate when considering the field's positions on the nature of childhood memory for traumatic events. On the one hand, some practitioners advocate repression theories, and on the other, some memory researchers maintain that repression contradicts everything that is known about memory. In response to this debate, the American Psychological Association formed a working group of three clinical psychologists (Alpert, Brown, and Courtois) and three memory researchers (Ceci, Loftus, and Ornstein) to investigate memories of childhood abuse. The final conclusions of the report (Alpert et al., 1996) indicated that the two factions agree that childhood sexual abuse is a pervasive societal problem, that most victims of abuse remember their experiences (although forgetting is possible), and that false-memory creation is possible. However, the clinicians and the scientists candidly admitted that they disagreed on the mechanisms that underlie memory, the privileged status afforded to memories of traumatic events, the relevance of research to understanding memory for traumatic events, the pervasiveness of false-memory creation, and the degree to which true memories can be distinguished from false memories. Although the social environment has changed considerably over the past 5 years or so, the critical issues have not been settled. It is our hope that in the future therapists and scientists can more easily share their ideas and data in an environment that is free from the polarizing polemics that characterized the previous decade.

REFERENCES

Alpert, J. L., Brown, L. S., Ceci, S. J., Courtois, C. A., Loftus, E. F., & Ornstein, P. A. (1996). *Working Group on Investigation of Memories of Childhood Abuse: Final report.* Washington, DC: American Psychological Association.

Baker-Ward, L., Ornstein, P. A., & Gordon, B. N. (1993). A tale of two settings: Young children's memory performance in the laboratory and the field. In G. M. Davies & R. H. Logie (Eds.), *Memory in everyday life* (pp. 13–41). Amsterdam: North-Holland/Elsevier.

Bass, E., & Davis, L. (1988). *The courage to heal.* New York: Harper & Row.

Bauer, P. J. (1996). What do infants recall of their lives? Memory for specific events by 1- to 2-year-olds. *American Psychologist, 51,* 29–41.

Belluck, P. (1997, November 6). "Memory" therapy leads to a lawsuit and big settlement. *The New York Times,* pp. A1, A10.

Binet, A. (1900). *La suggestibilité.* Paris: Schleicher Frères.

Bjorklund, D. F. (2000). *Children's thinking: Developmental function and individual differences* (3rd Ed.). Belmont, CA: Wadsworth.

Bjorklund, D. F., Bjorklund, B. R., Brown, R. D., & Cassel, W. S. (1998). Children's susceptibility to repeated questions: How misinformation changes children's answers and their minds. *Applied Developmental Science, 2,* 99–111.

Blume, E. S. (1990). *Secret survivors.* New York: Ballantine.

Brainerd, C. J., & Poole, D. A. (1997). Long-term survival of children's false memories: A review. *Learning and Individual Differences, 9,* 125–152.

Brainerd, C. J., & Reyna, V. F. (1990). Gist is the grist: Fuzzy-trace theory and the new intuitionism. *Developmental Review, 10,* 3–47.

Brainerd, C. J., & Reyna, V. F. (1998). Fuzzy-trace theory and children's false memories. *Journal of Experimental Child Psychology, 71,* 81–129.

Brainerd, C. J., Reyna, V. F., & Brandse, E. (1995). Are children's false memories more persistent than their true memories? *Psychological Science, 4,* 141–148.

Bruck, M., & Ceci, S. J. (1995). Amicus brief for the case of state of New Jersey v. Michaels presented by committee of concerned social scientists. *Psychology, Public Policy, and Law, 1,* 272–322.

Bugental, D. B., Blue, J., Cortez, V., Fleck, K., & Rodriguez, A. (1992). The influence of witnessed affect on information processing in children. *Child Development, 63,* 774–86.

Cassel, W. S., & Bjorklund, D. F. (1995). Developmental patterns of eyewitness memory and suggestibility: An ecologically based short-term longitudinal study. *Law and Human Behavior, 19,* 507–532.

Cassel, W. S., Roebers, C., & Bjorklund, D. F. (1996). Developmental patterns of eyewitness responses to repeated and increasingly suggestive questions. *Journal of Experimental Child Psychology, 61,* 116–133.

Ceci, S. J., & Bruck, M. (1993). Suggestibility of the child witness: A historical review and synthesis. *Psychological Bulletin, 113,* 403–439.

Ceci, S. J., & Bruck, M. (1995). *Jeopardy in the courtroom: A scientific analysis of children's testimony.* Washington, DC: American Psychological Association.

Ceci, S. J., & Bruck, M. (1998). Children's testimony: Applied and basic issues. In W. Damon (Series Ed.) & I. E. Sigel & K. A. Renninger (Vol. Eds.), *Handbook of child psychology: Vol. 4. Child psychology in practice* (5th ed., pp. 713–774). New York: Wiley.

Ceci, S. J., Crotteau-Huffman, M., Smith, E., & Loftus, E. F. (1994). Repeatedly thinking about non-events. *Consciousness and Cognition, 3,* 388–407.

Ceci, S. J., Loftus, E. F., Leichtman, M. D., & Bruck, M. (1994). The role of source misattributions in the creation of false beliefs among preschoolers. *International Journal of Clinical and Experimental Hypnosis, 62,* 304–320.

Ceci, S. J., Toglia, M. P., & Ross, D. F. (1990). The suggestibility of preschoolers' recollections: Historical perspectives on current problems. In R. Fivush & J. Hudson (Eds.), *Knowing and remembering in young children* (pp. 285–300). New York: Cambridge University Press.

Christianson, S. A., & Nilsson, L. (1989). Hysterical amnesia: A case of aversively motivated isolation of memory. In T. Archer & L. Nilsson (Eds.), *Aversion, avoidance, and anxiety: Perspectives on aversively motivated behavior* (pp. 289–310). Hillsdale, NJ: Lawrence Erlbaum Associates.

Courtois, C. (1992). The memory retrieval process in incest survivor therapy. *Journal of Child Sexual Abuse, 1,* 15–29.

Davis, L. (1991). *Allies in healing.* New York: HarperCollins.

Dawes, R. (1992). Why believe that for which there is no good evidence? *Issues in Child Abuse Accusations, Fall,* 214–218.

Eisen, M. L., Goodman, G. S., & Qin, J. J. (1995, April). *Eyewitness testimony in victims of child maltreatment: Stress, memory, and suggestibility.* Paper presented at the symposium of the Society for Applied Research on Memory and Cognition, Vancouver, Canada.

Fivush, R. (1988). The functions of event memory: Some comments on Nelson and Barsalou. In U. Neisser & E. Winograd (Eds.), *Remembering reconsidered: Ecological and traditional approaches to the study of memory* (pp. 277–282). New York: Cambridge University Press.

Foley, M. A., Santini, C., & Sopasakis, M. (1989). Discriminating between memories: Evidence for children's spontaneous elaborations. *Journal of Experimental Child Psychology, 48,* 146–169.

Forward, S. (1989). *Toxic parents.* New York: Bantam.

Forward, S., & Buck, C. (1978). *Betrayal of innocence: Incest and its devastation.* New York: Penguin.

Fredrickson, R. (1992). *Repressed memories: A journey to recovery from sexual abuse.* New York: Simon & Schuster.

Freud, S. (1957). Repression. In J. Strachey (Ed. and Trans.), *The standard edition of the complete psychological works of Sigmund Freud* (Vol. 14, pp. 66–89). London: Hogarth Press. (Original work published 1915)

Freud, S. (1963). *An outline of psycho-analysis.* New York: Norton. (Original work published 1940)

Freyd, P. (1997, February). [Letter]. *False Memory Syndrome Newsetter, 6*(2), 1.

Goldstein, E. (1997). False memory syndrome: Why would they believe such terrible things if they weren't true? *The American Journal of Family Therapy, 25,* 307–317.

Goldstein, E., & Farmer, K. (1993). *True stories of false memories.* Boca Raton, FL: Upton.

Goodman, G. S., Aman, C., & Hirschman, J. E. (1987). Child sexual and physical abuse: Children's testimony. In S. J. Ceci, M. P. Toglia, & D. F. Ross (Eds.), *Children's eyewitness memory* (pp. 1–23). New York: Springer-Verlag.

Goodman, G. S., & Clarke-Stewart, A. (1991). Suggestibility in children's testimony: Implications for child sexual abuse investigations. In J. L. Doris (Ed.), *The suggestibility of children's recollections* (pp. 92–105). Washington, DC: American Psychological Association.

Goodman, G. S., Emery, R. E., & Haugaard, J. J. (1998). Developmental psychology and law: Divorce, child maltreatment, foster care, and adoption. In W. Damon (Series Ed.) & I. E. Sigel & K. A. Renninger (Vol. Eds.), *Handbook of child psychology: Vol. 4. Child psychology in practice* (5th ed., pp. 775–874). New York: Wiley.

Goodman, G. S., Hirschman, J. E., Hepps, D., & Rudy, L. (1991). Children's memory for stressful events. *Merrill-Palmer Quarterly, 37,* 109–158.

Goodman, G. S., Quas, J. A., Batterman-Faunce, J. M., Riddlesberger, M. M., & Kuhn, J. (1994). Predictors of accurate and inaccurate memories of traumatic events experienced in childhood. *Consciousness and Cognition, 3,* 269–294.

Goodman, G. S., Quas, J. A., Batterman-Faunce, J. M., Riddlesberger, M. M., & Kuhn, J. (1997). Children's reactions to and memory for a stressful event: Influences of age, anatomical dolls, knowledge, and parental attachment. *Applied Developmental Science, 1,* 54–75.

Harvard Law Review Notes. (1985). The testimony of child sex abuse victims in sex abuse prosecutions: Two legislative innovations. *Harvard Law Review, 98,* 806–827.

Herman, J. L. (1981). *Father–daughter incest.* Cambridge, MA: Harvard University Press.

Herman, J. L., & Schatzow, E. (1987). Recovery and verification of memories of childhood sexual trauma. *Psychoanalytic Psychology, 4,* 1–14.

Howe, M. L., & Courage, M. L. (1993). On resolving the enigma of infantile amnesia. *Psychological Bulletin, 13,* 305–326.

Howe, M. L., Courage, M. L., & Peterson, C. (1995). Intrusions in preschoolers' recall of traumatic childhood events. *Psychonomic Bulletin and Review, 2,* 130–134.

Hyman, I. E., Husband, T. H., & Billings, F. J. (1995). False memories of childhood experiences. *Applied Cognitive Psychology, 9,* 181–197.

Johnson, M. K., Hashtroudi, S., & Lindsay, D. S. (1993). Source monitoring. *Psychological Bulletin, 114,* 3–28.

Kaminer, W. (1992). *I'm dysfunctional, you're dysfunctional.* Reading, MA: Addison-Wesley.

Leichtman, M. D., & Ceci, S. J. (1993). The problem of infantile amnesia: Lessons from fuzzy-trace theory. In M. L. Howe & R. Pasnak (Eds.), *Emerging themes in cognitive development: Vol. 1. Foundations* (pp. 195–213). New York: Springer-Verlag.

Lindsay, D. S., & Read, J. D. (1994). Psychotherapy and memories of childhood sexual abuse: A cognitive perspective. *Applied Cognitive Psychology, 8,* 281–338.

Lipmann, O. (1911). Pedagogical psychology of report. *Journal of Educational Psychology, 2,* 253–260.

Loftus, E. F. (1979). The malleability of memory. *American Scientist, 67,* 312–320.

Loftus, E. F. (1993). The reality of repressed memories. *American Psychologist, 48,* 518–537.

Loftus, E. F., & Ketchum, K. (1994). *The myth of repressed memory.* New York: St. Martin's Press.

Loftus, E. F., & Pickrell, J. E. (1995). The formation of false memories. *Psychiatric Annals, 25,* 720–725.

Loftus, E. F., Polonsky, S., & Fullilove, M. T. (1994). Memories of childhood sexual abuse: Remembering and repressing. *Psychology of Women Quarterly, 18,* 67–84.

Lynn, S. J., Lock, T. G., Myers, B., & Payne, D. G. (1997). Recalling the unrecallable: Should hypnosis be used to recover memories in psychotherapy? *Current Directions in Psychological Science, 6,* 79–83.

Malinoski, P., Lynn, S. J., Martin, D., Aronoff, A., Neufeld, J., & Gedeon, S. (1995, August). *Individual differences in early memory reports: An empirical investigation.* Paper presented at the 103rd Annual Convention of the American Psychological Association, New York.

Masson, J. M. (1992). *The assault on truth: Freud's suppression of the seduction theory.* New York: HarperCollins.

Mazzoni, G. (1998). Memory suggestibility and metacognition in child eyewitness testimony: The roles of source monitoring and self-efficacy. *European Journal of Psychology of Education, 13,* 43–60.

McCloskey, M., & Zaragoza, M. (1985). Misleading postevent information and memory for events: Arguments and evidence against the memory impairment hypothesis. *Journal of Experimental Psychology: General, 114,* 1–16.

Meltzoff, A. N. (1995). What infant memory tells us about infantile amnesia: Long-term recall and deferred imitation. *Journal of Experimental Child Psychology, 59,* 497–515.

Merritt, K. A., Ornstein, P. A., & Spicker, B. (1994). Children's memory for a salient medical procedure: Implications for testimony. *Pediatrics, 94,* 17–23.

Montoya, J. (1992). On truth and shielding in child abuse trials. *Hastings Law Journal, 43,* 1259–1319.

National Committee for the Prevention of Child Abuse. (1996, December). *Child sexual abuse* (No. 19) [Brochure]. Chicago: Author.

Nelson, K. (1996). *Language in cognitive development: The emergence of the mediated mind.* New York: Cambridge University Press.

NOW Legal Defense and Education Fund. (1992). *Legal remedies for adult survivors of incest and child sexual abuse* (Legal Resource Kit: Incest and Child Sexual Abuse). New York: Author.

Oates, K., & Shrimpton, S. (1991). Children's memories for stressful and nonstressful events. *Journal of Science, Medicine and the Law, 31,* 4–10.

Ofshe, R., & Watters, E. (1994). *Making monsters: False memories, psychotherapy, and sexual hysteria.* New York: Scribner's.

Ornstein, P. A., Ceci, S. J., & Loftus, E. F. (1996). Reply to the Alpert, Brown, and Courtois document: The science of memory and the practice of psychotherapy. In J. L. Alpert, L. S. Brown, S. J. Ceci, C. A. Courtois, E. F. Loftus, & P. A. Ornstein, *Working Group on Investigation of Memories of Childhood Abuse: Final report* (pp. 106–130). Washington, DC: American Psychological Association.

Ornstein, P. A., Shapiro, L. R., Clubb, P. A., Follmer, A., & Baker-Ward, L. (1997). The influence of prior knowledge on children's memory for salient medical experiences. In N. Stein, P. A. Ornstein, B. Tversky, & C. J. Brainerd (Eds.), *Memory for everyday and emotional events* (pp. 83–112.). Mahwah, NJ: Lawrence Erlbaum Associates.

O'Sullivan, J. T., Howe, M. L., & Marche, T. A. (1996). Children's beliefs about long-term retention. *Child Development, 67,* 2989–3009.

Peters, D. P. (1991). The influence of stress and arousal on the child witness. In J. Doris (Ed.), *The suggestibility of children's recollections: Implications for eyewitness testimony* (pp. 60–76). Washington, DC: American Psychological Association.

Pezdek, K., & Hodge, D. (1999). Planting false childhood memories: The role of event plausibility. *Child Development, 70,* 887–895.

Pillemer, D. B., & White, S. H. (1989). Childhood events recalled by children and adults. In H. W. Reese (Ed.), *Advances in child development and behavior* (Vol. 21, pp. 297–340). San Diego, CA: Academic Press.

Poole, D. A., & White, L. T. (1995). Tell me again and again: Stability and change in the repeated testimonies of children and adults. In M. S. Zaragoza, J. R. Graham, G. C. N. Hall, R. Hirschman, & Y. S. Ben-Porath (Eds.), *Memory and testimony in the child witness* (pp. 24–43). Thousand Oaks, CA: Sage.

Qin, J. J., Quas, J. A., Redlich, A. D., & Goodman, G. S. (1997). Children's eyewitness testimony: Memory development in the legal context. In N. Cowan (Ed.), *The development of memory in childhood* (pp. 301–341). Hove East Sussex, UK: Psychology Press.

Reyna, V. F. (1994). Interference effects in memory and reasoning: A fuzzy-trace theory analysis. In F. N. Dempster & C. J. Brainerd (Eds.), *New perspectives on interference and inhibition processes in cognition* (pp. 29–59). San Diego, CA: Academic Press.

Reyna, V. F., & Brainerd, C. J. (1995). Fuzzy-trace theory: An interim synthesis. *Learning and Individual Differences, 7,* 1–75.

Rovee-Collier, C. (1995). Time windows in cognitive development. *Developmental Psychology, 31,* 147–169.

Rovee-Collier, C., & Gerhardstein, P. (1997). Studies in developmental psychology. In N. Cowan (Ed.), *The development of memory in childhood* (pp. 5–39). Hove East Sussex, UK: Psychology Press.

Rush, F. (1980). *The best kept secret: Sexual abuse of children.* Englewood Cliffs, NJ: Prentice-Hall.

Steinem, G. (1992). *Revolution from within: A book of self-esteem.* Boston: Little, Brown.

Stern, W. (1910). Abstracts of lectures on the psychology of testimony and on the study of individuality. *American Journal of Psychology, 21,* 270–282.

Steward, M. (1989). *The development of a model interview for young child victims of sexual abuse* (Tech. Rep. No. 90CA1332). Washington, DC: U.S. Department of Health and Human Services.

Tizon, A. (1996, June 28). Wenatchee braces for sex-ring lawsuits. *The Seattle Times,* p. A1.

van der Kolk, B. A., & Fisler, R. E. (1995). Dissociation and the fragmentary nature of traumatic memories: Overview and exploratory study. *Journal of Traumatic Stress, 8,* 505–525.

Welch-Ross, M. K. (1995). An integrative model of the development of autobiographical memory. *Developmental Review, 15,* 338–365.

Zaragoza, M. (1991). Preschool children's susceptibility to memory impairment. In J. L. Doris (Ed.), *The suggestibility of children's recollections* (pp. 27–39). Washington, DC: American Psychological Association.

CHAPTER TWO

Current Directions
in False-Memory Research

Amy Tsai
Elizabeth Loftus
Danielle Polage
University of Washington

In commenting on John Dean's testimony in the investigation of Watergate and how it compared with the audiotapes that were later produced, Neisser (1982) stated, "The circumstances and the man conspired to favor exaggeration. . . . His ambition reorganized his recollections" (p. 157). Research has repeatedly shown that the imposition of forces both internal and external can serve to influence one's memory of events. Unlike the Watergate investigation, most researchers cannot use naturalistic observation, nor can they rely on a coincidence such as finding audiotapes to later verify whether events occurred as recalled. Experimental research on false memories has used several strategies for verification, such as testing memory using specific controlled stimuli, having participants keep accurate records of events for later testing, querying about memories before the age of 3 when childhood amnesia would prevent the recall of any true memories, or attempting to corroborate facts about the memory from other sources.

Armed with knowledge of which events are likely to be true, researchers have used these strategies to study how people might come to remember events that are false. The techniques used to test whether a false memory can be manufactured can be grouped into several main categories. Misinformation studies manipulate memory for particular details of an event by subtly suggesting that erroneous information is true. The misinformation studies were a springboard to a second class of studies testing memories for whole (complex) events. In the complex event literature, there have been a variety of techniques used to test whether false memories can be manufactured, including suggestive interviews (of adults and children), imagination exercises, use of bizarre items, and diary keeping.

All of these techniques rely on the use of a suggestive environment for stimulating memory creation, often with repetitive suggestion over time, and often in the presence of an authoritative source for the misleading information. Studies have been conducted on both adults and children. In this chapter, we review the memory creation techniques that have been used, their successfulness, and potential implications.

THE ORIGINAL MISINFORMATION STUDIES

Although psychologists have long looked at the question of what memories are and how to distinguish real memories from erroneous ones, false-memory research really took off with the advent of the misinformation technique. This technique used subtle false suggestion to encourage later faulty recall. (For a recent review of misinformation studies, see Ayers and Reder, 1998.)

In misinformation studies, first an event is observed, then false information is introduced, and then memory for the observed event is tested for distortion on the basis of the intervening misinformation. For example, Loftus, Miller, and Burns (1978) ran a series of experiments in which undergraduates watched slides depicting an automobile–pedestrian accident. When misleading information was introduced, participants' recognition of facts was worse than when either consistent or irrelevant information was introduced, particularly when the misleading information was introduced just before testing, rather than immediately following the slides.

Perhaps spurred by the increasing numbers of court cases in which a false childhood memory could have a disastrous effect (e.g., in cases involving possible repression of childhood trauma), later researchers in false memory studied the suggestibility of childhood memories. Ceci, Ross, and Toglia (1987) found that young children (3 to 4 years old) were particularly susceptible to suggestion, and furthermore, the effects were greater when the source of the misinformation was an adult rather than another child. Thus, early on, authority figures played an important role in the creation of memory distortions.

One consideration in the misinformation design is that it attempts to change memory for details of an event, rather than creating a whole event itself. Thus the next set of studies tried to push the boundaries of memory distortion and plant whole false memories.

COMPLEX FAMILY EVENTS: REPETITIVE SUGGESTION

Loftus and Coan (as described in Loftus & Pickrell, 1995) induced a person to remember a complex childhood event that did not occur. A 14-year-old boy was instructed to recall details over 5 days regarding four events involving his mother and older brother, of which one was false (as verified by his family). The fictitious event involved the boy having been lost in a particular shopping mall when he was 5 years old and being rescued by an elderly man. Over time, even though given an option to state that he could not remember, the boy began to recall more and more details about the fictitious event in his writings. In a subsequent interview, he rated the false event as more likely to have occurred than all but one of the true events and was unable to identify which event was the false one. During debriefing, he was reluctant to believe the truth.

Using a similar methodology, Loftus and Pickrell (1995) gave undergraduate students a mix of true and false events and asked them to recall details over several days. They found that 6 out of 24 participants erroneously believed part or all of the false event. These investigators also showed that descriptions for the true events tended to have more words than the false event did.

Researchers in complex event creation have also studied whether more bizarre events can be falsely recalled. Choosing events that were less likely to have occurred, Hyman, Husband, and Billings (1995), in the second of two experiments, used three unusual events: spilling a punch bowl at a wedding reception, evacuating a grocery store when sprinklers went off, and releasing the parking brake of a car in a parking lot and hitting something. Introductory psychology students participated in three interviews every other day during which they were asked to remember and describe three to five true events (again, solicited from parents) and one of the three false events. Recall was defined as the point at which participants' descriptions included some false information or elaborations consistent with the false information. Hyman et al. found that there was high recall for true events, increasing from 89% to 95% of events recalled by the third interview. Recall was considerably less for false events but had some success nevertheless. For false events, there was no erroneous recall after the first interview, but it increased to 25% by the third interview.

Some researchers have used even more extreme events to more closely simulate the kinds of situations one might falsely recall in real court settings. Pezdek, Finger, and Hodge (1997) asked adolescents to recall details about true and false events. For the false events, they suggested to the participants that they had engaged in religious activities that were consistent or inconsistent with their denomination (Jewish or Catholic) when they were 8 years old. Ten out of 29 Catholics and 3 out of 22 Jews remembered at least one false event. It is also notable that 3 participants (all Catholic) falsely recalled the implausible event involving the inconsistent denomination. Those who recalled a false event used more words for the true events and rated the true events higher on clarity and confidence than the false events.

These types of suggestive interview studies rely on a family member to provide an authoritative source of corroboration for the false event, and the participant is then pressured to believe the false event over multiple sessions. This technique has also been successfully applied to children, which extends the usefulness of this research to the veracity of child witnesses, who could be particularly susceptible to leading questions from adult figures.

In investigating the effects of suggestion on children, Ceci, Huffman, and Smith (1994) repeatedly interviewed children over 10 weeks and asked them to recall details about events that their mothers had allegedly supplied (in fact, some of the events were false). Ceci et al. (1994) found that 58% of the children recalled details about one or more false events, with 25% of the children recalling a majority of the false events.

A field test of the suggestive interview was conducted by Ofshe (see Wright, 1994) in the case of Paul Ingram. Ingram was convicted of raping his daughters following their recovery of memories of the abuse and a confession by Ingram. Although working for the prosecution, Ofshe questioned the veracity of the confession because it was written after intensive interrogations that followed dissociative relaxation techniques, hypothetical imaginings, and extreme pressure by the interrogators to recall the abuse. To test his theory, Ofshe invented a scenario in which Ingram had made his son and daughter have sex together while he watched. Unaware that the event was false and that he was participating in an experiment, Ingram was told to imagine the scene. He came back with many details about the event the next day. In a second phase of the experiment that tested his confidence and the truthfulness of his belief in the memories, Ingram was confronted for several hours. The confrontation was "intense" and Mr. Ingram would not agree that the invented event was false. Because this study could not ever be replicated in a laboratory setting, the Ingram case provides one extreme example of how repeated suggestive interviews can have drastic effects on memories with significant real-world implications.

These studies show that repeated suggestive conversation by authoritative and credible figures can lead to the creation of memories for false events. Other researchers have sought to test the boundaries of this phenomenon by exploring whether milder, less drastic measures can also work to create false memories.

IMAGINATION INFLATION

Telling someone that his or her mother provided descriptions of events from his or her childhood when in fact the events never occurred might be considered a strong suggestion, and research substantiates that this scenario can effectively lead to the creation of false memories. Could less drastic steps make a person remember something that never happened to them? Researchers have investigated whether simply having people imagine that they had experiences that they previously denied having can effect a change in memory.

Researchers studying imagination inflation first ask participants to rate the likelihood that certain events happened to them when they were young. Participants are asked to imagine some of the events that they believe did not happen, much like the original complex event studies had participants generate details (and therefore think) about the events and write them down. Then they again rate the likelihood that the events happened. The main difference from the original complex event studies is that the imagination inflation technique makes it easier to ask about multiple false events, and the imagination takes place in fewer sessions. In addition, the end goal is to change perception of the likelihood that the events happened, rather than measuring the amount of information recalled about the fictitious event.

The first study in which researchers used imagination inflation illustrates the basic design. Garry, Manning, Loftus, and Sherman (1996) had participants take a Life Events Inventory (LEI), which asked them to indicate the likelihood that certain events had happened to them before the age of 10. Two weeks later, a participant was told to "picture" some of the events and answer questions about them. They then filled out the LEI again under the pretext of the initial survey having been lost. Garry et al. found that most scores did not change, but likelihood ratings were more likely to increase for imagined versus not-imagined items (34% vs. 25%, respectively).

Garry et al. (1996) posited several explanations for the imagination inflation effect. First, under an availability hypothesis, if cueing the false event makes it more readily accessible, then the person may mistake ease of accessibility for a real memory. Imagination inflation is consistent with findings that imagination can increase people's sense of probability for future events, just as it affected the likelihood estimates of past events in this study. As noted by Johnson and Sherman (as cited in Garry et al., 1996), the future is tied to a changing past, thus even though predicting the probability of future events does not require memory, to a certain extent it may rely on memory just as estimates of past events do. Second, it is possible that participants interpreted the question more broadly the second time it was asked, thereby including the imagined event within the purview of the question whereas earlier they might have considered it not to be. A third possibility is the phenomenon of hypermnesia, in which people tend to recall more information over successive tests. Thus, the design may encourage increasingly accurate recall of past childhood events. Whichever explanation may be the correct one, Garry et al. noted a need for caution in situations such as police interrogations or sexual abuse therapy, in which repeated imagining of a scenario could erroneously increase a person's belief that a certain event happened.

The initial imagination inflation researchers asked about the likelihood of childhood events. Can imagination also create memories for things that happened a short time ago? Goff and Roediger (1998) conducted two experiments in which undergraduate students heard statements describing 96 simple actions, and then some participants performed or imagined performing the action. At varying intervals later (24 hours in the first experiment and from 10 minutes up to 2 weeks in the second experiment), subjects imagined performing the actions one, three, or five times. Two weeks after the first session, participants had to identify actions from the first day and identify their source (heard, done, or imagined). As number of imaginings per item increased, participants were more likely to recall that they had performed an action in the first session when in fact they had not, regardless of whether the statement had even been heard or not. Thus, imagining recent activities can increase belief in having done those activities.

Thomas and Loftus (1998) took Goff and Roediger's (1998) multiple-task approach and addressed the question of whether imagination of bizarre events or actions could create false memories. They presented action statements to 210 undergraduate students who performed or imagined them during an initial encoding phase. The statements described actions that were either familiar or bizarre. In a second session, 24 hours later, the participants imagined performing a series of actions. Finally, 2 weeks after the second session, they were tested on their memory of the original actions. Thomas and Loftus found that the more times subjects imagined an action in Session 2, the more likely they were to erroneously report that they performed the action in Session 1. This result was apparent for both familiar and bizarre actions. Secondary results revealed that other measures of memory did demonstrate differences between familiar and bizarre actions. Thus, Thomas and Loftus met with some success in affecting memories for more recent bizarre events.

Dream Experiences

Researchers using the imagination technique have also used dream interpretation as the suggestive influence. In an initial study, Mazzoni and Loftus (1996) analyzed the suggestibility of dream material using a word list. First, participants brought in a description of one of their dreams and were given a list of words to study. On the following day, participants were told that the original list had been lost, and 14 possible words had been gleaned from other participants. In this list were embedded two words from the participant's dream report and two from another participant's dream report. The participant was asked to indicate which words he or she thought was on the original list. In a third session the next day, participants were presented with a new list taking the 14 words and adding two more from each of the two dream reports. Participants then had to recall which words were on the original list. Mazzoni and Loftus (1996) found high false recognition for dream words that sometimes even matched the recognition of true words. Participants also reported remembering the words from their own dream that were on the list rather than just knowing the words were on the list (words from other people's dreams tended to receive the "knowing" response more often). Further testing showed that self-generated stories have a similar effect on memory, but the effect is not as strong as with dream material (Mazzoni, Vannucci, & Loftus, 1999).

Realizing that dreams could be powerful suggestive material, the researchers extended dream work to the imagination inflation design. Mazzoni, Lombardo, Malvagia, and Loftus (described in Mazzoni & Loftus, 1998) had participants complete an LEI, allegedly to study early childhood memories. The LEI contained three critical items: getting lost in a public space, being abandoned by parents, finding oneself lonely and lost in an unfamiliar place. Participants who rated the critical items more unlikely were brought back 3 to 4 weeks later and completed an identical LEI. In a typical imagination inflation study, participants are asked to imagine the events occurred. Instead, Mazzoni and Loftus (1998) used alleged dream therapy for the imagination session. Between the two LEI sessions, some participants were solicited to participate in an allegedly completely different experiment on sleep and dreaming with a different experimenter. Participants brought a description of a dream to a 30-minute therapy session with a clinical psychologist. The psychologist (a well-known practicing clinical psychologist in Italy) interpreted the dream by indicating that the critical events from the LEI were likely to have occurred. As part of this suggestive interpretation, the psychologist related specific dream items to possible feelings, tried to induce the participant's agreement of his interpretation, provided a global interpretation of dream meaning, and suggested that childhood events were commonly associated with the participant's kind of dream report (the critical items in particular). He then suggested that other individuals' dreams have indicated that those events occurred, tried to again induce agreement, and finally stated that the events may have happened to the participant (if the event was not recalled, he suggested it was due to the unpleasant nature of the event). Mazzoni and Loftus (1998) found strong support for a dream effect. More participants who underwent the dream therapy session increased the likelihood ratings of all three critical items on the LEI than did control participants who did not have the dream therapy. Of those ratings that increased, the strongest item was getting lost in a public place, with 88% of dream and only 43% of nondream participants increasing that rating.

Like other false-memory research, dream interpretation has also been tested with more bizarre events to address the concern that the critical items were too commonplace and easily suggested. In a follow-up study, Mazzoni, Lombardo, Malvagia, and Loftus (1999) extended the time between dream therapy and the second LEI to 4 weeks instead of 2, and added three critical items that were more unusual: going through a very dangerous situation, having one's life severely threatened, and being rescued from a dangerous situation. Results showed that confidence of occurrence was again increased for each critical event. The biggest difference was in the situation of one's life being severely threatened: 66% of dream participants increased their likelihood ratings compared with 12% of nondream participants. Thus, a single session with an authoritative therapist using suggestible dream material can have a significant impact on the creation of false memories that lasts at least 4 weeks. In the future, researchers might test the duration of the effects of imagination inflation using the standard imagination sessions.

Changing Behaviors

Researchers have also used imagination effects to effect positive change in behaviors. For example, Mickel, Manning, and Loftus (see Mickel, 1997) investigated whether repeatedly imagining healthy behaviors would lead to an increase in estimates of performance. After indicating how often they performed certain healthy behaviors in the past week and on average, participants were brought back 3 to 5 weeks later and imagined two of three critical healthy behaviors. Then, after another week, they imagined one of the items a second time (repeated imaginings condition) and then restated how often they performed the healthy behaviors. Imagining increased estimates of two of the three critical items, flossing and eating vegetables, particularly for past week estimates. Although one cannot tell whether behavior actually changed in the second week, the results show that participants were at least more likely to think it did after imagining the events.

Hannula (1998) conducted an honors project at the University of Washington that similarly investigated the influence of imagination on behavior but from the standpoint of decreasing negative behaviors. First, participants filled out a 30-item health habits questionnaire indicating past week and month and average week and month behaviors, with caffeine consumption as the critical item. Participants who rated the caffeine critical item between 5 and 15 returned for the imagination session approximately 2 weeks later and then for another imagination session 1 week after that. Imagination exercises were either long or short and specifically suggested a replacement for caffeinated drinks or just a general suggestion to replace it with a healthy alternative. Two weeks later, the participants returned to complete the health habits questionnaire again. In this final session, participants were asked whether they thought their behavior had changed and how often they expected to perform each task in an average week, and then if their estimates differed from their original responses, they were asked why. The control group filled out the health habits questionnaires and the posttest questions but did not have any intervening imagination sessions.

For estimates of caffeine consumption in an average week, the imagination groups were more likely to report a decreased amount than the control group. Although the imagination groups behaved in a consistent direction with past week estimates, they were not significantly different from controls who also tended to decrease consumption estimates. Among the imagination scripts, the long script had the greatest effect on past week estimates, and the short script with general recommendations showed the least decrease. Unexpectedly, the short script with a recommendation resulted in the greatest decrease for caffeinated beverage consumption in an average week. Because both past week and average week consumption decreased for the imagination group, it could not be ascertained whether the behaviors actually decreased or whether participants only thought they did (perhaps because they mistook the imagined events for real behavior); a third possibility is that participants were giving a socially desirable response.

DIARY KEEPING

A similar technique to the repeated suggestive interview discussed earlier relies instead on participants keeping their own diaries of the events. In this way, the problem of whether memory estimates of behavior differ from actual behavior is eliminated. Whereas in suggestive interviews, investigators have questioned participants about childhood events, in the more recent diary studies, researchers have investigated the ability to distort recent events in a person's history. Loftus and Polage (1999) compared participants' actual renditions of recent events as described in a diary with the participants' memory for these events after imagining alternate outcomes. Participants in this experiment were told that the purpose of the study was to investigate how people evaluate situations that were experienced firsthand versus situations that were experienced by others. They signed up in pairs and were asked to keep a diary for 1 week. Participants were asked to provide actual events that happened that day, a realistic wish for that day, an event that they wished had not happened but did and a preferred outcome for that event, and an event that happened to their partner. The focus of this paper was the wish-had-nots; the rest of the data is currently being analyzed. Participants returned for a second session in which they imagined that several events had happened to them. The experimenter guided them through imagery by asking probing questions. They were told the experimenters were interested in how they felt about events that had happened to them versus events that had happened to other subjects. They were asked to involve themselves in the imagery and to close their eyes if it facilitated image creation. Participants were reminded that several of the events might seem familiar to them because they were taken from their journals. They were also reminded that the experimenters had included their partner's excerpts about them (which was not true) so they might recognize an event as theirs, even though they didn't remember writing about it in their journal. They were asked to immerse themselves in the images, to imagine the event in first person as if it had happened to them, and to use as many personal references as possible. If the image was one they recognized as true from their own journals, they were asked to use details consistent with those written in their journal. After each imagination, participants were asked to summarize their images. After a filler task, they were asked to fill out a questionnaire that included the true events, in addition to the preferred outcomes for the wish-had-nots, and they were asked to indicate which events had happened to them the week they kept a journal.

From their journals, four of the wish-had-not items were chosen, two of which were imagined as if the preferred outcome had happened and two of which were controls. The primary experimenter designed questionnaires and imagination sessions individually for each participant. Overall, imagining the preferred event decreased the likelihood of participants responding "yes" to the original event (88% "yes" for controls vs. 68%) and increased the likelihood of their responding "yes" to the preferred event (45% "yes" for controls vs. 53%). In addition, participants who said "yes" to the preferred event happening and "no" to the actual event happening occurred in 20% of the imagination participants and less than 3% in controls. Following is a sample of one participant's response as recorded in her original diary entry: "Today our church celebrated a couple of birthdays and then we had some cake and cookies. I ate some of the treats to celebrate with them, but wish I had not because I am trying to watch what I eat. If I hadn't eaten them I would have felt better, healthier." In the imagination session, the participant imagined the event as she wished it had happened (but in reality had not): "Your church celebrates some people's birthdays and they have lots of cake and cookies. You decide not to eat any because you are watching what you eat." In a recognition test, the participant rated the original event as false and the imagined version as true. When she was presented with the contradiction of two questions referring to the same event, one of which was written about in her journal, and asked to clarify which event had actually occurred, the participant responded, "I was at my church and was celebrating bdays. There were cake and cookies and I had not eaten any to watch my weight. I remember it because I enjoy spending time with them especially for special occasions." So, it seems that it is not only possible to convince people of things that have happened in the distant past but also to alter their recollections of the recent past. It seems that participants remembered events in ways that were consistent with the way they wished things had happened instead of in the way they actually did.

Other researchers have used a diary technique to investigate whether recall of past events can change future behavior. For example, Tsai, Polage, and Loftus (1997) began studies in which participants kept track of their eating and drinking behavior for a week in diaries. Participants then returned to the laboratory where half of them underwent an imagination exercise, followed by everyone answering a memory questionnaire of the food and drink consumed during the past week. This activity was followed by another week of journal keeping to track any changes in future behavior following the imagination manipulation. In this particular study, participants who imagined drinking water were significantly more likely to inflate their estimates of how many times they drank water in the previous week compared with nonimagination controls. Unfortunately, this result was not consistent across other consumption measures (such as amount of fruit eaten), nor were there consistent patterns of change in future behavior observed in Week 2.

Nevertheless, the advantage of the journal-keeping technique is that one can have a relatively accurate record of actual behaviors, rather than having to presume that the original measurement of the event (such as the LEI or parents' confirmation of childhood events) is an accurate one.

SUMMARY OF FALSE MEMORY TECHNIQUES

Suggestive interviews, being the strongest suggestive environment, have shown that if the suggested false information comes from an authoritative source, and pressure to recall that information is applied repetitively from a third party, then memory distortion can occur strongly and reliably. Taking each of the components of the suggestive interview apart, we note that other techniques shed light on which aspects may be necessary or sufficient for false-memory creation to occur. In diary studies, we see that the repetitive suggestions do not have to come from an authoritative third party; they can be internally generated. In the imagination studies, we see that the false events do not have to be suggested by an authoritative source such as one's parents; merely imagining the event can change one's assessment of the likelihood of that event. Finally, the recent dream study shows that a one-trial suggestive interview from a powerful therapist figure can sway one's assessment of the likelihood of childhood events.

Thus, the most effective situation for the creation of a false memory appears to be one in which the person is given a reason to believe the event happened (because a relative backs up the story or because a therapist says it must have happened) and is then pressured over multiple sessions to believe the memory (either through interviews or diary keeping). However, milder forms of pressure, such as the act of imagining the false event, can sway assessments of the likelihood of the event; repetitive sessions can be done by self-report diaries or by a third party; and in the absence of repetitive sessions, a single strong authoritative source can be sufficient to create belief in false events.

CONCLUSION

It is clear that false memories have been created in the laboratory. One might argue that they are the result of social desirability, in which the subject claims to have a memory of an event only because he or she believes the experimenter desires that response. Or one might argue that participants are agreeing that the false circumstances are possible without having an actual memory of the event (they might "know" it happened rather than "remember" it happened). Nevertheless, it is indisputable that people's memories can be affected by suggestion presented in various forms from various sources.

REFERENCES

Ayers, M. S., & Reder, L. M. (1998). A theoretical review of the misinformation effect: Predictions from an activation-based memory model. *Psychonomic Bulletin & Review, 5,* 1–21.

Ceci, S. J., Huffman, M. L. C., & Smith, E. (1994). Repeatedly thinking about a non-event: Source misattributions among preschoolers. *Consciousness & Cognition: An International Journal, 3,* 388–407.

Ceci, S. J., Ross, D. F., & Toglia, M. P. (1987). Suggestibility of children's memory: Psycholegal implications. *Journal of Experimental Psychology: General, 116,* 38–49.

Garry, M., Manning, C. G., Loftus, E. F., & Sherman, S. J. (1996). Imagination inflation: Imagining a childhood event inflates confidence that it occurred. *Psychonomic Bulletin & Review, 3,* 208–214.

Goff, L. M., & Roediger, H. L. (1998). Imagination inflation for action events: Repeated imaginings lead to illusory recollections. *Memory & Cognition, 26,* 20–33.

Hannula, D. (1998). *Does imagination influence behavior or only our perception of behavior?* Unpublished honor's thesis, University of Washington.

Hyman, I. E., Husband, T. H., & Billings, F. J. (1995). False memories of childhood experiences. *Applied Cognitive Psychology, 9,* 181–197.

Loftus, E. F., Miller, D. G., & Burns, H. J. (1978). Semantic integration of verbal information into a visual memory. *Journal of Experimental Psychology: Human Learning & Memory, 4,* 19–31.

Loftus, E. F., & Pickrell, J. E. (1995). The formation of false memories. *Psychiatric Annals, 25,* 720–725.

Loftus, E. F., & Polage, D. C. (1999). Repressed memories: When are they real? How are they false? *The Psychiatric Clinics of North America, 22,* 61–71.

Mazzoni, G. A. L., & Loftus, E. F. (1996). When dreams become reality. *Consciousness & Cognition, 5,* 442–462.

Mazzoni, G. A. L., & Loftus, E. F. (1998). Dreaming, believing, and remembering. In J. De-Rivera & T. R. Sarbin (Eds.), *Believe in Imaginings* (pp. 145–156). Washington, DC: American Psychological Association.

Mazzoni, G. A. L., Lombardo, P., Malvagia, S., & Loftus, E. F. (1999). Dream interpretation and false beliefs. *Professional Psychology: Research and Practice, 30,* 45–50.

Mazzoni, G. A. L., Vannucci, M., & Loftus, E. F. (1999). Misremembering story material. *Legal and Criminological Psychology, 4,* 93–110.

Mickel, N. (1997). *Does imagining healthy behaviors increase estimates of performance?* Unpublished Master of Arts thesis, University of Washington.

Neisser, U. (1982). John Dean's memory: A case study. In U. Neisser (Ed.), *Memory observed: Remembering in natural contexts* (pp. 139–159). New York: Freeman.

Pezdek, K., Finger, K., & Hodge, D. (1997). Planting false childhood memories: The role of event plausibility. *Psychological Science, 8,* 437–441.

Thomas, A. K., & Loftus, E. F. (1999). *Imagination inflation for familiar and bizarre action statements.* Unpublished manuscript, University of Washington.

Tsai, A. C., Polage, D. C., & Loftus, E. F. (1997). *Food for thought: Effect of imagining on memory and future performance.* Unpublished research, University of Washington.

Wright, L. (1994). *Remembering Satan.* New York: Knopf.

CHAPTER THREE

The Changing Face of Memory and Self

MARK A. OAKES
IRA E. HYMAN, JR.
Western Washington University

> *To say to him "change yourself" means to demand that every-*
> *thing should change, even the past.*
> —Nietzche

Who am I? At some point all of us have asked this question, looking for answers in all the obvious places: Am I a product of my environment, my genes, my family, or my friends? Part of who we are is defined by our past and our memories of our past. Using a narrative framework, people can express their diverse and complicated identities through the stories they tell. With one story, people can communicate their past, present, and future. They can describe their goals, their loves, their philosophy of life, and the moral guidelines they follow. Through this system, people can string together several categories of self-representation into a single tale or multiple stories that they share with others. To create these identity narratives, people must be able to access a vast network of information about their lives. Thus, memories play a vital role in the search for self. Clearly, memory and narrative do not encompass the entire definition of self. James (1890) and Neisser (1988), among many others, have argued that the self is composed of a variety of information garnered from several sources. Nonetheless, the remembered self becomes the basic fabric of self that is communicated to others and used to plan for the future.

But memory is an unreliable foundation on which to build an identity. People forget events. The retrieval of memories is dependent on current circumstances. Memories may be distorted by additional information. In addition, people may create entirely false memories. Remembering is a constructive process, and although the self is constructed through memories, the construction of memories is also influenced by the self. An individual's self-concept may drive the selection of memories that are recalled and may contribute to the distortion of the past. For example, an individual may think of himself or herself as hard working. When describing the past, that person will retrieve events that fit with that description and not events that suggest laziness. Other events may be modified to fit with the hard-working description. Consequently, the types of memories that we remember and how we tell our self narratives may be altered to reflect the life themes that we have adopted. Thus, the relationship between memories and self is circular: Memories define and shape the self while the self shapes the memories that are retrieved.

Imagine what happens if an individual suddenly remembers a past event that does not correspond with the self concept. Would this new piece of the puzzle change the life narrative, the identity, the self? Would the person reject the memory and deny the reality? Consider an example from a work of fiction, *A Thousand Acres,* by Jane Smiley (1991). Ginny, the main character, is suddenly informed by her sister, Rose, that they were both sexually abused by their father. Ginny, however, does not remember any abuse and contests her sister's suggestions. Rose counters by reciting details of how she used to watch their father go into Ginny's room at night for extended periods of time, using her clock to check when he entered and left. Ginny resisted and claimed memory for shorter visits than what Rose reports. Later, however, during a visit to her father's house, Ginny laid down on the same bed she used as a child. With a flash of emotional clarity, Ginny's memory flooded back to her: "Lying here, I knew that he had been in there with me, that my father had lain with me on that bed, that I had looked at the top of his head, at his balding spot in the brown grizzled hair . . ." (Smiley, 1991, p. 229). Eventually Ginny rose from the bed and left her parents' house, and she thought to herself that "a new life, yet another new life, had begun early in the day" (p. 229). Smiley's account of Ginny's memory highlights the relationship between memory and identity. Her new life begins with the recovery of a memory. Thus, the change in memory can affect an individual's entire understanding of self. A change in the past changes the present. In Smiley's story, not only did the revelation affect Ginny's sense of self, but it also affected her relationship with her sister, Rose, who had always thought that the abuse, even when not part of the conversation, was an experience that they shared. Thus, memories define not only the self but also the relationship of the individual to others, defining families, friends, social groups, and culture. When memory changes, people change how they conceive of themselves and their relationships with others.

Although Ginny and her memories are the fictional creation of Jane Smiley, like much fiction they represent the experiences that many real individuals have. As has been documented several times recently, people discover memories for events of which they believe they were previously unaware. This can even happen with traumatic experiences such as child abuse (Schooler, Bendiksen, & Ambadar, 1997; Williams, 1995). When people discover such experiences in their past, it affects their current understanding of self, alters their plans for the future, and impacts the most important relationships in their lives.

The impact of the discovered memories will be felt whether the events truly were experienced, forgotten, and only recently remembered, or whether the memories have been created through memory construction. This idea is important to note, for just as people can recover memories of traumatic childhood experiences, they can also create false memories. Pendergrast (1995) has told the stories of individuals who have discovered memories that were later confirmed by external sources and of individuals who recovered memories that they eventually came to believe were false. In both cases, the self concept was dramatically affected as people began to think of themselves as abuse survivors. In both cases, relationships with family members were affected. People cannot easily and reliably distinguish between recovered true memories and created false memories (Hyman & Pentland, 1996). What people know is that the memories are their memories—thus, they act on the memories they possess, and the self and family relationships are reshaped.

In this chapter, we review the recent research on creating complete false memories, outline a theory of the processes involved in memory creation, describe some new research on those processes, and finally return for a discussion of ramifications of false memories on the self concept. If self and memory codetermine each other, how comfortable can anyone feel in the conceptualization of self, knowing that some of the memories that create the self may be false?

RESEARCH ON FALSE CHILDHOOD MEMORIES

Memory researchers have studied errors in memory for a variety of materials: word lists (Roediger & McDermott, 1995), short stories (Bartlett, 1932), songs (Hyman & Rubin, 1990), and personal experiences (e.g.,

Barclay & DeCooke, 1988; Neisser, 1982). Some of the classic research on memory errors has investigated eyewitness memory and the misinformation effect (e.g. Belli, 1989; Lindsay, 1990; Loftus, 1979; Loftus, Donders, Hoffman, & Schooler, 1989; McCloskey & Zaragoza, 1985; Zaragoza & Lane, 1994). The *misinformation effect* is defined as the process by which people first experience an event (e.g., they watch a video of a car accident), then they are given misleading postevent information or misinformation (they are told the car went past a stop sign when it actually was shown passing a yield sign), and finally they incorporate the misinformation into their recollections of the event when they are later tested. These studies illustrate that misinformation provided after the event occurred can alter what people remember about an event.

The results of these misinformation studies have been applied to therapy situations in which suggestions about the past are made (Lindsay & Read, 1994; Loftus, 1993). For example, consider a person who has experienced a benign childhood (the original event). Several years later someone suggests that abuse may have occurred during childhood (the misinformation). Eventually, after several such suggestions, the person includes abuse as a part of the story of childhood. In Jane Smiley's fictional example with Ginny, Rose's suggestions of abuse could have been strong enough to mislead her sister into creating a memory. In addition, Ginny was in her childhood house, a place that cued numerous childhood memories. When Ginny's growing animosity toward her father and Rose's suggestions about sexual abuse are combined with true childhood memories, Ginny entered a state of mind that was very conducive to memory creation.

Such misinformation studies, however, did not provide clear evidence that a false memory of a complete event can be created through recurring suggestions. There are several differences between misinformation experiments and the creation of false childhood memories that make this comparison risky (Hyman, Husband, & Billings, 1995). First, misinformation experiments demonstrate that aspects of an event can be created in response to misleading suggestions, but not that entire life events can be created in response to misleading suggestions. In addition, in most of the misinformation studies, the event is not related to the self nor is the self involved in the event, whereas for false childhood memories, the self is intimately involved. Finally, in misinformation studies, the participants usually have little or no emotional involvement with the event, whereas in the creation of false childhood memories, the event may be very emotional. All of these differences make the creation of false childhood memories less likely than the introduction of errors to a memory.

In response to these concerns in generalizing the misinformation effect studies, several researchers have altered the misinformation methodology and come to a general working method for studying false memories (Ceci, Huffman, Smith, & Loftus, 1994; Ceci, Loftus, Leichtman, & Bruck, 1994; Hyman & Billings, 1998; Hyman et al., 1995; Hyman & Pentland, 1996; Loftus & Pickrell, 1995; Pezdek, Finger, & Hodge, 1997). For the most part, researchers request from family members information about events that occurred during the participant's childhood. The participant is then asked to try to recall these true events along with a false event—an event that the researchers are fairly sure did not happen to the participant. During a series of interviews, the false event is presented as if it is also a true event that was obtained from the initial family solicitation. The participants are usually interviewed repeatedly about both the true and false events and told their memories will improve over time. The most meaningful result of this sort of study is how the participants respond to the false event: Do the participants come to believe that the event took place sometime during their childhood? Do they elaborate on the false event by importing details not contained in the original presentation of the false event? Do they contend the event is a personal memory? If this is the case, it would be evidence for the creation of an entire, self-involved, and somewhat emotional memory.

For example, Hyman et al. (1995) used this methodology in a study involving the childhood memories of college students. Through surveys sent to the students' parents, the researchers obtained descriptions of true childhood events involving the students. When the surveys were returned, the researchers asked the students to participate in a series of interviews investigating their memory for early childhood experiences. In each of three interviews (separated by 1 day), the students were asked to remember several true events plus one false event. For all the events, the interviewer provided the students with a basic description (including the age at which the event occurred, the event, a few actions, other people involved, and a location) and asked the students what they remembered about the event. Three different false events were used in this study. For example, one was called the *punch bowl event:* When you were 6 years old, you were at the wedding of a friend of the family. You were running around with some other kids when you bumped into the table the punch bowl was sitting on, and it spilled on the parents of the bride. All of the false events were self-involving and would have been somewhat emotional at the time of the event, although none were traumatic events.

In general, the results of the this study showed that participants recalled a majority of the true events in the first interview and remembered even more of the true events over time. There are two ways to explain the increased recall of the true events. First, by thinking about the events over a period of time, the students provided themselves with additional memory cues that led to the recollection of previously unretrieved memories. Another possibility is that the participants created, rather than recalled, memories that matched the cues provided in the interviews. One cannot say whether this recovery of memory for the true experience represents actual memories or the creation of memories.

Regarding the false events, no participants remembered the false event on its initial presentation; however, by the third interview, 25% of the students (13 students) reported remembering the event. Six students reported memories that were very clear and included the critical information (such as turning over the punch bowl) as well as consistent elaborations (such as their parents being upset). Five of the reports were less clear; the students included little of the critical suggested information although they elaborated in a consistent fashion. Two of the students created clear images, but they were not positive about whether they were remembering or simply imagining the events that had been suggested to them.

Although Hyman et al. (1995) used only college students in their study, other researchers have studied varying populations (e.g., preschool children, adults, teenagers) and different false events and have found similar results (Ceci, Huffman, et al., 1994; Ceci, Loftus, et al., 1994; Loftus & Pickrell, 1995; Pezdek et al., 1997). Still other researchers have shown that suggestions that are not based on parent or family information have the necessary demand characteristics to create false memories (Kelley, Amodio, & Lindsay, 1996; Lindsay, 1997; Loftus, 1997). People will create false memories of childhood experiences. These false memories can be clear, somewhat emotional, self-involved, and holistic.

Nonetheless, questions of generalizability still remain. Spilling a punch bowl at a wedding is not the same as being sexually abused. To this point, no researcher has attempted to have participants create memories of being sexually abused. For ethical reasons, it is unlikely that anyone ever will: If memories impact one's self-concept and family relationships whether the memories are true or false, then experimentally inducing such memories would be atrocious. Although this fact makes generalizing to sexual abuse memories difficult, it is not impossible. First, real-world cases often provide dramatic evidence that individuals can create memories of a great variety of events. For example, two boys in Chicago recently confessed to murdering another child after being aggressively interviewed by police. Physical evidence that was discovered later indicated that the boys could not have committed the crime. Second, an understanding of the factors that affect memory creation and the processes involved in memory creation will allow some generalization to situations that share characteristics.

FACTORS CONTRIBUTING
TO FALSE-MEMORY CREATION

Thus, research on false memories has moved to the study of factors that make memory creation more or less likely to occur. First, Hyman and his colleagues (Hyman & Billings, 1998; Hyman et al., 1995) found that students' responses in an initial interview predicted who would eventually create false memories. Individuals who talked about related self-knowledge were more likely to create false memories than individuals who did not describe self-knowledge. This fact indicates that individuals construct false memories by combining the false suggestions with true information from their own pasts, which makes it difficult to identify a false memory because it contains some true information. Second, Hyman and Pentland (1996) ascertained that mental imagery increases the probability of creating a false memory. Individuals who created and described images of false events were more likely to create false memories. In addition, individual differences among participants also plays a part in the creation of false childhood memories. Hyman and Billings (1998) found that false-memory creation is related to the Dissociative Experiences Scale ($r = .48$) and the Creative Imagination Scale ($r = .38$). Pezdek et al. (1997) found that the plausibility of the event also plays a role. Participants are more likely to create false memories of events that match their self-schemas and are thus more plausible.

These researchers all relied on the basic methodology of false childhood memory research. Unfortunately, this methodology is both difficult to perform and intrusive. Thus, psychologists have been exploring a variety of different methods that allow the investigation of the processes involved in false-memory creation.

A THEORY OF FALSE-MEMORY CREATION

Hyman and Kleinknecht (1999) suggested three processes that are involved in the creation of false childhood memories: plausibility judgments, memory construction, and source-monitoring errors of claiming the constructed narrative as a personal memory. For a person to create a false memory, the suggested event needs to be plausible. In other words, the event needs to be something that the person is willing to believe could have happened to him or her. For example, some participants in Hyman's studies (Hyman & Billings, 1998; Hyman et al., 1995; Hyman & Pentland, 1996) did not create memories of spilling a punch bowl at a wedding because they believed that they had never attended a wedding as child. They refused to accept the event as a plausible personal experience. Similarly, Pezdek et al. (1997) found that less plausible events are less likely to lead to memory creation. Plausibility is not, however, something that is automatically associated with an event. Instead, it is a judgment that people make on the basis of various information.

Because plausibility is a judgment, several factors may influence whether a person sees an event as plausible. For example, the source of the suggestion will affect plausibility assessments. In the typical false-memory experiment, the suggested event is presented by an experimenter, and the information is based on information supposedly from the participant's parents—these are two generally reliable sources of information (although students would occasionally question their parents' accuracy). Not only will the source affect whether a person views an event as plausible, but the event itself will determine whether a person views this event as something that actually happened. For instance, most people may not consider abduction by extraterrestrials a likely event, whereas, others may consider this event common. Spanos, Cross, Dickson, and DuBreuil (1993) found that belief in alien visitations was the primary variable that differentiated people who claimed to have memories of UFO experiences from individuals who did not claim such experiences. Thus, judgments about the general frequency of an event will influence plausibility judgments. In addition, suggestions that the experience is not only generally likely but also personally likely will increase a person's willingness to believe an event may have occurred. For example, studies using false feedback (e.g., Kelley et al., 1996) have been effective in part because the researchers provided reasons for the participants to believe that an experience occurred to them.

Group membership also may affect plausibility and thus the creation of false memories. If new people are introduced to a group that is similar to themselves on some dimensions (e.g., common problems, experiences, world views, etc.) and if all of the other members of the group share common memories of an experience that the new members lack, then the experience may be more plausible for the new members. This increase of plausibility seems particularly likely if the experience is important for the group. In this case, the group's memories act as feedback, indicating that people who share common characteristics are likely to have had a certain class of experiences. In this way, an individual without memories of abuse who participates in a group of survivors of sexual abuse may receive feedback that sexual abuse is a very probable experience for him or her.

In addition, Garry, Manning, Loftus, and Sherman (1996) showed that imagining an event influences plausibility judgments. They asked participants to imagine events that they previously stated did not occur. When participants later rated the events, their ratings indicated an increased acceptance that the event may have happened.

The point here is that researchers can manipulate people's impression of the likelihood of a suggested event having occurred. For example, consider again those students who doubted they attended a wedding and thus refused to see spilling a punch bowl as likely. In such a case, the experimenter could manipulate the participant's judgment of the event plausibility by suggesting some reasons for this belief: Perhaps the student repressed memories of weddings, or perhaps the parents were embarrassed and thus never talked about it.

A person can believe that an event is likely or even that the event occurred but must still construct a memory—an image with a narrative. Since the time of Bartlett (1932), researchers have studied memory construction. Memory is not like videotape—people do not simply retrieve a memory and replay the experience. Instead, people construct a memory by combining schematic knowledge from various sources with personal experiences, suggestions, and current demands. All memories are constructions.

Several activities may make false-memory construction more likely. For example, tying a false event to self-knowledge will encourage false-memory creation (Hyman & Billings, 1998; Hyman et al., 1995). In this situation, when the person thinks again about the false event, the person will construct a memory combining the suggestion and self-knowledge. The image a person constructs will likely involve some true information. In addition, encouraging a person to construct and describe an image of a false event also leads to memory construction (Goff & Roediger, 1998; Hyman & Pentland, 1996). Probably any activity that encourages people to think about, image, or talk about events will lead to the construction of an image and narrative. Thus, activities such as keeping a journal and dream interpretation may lead to memory creation if the focus is on trying to remember events.

Even if a person believes an event is plausible and constructs an image of the event, he or she still may not think that the event is a memory. All of the participants in the imagery condition of Hyman and Pentland (1996) constructed an image of spilling the punch bowl at a wedding. Many, however, did not claim the image as a memory; instead they correctly monitored the source of the image. To have a false memory, the participants had to make a source-monitoring error—they had to claim the image as a personal memory. Many studies have shown that people experience difficulties remembering the source of information they have learned (see Johnson, Hashtroudi, & Lindsay, 1993). In addition, source misattribution has been suggested as a primary cause of the misinformation effect—people remember the misleading postevent information and incorrectly claim that the information was part of the original event (e.g., Zaragoza & Lane, 1994). The error for a false childhood memory is claiming the suggestion or constructed image or both as a personal memory.

Situational demands may affect whether a source-monitoring error occurs. For example, if a person shares an image and denotes that they are not sure whether it is a memory, others (an experimenter or members of a group) may tell the person that the image is a memory. Thus, social suggestions can alter the source-monitoring criteria people apply to their memories. The amount of time since a false suggestion was given may also affect source-monitoring errors because memory for the source of information fades more rapidly than memory for the content. In this fashion, over time people may remember the false suggestion, forget the source, and attribute the source to their own memory. In addition, Zaragoza and Mitchell (1996) recently found that repetition of false suggestions also increases the likelihood of source-monitoring failures.

Although the processes of plausibility judgment, memory construction, and source-monitoring error may occur in a linear fashion and be dependent on the preceding step, we suspect that the processes are somewhat interactive. For example, constructing a clear image may influence one's assessment of the plausibility of an event having occurred (Garry et al., 1996). It is more correct to state that all three processes are necessary for false-memory creation and that they are somewhat independent in the sense that different factors and individual differences may influence each process. Thus, in our recent research, we have focused on studying plausibility judgments and source-monitoring judgments separately.

PLAUSIBILITY JUDGMENTS

In our laboratory, we have investigated how plausibility judgments can be manipulated. Our basic goal has been to provide people with reasons to believe that certain events are likely to have occurred to them. We have done this by connecting childhood events that occur rarely to personality characteristics that we tell them they possess. Thus, our investigations of plausibility judgments have been based on an extension of the Barnum effect.

In a classic investigation of the Barnum effect, individuals take a personality test and are later provided feedback supposedly based on the test. The test used does not particularly matter because the feedback is not actually based on the personality test. Instead, all participants receive identical feedback containing statements that are vague, generally socially desirable, and positive. The typical finding is that most individuals rate the resulting personality description as describing them. The effect is powerful and can be used as a teaching tool to demonstrate how people blindly accept the results of psychological tests (Forer, 1949) and of horoscopes (Glick, Gottesman, & Jolton, 1989), which can lead into a discussion of ethics in research (Beins, 1993). In addition, the effect has been used to understand a variety of situations in which people accept test results as plausible and subsequently diagnose themselves (cf. Goodyear, 1990).

Hyman, Chesley, and Thoelke's (1997) research on plausibility judgments began as a type of Barnum study. They went into a large introductory psychology class and administered two personality tests: The Rotter Locus of Control Scale (Rotter, 1966) and the Eysenck Personality Inventory (Eysenck & Eysenck, 1968); the latter assesses neuroticism and extroversion and includes a Lie scale. These scales were used because researchers have found that acceptance of a Barnum description is related to an external locus of control and to higher scores on neuroticism. The researchers told students that they were investigating the relationships between personality and autobiographical memory. One week later, all the students were provided with a packet containing their individual feedback and a follow-up questionnaire on autobiographical memory. There were 104 students who completed the study (58 women and 46 men, *M* age = 19.05, *SD* = 1.09). The students were asked to read their personality description and rate how well it described them on a scale from 1 (*does not describe me*) to 7 (*describes me very well*). To this point, the experiment was a standard Barnum-effect demonstration.

After the students had rated the personality description, they were asked to respond to the autobiographical memory questionnaire, which was the extension the researchers added to the standard Barnum methodology. All students were told that the autobiographical memory questionnaire included some events that were likely to have happened to them and other events that were unlikely to have happened to them on the basis of their personality type—thus tying together the suggested events and personality descriptions and giving the students a reason to believe the events were personally plausible. All students were given 10 events that the researchers told them were likely to have occurred on the basis of their personality type and 10 that were unlikely on the basis of their personality type. The events were counterbalanced across packets so that half the students received one set of 10 likely and unlikely events, and these were reversed for the remainder of the students. The students rated each event on a scale from 1 (*did not happen*) to 7 (*did happen*).

The events were selected on the basis of a pilot survey to find events that were unlikely to have occurred to our population of students. In the pilot survey, 45 college students reported whether each of 70 events had happened to them before the age of 10. The researchers selected the events on the basis of their impression of low-likelihood events—events such as climbing on the roof and jumping off. They then selected 20 events that had happened to less than 30% of the sample.

Hyman et al.'s (1997) goals were multiple. First, they expected to replicate the Barnum effect and find that most students would accept the feedback as describing themselves. Second, they thought that the acceptance of feedback by the students would lead them to believe that the events that were tied to the personality description were more likely to have happened than the events that the researchers said were unlikely to have occurred. This would not be the creation of a false memory but rather the first step in the process: the step of agreeing that certain events may have happened. Third, they suspected that individuals who were more accepting of the personality description would also be more likely to rate the likely events as having happened to them and that these individual differences would be tied to both locus of control and neuroticism.

The first thing to note is that most of the students rated the personality description as a good fit. The mean rating on the 7-point scale was 5.27 ($SD = 1.13$), and the distribution was negatively skewed so that 84 students rated the description as a 5 or higher and only 2 individuals gave the rating of 1 or 2.

Although there was an overall tendency for individuals to rate the events they were told were likely as more plausible than the events they were told were unlikely, the effect was more clear for individuals who accepted the personality description. There was a significant correlation, such that individuals who rated the description as a better description of themselves rated the events they were told were more likely as more plausible ($r = .32$, $p = .001$). To put this another way, Hyman et al. (1997) categorized the individuals on the basis of how completely they accepted the

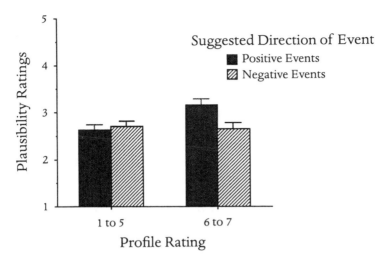

FIG. 3.1 Plausibility ratings based on profile acceptance and feedback that events were and were not related to the personality profile.

personality description: less acceptance for those who rated the profile a 5 or less ($n = 55$) and higher acceptance for those with ratings of 6 or 7 ($n = 49$). The researchers then conducted a 2 × 2 analysis of variance investigating the effects of profile acceptance and the feedback that events were likely or unlikely on the students' plausibility ratings. The investiators found no overall effect of profile acceptance, a marginal overall effect of feedback, $F(1, 102) = 4.14$, $p = .045$, $MSE = 0.51$, and a significant interaction of the two, $F(1, 102) = 8.27$, $p = .005$. As can be seen in Fig. 3.1, those who did not accept the profile were unaffected by the connection of certain events to their personality profile, whereas those who accepted the personality profile rated the events they were told were connected to their profile as more plausible. There was no effect for the events they were told were unlikely to have occurred, most likely because the events were selected because they were unlikely for everyone.

Hyman et al. (1997) also found that acceptance of the personality profile and the ratings of events they were told were likely on the basis of the profile were correlated with some of the actual personality measures. Acceptance of the personality profile was significantly correlated with neuroticism ($r = .32$, $p = .001$). The plausibility ratings of the events they were told were likely on the basis of their personality were related to the Rotter Locus of Control Scale (Rotter, 1966), such that scores closer to the external end of the scale were related to higher plausibility ratings ($r = .19$,

$p = .049$). In addition, the plausibility ratings of the likely events were also related to neuroticism ($r = .32$, $p = .001$) and negatively related to the lie index ($r = -.19$, $p = .049$).

These findings indicate that plausibility judgments can be manipulated. If childhood events are connected to personality characteristics, then people may begin to believe that the events happened—whether or not they remember the events. It is important to note that the personality characterisitics need not be accurate—it may only be necessary for individuals to believe the personality descriptions. The acceptance of events as plausible is a step in all memory error studies: All studies work to ensure that the false suggestions are plausible to the participants. Further systematic exploration of factors that affect plausibility is still needed.

MEMORY CONSTRUCTION AND SOURCE MONITORING

To study source-monitoring judgments, researchers have explored how people make "remember" and "know" judgments for autobiographical memories. In 1985, Tulving described a basic distinction between types of memory assessments individuals make about past experiences. Tulving argued, in part on the basis of his categories of episodic memory and semantic knowledge, that there are two basic forms of awareness associated with memory: *remember* and *know*. When people remember, the event is reexperienced as a personal memory encompassing both self-awareness and an awareness of some of the original sensory impressions. To remember an event is to claim that the source of one's memory is a personal recollection. When a past experience comes to mind in the know state of awareness, the event is recognized on the basis of some source of knowledge without the sense of a personal memory. When applied to word lists, this recognition is often described as familiarity absent any personal memory of hearing the word presented. For autobiographical knowledge, other sources include external knowledge such as general self-schematic knowledge and information from parents, friends, pictures, and diaries. People can know that an event occurred to them without remembering the event.

A remember–know judgment of an autobiographical recollection is a type of source-monitoring judgment. When knowledge about or an image from a past experience comes to mind, what is the source of the information? Is it a personal memory or something known from another source? This is a judgment people may regularly face when recollecting childhood experiences: Is this my memory or is this based on the family story or family pictures? This is also the judgment people make if some recollection is developed in response to suggestions from other people: Is this my memory or something produced in response to the suggestions?

Thus, Hyman, Gilstrap, Decker, and Wilkinson (1998) explored how people make the remember versus know judgment in autobiographical memories. If this judgment is a source-monitoring judgment, then the quality of the memory for events that people remember should differ from those associated with events they only claim to know. Johnson, Foley, Suengas, and Raye (1988) found that childhood events people remembered differed in many ways from childhood experiences they imagined. The events people remembered generally included much more sensory details of various sorts, whereas the imagined events included information on the cognitive operations of constructing the image. Johnson et al. (1988) argued that the quality of the memory determined the source judgment: The more sensory detail, the more indicative these recollections are of personal memories. Thus, if the distinction between remembered and known events matched that between remembered and imagined events, this would support the claim that the remember–know judgment is a source-monitoring judgment.

In Hyman et al.'s (1998) first experiment, participants first learned the definitions of remember and know. After the participants understood the definitions, they wrote a description of a childhood event (that occurred before the age of 10) for each of three categories: remember, know, and unsure if remembered or known. After they described all three events, they were asked to rate each memory on eight dimensions, including visual detail, other sensory detail, clarity of location, clarity of time, amount of emotion, doubts about accuracy, frequency of thinking about the event, and whether the event had serious implications. These dimensions were based on the Memory Characteristics Questionnaire used by Johnson et al. (1988).

Hyman et al. (1998) found that childhood events people claimed to remember differed from events they claimed to only know on a variety of measures of memory quality, including the amount of visual and other sensory details, the clarity of location and time knowledge, the amount of emotion, and confidence. In essence, the remembered events were clearer and contained more information. These results, for the most part, mirrored the Johnson et al. (1988) results and therefore can be viewed as evidence for the remember–know judgment being a type of source-monitoring judgment.

One way of explaining these results is that the events people know happened but can not remember are not a product of a personal recollection. Instead, known memories are the result of thinking about the event, hearing about the event, or imagining what took place during that experience. Thus, the source of a memory determines the quality of the memory; one has access to greater event elaboration for things one remembers.

On the other hand, this relationship could run in the opposite direction: The quality of the memory could determine the source to which someone attributes their memory. That is, if the memory is recalled with greater visual clarity, emotion, and sensory details, then one might label it as a personal memory rather than a memory that is simply known. This idea is congruent with Johnson's description of the source-monitoring process (Johnson et al., 1988; Johnson et al., 1993). People make a source judgment in part on the basis of the qualities of the constructed memory. If people construct a more elaborate recollection, they should be more likely to attribute the recollection to personal memory, to something they remember. Thus, asking people to imagine a false childhood experience (Hyman & Pentland, 1996) and repeatedly imagining an event (Goff & Roediger, 1998) increases false memories because people create more elaborate representations of the experiences.

In keeping with this view, adding more memory qualities to a known event should result in people being more likely to claim they remember the experience. Therefore, the goal of further research exploring remember–know judgments in autobiographical memories has been to determine what factors lead people to alter their source judgment for autobiographical recollection. In two additional experiments, Hyman et al. (1998) had people start with a childhood experience they claimed to know but not remember. They then asked the participants to form mental images of the experience and answer questions based on their images. Finally, individuals rated their recollection on a scale from 1 (*know*) to 7 (*remember*). Compared with a control group, individuals who imagined and described a known experience did rate their previously known memories further from the know end of the scale and toward the remember end, resulting in an unsure (middle) rating.

Wilkinson and Hyman (1998) used the same basic methodology to explore individual differences in source-monitoring judgments. As in Hyman et al. (1998), they asked participants to start with a known childhood experience and imagine the experience in more detail. They found that individuals who showed more change in their source judgments tended to score higher on the Dissociative Experiences Scale but were no more likely to make memory errors in remembering word lists of semantically related words (Roediger & McDermott, 1995).

In summary, it appears that the remember–know distinction is a valuable tool for exploring source-monitoring decisions for autobiographical experiences. In future research, we plan to explore how other factors influence this judgment. For example, will adding other characteristics to known events also lead people to claim to remember the event? Hyman et al. (1995) noted that making connections to self-relevant knowledge was related to the creation of false childhood memories. If people start with an event they know, focusing on the role of the self in the memory (e.g., imagining their own thoughts and emotional responses during the event) may add information unavailable from external sources (Hyman & Neisser, 1992), which may lead to claims of remembering the experience (Conway & Dewhurst, 1995). In addition, this method may also be valuable for exploring how social pressures affect the source-monitoring criterion that people apply to their memories. It may also be possible to use similar methodologies to convince people that they do not remember something but only know it instead. Perhaps causing people to focus on the other possible sources of their knowledge of an experience will lead to claims of knowing rather than remembering.

Deciding whether a recollection is something remembered or something known is a source-monitoring decision; this fact points to an additional concern—the difficulty in reliably discriminating true from false memories. The distribution of true and false memories in terms of sensory details will overlap: Some true memories will be vague, some false memories will use true sensory information in the construction of the recollection, and some false memories will have been rehearsed and elaborated. Nonetheless, in general, true memories should contain more sensory details than false memories because they are derived from real experiences. Johnson et al. (1988) found that memories contained more sensory information than imagined experiences, and Hyman et al. (1998) found that remembered events contained more sensory information than known events. Thus, many researchers have been able to find an overall difference between true and false memories in several ratings (Hyman & Pentland, 1996), in remember–know judgments (Conway, Collins, Gathercole, & Anderson, 1996), and in the content of the verbal descriptions (Pezdek et al., 1997).

However, the overall difference masks two important questions: First, can recovered true memories be discriminated from false memories? Second, can false memories that have been repetitively elaborated be discriminated from true memories? Hyman and Pentland (1996) had individuals recover true memories and create false childhood memories over the course of the three interviews. When they asked individuals to rate all their memories, they found that the true memories that they could recall throughout the sessions were the most clearly and confidently remembered. They also found that recovered true memories (events not recalled in the first session and later remembered) and false memories were both rated lower than the always remembered true memories. In addition, recovered true memories and created false memories were not reliably different from one another. Hence, there may be no way to discern recovered from false memories. To our knowledge, no one has looked at how false memories that are held for an extended time compare to true memories. We suspect that as sensory information is added to false memories, they will become more difficult to discern from true memories.

FALSE MEMORIES, FALSE SELF

People create false memories. Sometimes the errors will be small: adding someone to a party who wasn't actually there, thinking one's role was larger than it actually was (Ross & Sicoly, 1979), remembering the pain as more severe than it was (Ross, 1989), or downplaying personal foibles and inflating one's value (Greenwald, 1980). Sometimes the errors will be larger: forgetting events that were previously important for self-definition (Hirst, 1994; Usita, Hyman, & Herman, 1998), creating an entire event in one's childhood (e.g., Hyman et al., 1995), or creating an adult experience (Kassin, 1997; Kassin & Kiechel, 1996). Because the self is constructed from memories, the self will be a false self, based on beliefs and memories that do not accurately represent the past.

Although many of these changes may simply serve the goal of preserving a confident ego (Greenwald, 1980), others may be more damaging. If a person comes to believe that he or she was abused as a child, this change may have negative effects on the ego. It could alter anyone's self conception—even individuals who experienced a less than ideal childhood may find child abuse a qualitative change in their understanding of their past. This concept is clear when considering the narratives of individuals who recover memories of abuse (e.g., Bass & Davis, 1988; Pendergrast, 1995). The abuse becomes a part of how these people define themselves, something they must integrate with their life stories. In Jane Smiley's fictional case of Ginny, the new memory changed her life to such a degree that she indicated life as she knew it had ended and a new life began. These changes may be difficult to reconcile with previous self-conceptions for some individuals but may provide a narrative that accounts for many previously unexplained instances in one's life.

Memories that include abuse not only affect self-definition but also affect an individual's interactions with others. If the accused perpetrator is a member of the family or a family friend, the memories will likely cause schisms in the relationships. The memories may force a person to reevaluate the types of social interactions she or he has with others.

These changes in self-concept and relationships with others are justified when the recovered memories are of events that actually happened. In contrast, if the individual has created false memories, then the changes are a catastrophic error. The individual develops a false sense of self based on events that never occurred. The individual interrupts relationships with important individuals for a false cause.

This is the argument that has been played out in many families and in court cases across the country for the past several years. Individuals recover memories of abuse. They rewrite their personal narrative and change their relationships on the basis of the memories. Families often contend that the memories are false—that they are the result of suggestions and social pressure. Families argue that they have been wrongfully cut off from children, siblings, and grandchildren. In the absence of some evidence external to memory, it is difficult, if not impossible, to know which narrative corresponds to historical truth.

Although these cases are dramatic, they exist because they are instances of how human memory functions. The inability to differentiate between false memories and historically accurate memories raises the question of how to balance historical and narrative truth (Spence, 1982). If a person believes that a memory is accurate, how is society to deal with this? Are we to accept that person's belief and focus on promoting health and welfare? Are we to question that belief and take an investigative role? This question is relevant for most memories discussed in therapy and not just memories of child abuse. As psychologists, we need to be concerned with distinguishing false and historically accurate memories, but we must not lose sight of the practical implications of individuals dealing with what they believe is their past.

Memory is always constructed. What people remember will be constructed from remaining materials and from general schematic knowledge structures. In addition, memory construction often takes place within a social context and in response to social pressures. Thus, the memories we construct reflect the suggestions and stories told by others. Many of our childhood memories may actually be stories that we heard others, such as parents or siblings, tell. We imagine the stories and perhaps eventually adopt the image and story as our own memory. Much of the past is constructed in a social environment, which may explain how individuals fail to remember abuse or come to mislabel abuse—they have adopted the story of the perpetrator (see Hyman & Kleinknecht, 1999). As Hyman and Pentland (1996) suggested, life is an ongoing misinformation experiment, and the outcome is that the self is memory's illusion.

The fact that memory is constructed also means that history is constructed. Consider the ongoing process of spin doctoring in the political area. The need to write a favorable interpretation of the present and the past to argue for a certain political viewpoint has inspired numerous version of political events. Consider the current effort to write the generally accepted version of President Clinton's affair with Monica Lewinsky. Did the president lie? Did he give honest but not particularly revealing answers? Is Independent Prosecutor Starr an honest public servant striving to uncover serious crimes? Is he instead a man with a political agenda out to discredit a president with whom he disagrees? Although everyone alive now has lived through these episodes, the eventual story that is developed will be dependent on which narrative is adopted. History is written by the victors, or perhaps the victors are those who write a version of history that becomes the accepted version. In essence, as a society, we are living the nightmare of George Orwell's (1949) *1984*. We may not be experiencing the negative totalitarian state described, but we certainly are experiencing the constant historical and personal revisions.

Nonetheless, there must be some limit on how malleable memory is. If memory were constantly being altered by the whims of individuals' most recent interactions, then surely these changes would be problematic. People would experience difficulties accurately tracking the world, and conversations would be constant miscommunication in which participants would have difficulties identifying experiences they shared. Hyman (1999) argued that the malleability of memory is an evolved trait that must balance opposing pressures. On one side are pressures favoring memory malleability—pressures such as updating memory to continue to recognize constancy in the face of small changes and pressures to change memory to better fit with social groups. On the other side are pressures for memory accuracy—pressures to be able to learn from the past and be able to recognize shared experiences. The outcome of these pressures appears to be a memory system that is generally reliable. The gist will generally be accurate, as will most remembered details. Nonetheless, the system needs to be integrative, which means that schematic intrusions will be seen. In addition, the memory system serves social interaction, and thus response to social pressure will also be observed. Therefore, extreme errors are possible, although most likely infrequent. Conversely, there should be times when memory is highly accurate. Thus, the self as defined by autobiographical memory will be generally resilient, providing individuals with some confidence in who they are and what they can become.

REFERENCES

Barclay, C. R., & DeCooke, P. A. (1988). Ordinary everyday memories: Some of the things of which selves are made. In U. Neisser & E. Winograd (Eds.), *Remembering reconsidered: Ecological and traditional approaches to the study of memory* (pp. 91–125). Cambridge, England: Cambridge University Press.

Bartlett, F. C. (1932). *Remembering: A study in experimental and social psychology.* Cambridge, England: Cambridge University Press.

Bass, E., & Davis, L. (1988). *The courage to heal: A guide for women survivors of child sexual abuse.* New York: Harper & Row.

Beins, B. C. (1993). Using the Barnum Effect to teach about ethics and deception in research. *Teaching of Psychology, 20,* 33–35.

Belli, R. F. (1989). Influences of misleading postevent information: Misinformation interference and acceptance. *Journal of Experimental Psychology: General, 118,* 72–85.

Ceci, S. J., Huffman, M. L. C., Smith, E., & Loftus, E. F. (1994). Repeatedly thinking about non-events. *Consciousness and Cognition, 3,* 388–407.

Ceci, S. J., Loftus, E. F., Leichtman, M. D., & Bruck, M. (1994). The possible role of source misattributions in the creation of false beliefs among preschoolers. *International Journal of Clinical and Experimental Hypnosis, 42,* 304–320.

Conway, M. A., Collins, A. F., Gathercole, S. E., & Anderson, S. J. (1996). Recollections of true and false autobiographical memories. *Journal of Experimental Psychology: General, 25,* 69–95.

Conway, M. A., & Dewhurst, S. A. (1995). The self and recollective experience. *Applied Cognitive Psychology, 9,* 1–19.

Eysenck, H. J., & Eysenck, S. B. G. (1968). *Eysenck Personality Inventory.* San Diego, CA: Educational and Industrial Testing Service.

Forer, B. R. (1949). The fallacy of personal validation: A classroom demonstration of gullibility. *Journal of Abnormal and Social Psychology, 44,* 118–123.

Garry, M., Manning, C. G., Loftus, E. F., & Sherman, S. J. (1996). Imagination inflation: Imaging a childhood event inflates confidence that it occurred. *Psychonomic Bulletin & Review, 3,* 208–214.

Glick, P., Gottesman, D., & Jolton, J. (1989). The fault is not in the stars: Susceptibility of skeptics and believers in astrology to the Barnum Effect. *Personality and Social Psychology Bulletin, 15,* 572–583.

Goff, L. M., & Roediger, H. L., III (1998). Imagination inflation for action events: Repeated imaginings lead to illusory recognition. *Memory & Cognition, 26,* 20–33.

Goodyear, R. K. (1990). Research on the effects of test interpretation: A review. *The Counseling Psychologist, 18,* 241–257.

Greenwald, A. G. (1980). The totalitarian ego: Fabrication and revision of personal history. *American Psychologist, 35,* 603–618.

Hirst, W. (1994). The remembered self in amnesiacs. In U. Neisser & R. Fivush (Eds.), *The remembering self: Construction and accuracy in the self-narrative* (pp. 252–277). New York: Cambridge University Press.

Hyman, I. E., Jr. (1999). Creating false autobiographical memories: Why people believe their memory errors. In E. Winograd, R. Fivush, & W. Hirst (Eds.), *Ecological approaches to cognition: Essays in honor of Ulric Neisser* (pp. 229–252). Mahwah, NJ: Lawrence Erlbaum Associates.

Hyman, I. E., Jr., & Billings, F. J. (1998). Individual differences and the creation of false childhood memories. *Memory, 6,* 1–20.

Hyman, I. E., Jr., Chesley, C. A., & Thoelke, R. S. (1997, November). *False memories: False personality feedback affects plausibility judgments.* Paper presented at the meeting of the Psychonomic Society, Philadelphia.

Hyman, I. E., Jr., Gilstrap L. L., Decker, K. L., & Wilkinson, C. L. (1998). Manipulating remember versus know judgments in autobiographical memories. *Applied Cognitive Psychology, 12,* 371–386.

Hyman, I. E., Jr., Husband, T. H., & Billings, F. J. (1995). False memories of childhood experiences. *Applied Cognitive Psychology, 9,* 181–197.

Hyman, I. E., Jr., & Kleinknecht, E. E. (1999). False childhood memories: Research, theory, and applications. In L. M. Williams & V. L. Banyard (Eds.), *Trauma and memory* (pp. 175–188). Thousand Oaks, CA: Sage.

Hyman, I. E., Jr., & Neisser, U. (1992). The role of the self in recollections of a seminar. *Journal of Narrative and Life History, 2,* 81–103.

Hyman, I. E., Jr., & Pentland, J. (1996). The role of mental imagery in the creation of false childhood memories. *Journal of Memory and Language, 35,* 101–117.

Hyman, I. E., Jr., & Rubin, D. C. (1990). Memorabeatlia: A naturalistic study of long-term. *Memory & Cognition, 18,* 205–214.

James, W. (1890). *Principles of psychology.* New York: Holt.

Johnson, M. K., Foley, M. A., Suengas, A. G., & Raye, C. L. (1988). Phenomenal characteristics of memories for perceived and imagined autobiographical events. *Journal of Experimental Psychology: General, 117,* 371–376.

Johnson, M. K., Hashtroudi, S., & Lindsay, D. S. (1993). Source monitoring. *Psychological Bulletin, 114,* 3–28.

Kassin, S. M. (1997). The psychology of confession evidence. *American Psychologist, 52,* 221–233.

Kassin, S. M., & Kiechel, K. L. (1996). The social psychology of false confessions: Compliance, internalization, and confabulation. *Psychological Science, 7,* 125–128.

Kelley, C., Amodio, D., & Lindsay, D. S. (1996, July). *The effects of "diagnosis" and memory work on memories of handedness shaping.* Paper presented at the International Conference on Memory, Padua, Italy.

Lindsay, D. S. (1990). Misleading suggestions can impair eyewitnesses' ability to remember event details. *Journal of Experimental Psychology: Learning, Memory, and Cognition, 16,* 1077–1083.

Lindsay, D. S. (1997). Increasing sensitivity. In D. Read & S. Lindsay (Eds.), *Recollections of trauma: Scientific research and clinical practice* (pp. 1–16). New York: Plenum.

Lindsay, D. S., & Read, J. D. (1994). Psychotherapy and memories of childhood sexual abuse: A cognitive perspective. *Applied Cognitive Psychology, 8,* 281–338.

Loftus, E. F. (1979). *Eyewitness testimony.* Cambridge, MA: Harvard University Press.

Loftus, E. F. (1993). The reality of repressed memories. *American Psychologist, 48,* 518–537.

Loftus, E. F. (1997). Dispatch from the (un)civil memory wars. In D. Read & S. Lindsay (Eds.), *Recollections of trauma: Scientific research and clinical practice* (pp. 171–194). New York: Plenum.

Loftus, E. F., Donders, K., Hoffman, H. G., & Schooler, J. W. (1989). Creating new memories that are quickly accessed and confidently held. *Memory & Cognition, 17,* 607–616.

Loftus, E. F., & Pickrell, J. E. (1995). The formation of false memories. *Psychiatric Annals, 25,* 720–725.

McCloskey, M., & Zaragoza, M. (1985). Misleading postevent information and memory for events: Arguments and evidence against memory impairment hypothesis. *Journal of Experimental Psychology: General, 114,* 3–18.

Neisser, U. (1982). John Dean's memory: A case study. In U. Neisser (Ed.), *Memory observed: Remembering in natural contexts* (pp. 139–159). San Francisco: Freeman.

Neisser, U. (1988). Five kinds of self-knowledge. *Philosophical Psychology, 1,* 35–59.

Orwell, G. (1949). *1984.* New York: Harcourt Brace Jovanovich.

Pendergrast, M. (1995). *Victims of memory: Incest accusations and shattered lives.* Hinesburg, VT: Upper Access, Inc.

Pezdek, K., Finger, K., & Hodge, D. (1997). Planting false childhood memories: The role of event plausibility. *Psychological Science, 8,* 437–441.

Roediger, H. L., III, & McDermott, K. B. (1995). Creating false memories: Remembering words not presented in lists. *Journal of Experimental Psychology: Learning, Memory, and Cognition, 21,* 803–814.

Ross, M. (1989). The relation of implicit theories to the construction of personal histories. *Psychological Review, 96,* 341–357.

Ross, M., & Sicoly, F. (1979). Egocentric biases in availability and attribution. *Journal of Personality and Social Psychology, 37,* 322–336.

Rotter, J. B. (1966). Generalized expectancies for internal versus external control of reinforcement. *Psychological Monographs, 91*(1, Whole No. 609).

Schooler, J. W., Bendiksen, M., & Ambadar, Z. (1997). Taking the middle line: Can we accommodate both fabricated and recovered memories of sexual abuse? In M. Conway (Ed.), *False and recovered memories* (pp. 251–292). Oxford, England: Oxford University Press.

Smiley, J. (1991). *A thousand acres.* New York: Knopf.

Spanos, N. P., Cross, P. A., Dickson, K., & DuBreuil, S. C. (1993). Close encounters: An examination of UFO experiences. *Journal of Abnormal Psychology, 102,* 624–632.

Spence, D. P. (1982). *Narrative truth and historical truth: Meaning and interpretation in psychoanalysis.* New York: Norton.

Tulving, E. (1985). Memory and consciousness. *Canadian Psychology, 26,* 1–11.

Usita, P. M., Hyman, I. E., Jr., & Herman, K. C. (1998). Narrative intentions: Listening to life stories in Alzheimer's Disease. *Journal of Aging Studies, 12,* 185–197.

Wilkinson, C., & Hyman, I. E., Jr. (1998). Individual differences related to two types of memory errors: Word lists may not generalize to autobiographical memory. *Applied Cognitive Psychology, 12,* S29–S46.

Williams, L. M. (1995). Recovered memories of abuse in women with documented child sexual victimization histories. *Journal of Traumatic Stress, 8,* 649–673.

Zaragoza, M. S., & Lane, S. M. (1994). Source misattributions and the suggestibility of eyewitness memory. *Journal of Experimental Psychology: Learning, Memory, and Cognition, 20,* 934–945.

Zaragoza, M. S., & Mitchell, K. J. (1996). Repeated exposure to suggestion and the creation of false memories. *Psychological Science, 7,* 294–300.

CHAPTER FOUR

Discriminating Between Accounts of True and False Events

KATHY PEZDEK
JENNIFER TAYLOR
Claremont Graduate University

In recent years, we have been interested in the conditions under which false memories are likely to be planted in adults and children and the conditions under which adults and children are more likely to be resistant to the implantation of false memories. In the process of accumulating results that address this research question (see, e.g., Pezdek, Finger, & Hodge, 1997; Pezdek & Hodge, 1999; Pezdek & Roe, 1994, 1997), we realized that we had a fairly large corpus of data on a different issue, that is, qualitative and quantitative differences between memories for true and false events. Although some of these data are included in the various articles that we have published, we decided that there was a need to synthesize these findings in one source, along with the findings of other researchers who have compared phenomenological qualities of memories for true and false events. This chapter was written for this purpose.

In the three sections of this chapter, we review three methods that have been proposed to differentiate between accounts of true and false events. Research on the effectiveness of these three methods is included as well. We should say up front that although some measures are more sensitive to differences between accounts of true and false events than others, we agree with Steve Ceci and others that there is no Pinocchio test for

determining whether accounts are true or false (cf. Ceci, Loftus, Leichtman, & Bruck, 1994). We mention this disclaimer here for those who approach this chapter with the anticipation that we offer some fail-proof
technique for assessing the veracity of reported memories. Such a technique is not available. Also, as we discuss in this chapter, the problem is
further complicated by the fact that the cognitive characteristics of memories for true events and false events are overlapping functions; memories
for true and false events share numerous features. Nonetheless, we suggest that a review and critical evaluation of the research on this topic has
utility for practitioners as well as for researchers investigating the nature
of memories for true and false events.

The first method to be discussed for differentiating between accounts
of true and false events is the Statement Validity Assessment (SVA) that
was developed by David Raskin and Max Steller and based on the early
work of Udo Undeutsch in Germany. In the second section, the method
derived from Marcia Johnson's model of reality monitoring is reviewed.
According to the reality monitoring framework, memories for real and
fictitious events will differ qualitatively. On the basis of this work, the
Memory Characteristics Questionnaire (MCQ) was developed (Johnson,
Foley, Suengas, & Raye, 1988) to assess the qualitative differences between
accounts of real and fictitious events.

In the third section of this chapter, a number of studies are considered
that have examined the conditions under which false memories are more
likely to be suggestively planted. Data have been collected on people's accounts of events that they believed to be real, although some were true
and some were false. Characteristics of the memory accounts for these
two types of events have been compared. The major difference between
the data generated in the reality monitoring research and data generated
in the false memory research is that the events for which memory was assessed in the reality monitoring research included real events that had occurred, and they were compared with, for example, memories for dreams,
fantasies, and unfulfilled intentions. On the other hand, in the false memory research, the events for which memory was assessed included similar
types of events that either had occurred (true events) or had not occurred
(false events.)

Several related areas of research are not included in this chapter. Our
goal in this chapter is to assist professionals in discriminating between
memories for true versus false events, both of which individuals believe to
be true. Thus, research on lie detection techniques, credibility assessment,
and malingering are not considered in this chapter. We have also avoided
much of the research comparing accounts of true and consciously fabri-

cated false events because consciously fabricated accounts are considered to be different from events that are erroneously believed to be true.

STATEMENT VALIDITY ASSESSMENT

Much of the early work on what is now known as SVA was conducted in Germany in the 1950s to assist the courts in differentiating between eye-witness accounts that were based on real events and those that were fabricated (see Undeutsch, 1989, for a history of this early work). This work was known as Statement Reality Analysis. The principle hypothesis underlying this work is that accounts of actual experiences differ in content and quality from accounts of experiences that were confabulated, suggested or imagined. Steller (1989) termed this the *Undeutsch hypothesis*. On the basis of this early work, much of which was conducted by Undeutsch, the Supreme Court of Germany ruled in 1955 that psychological assessments and interviews would be required to determine the credibility of child witnesses in most child sexual abuse cases. As a result of this ruling and a similar one at the time in Sweden, a rash of content criteria was developed to assess the credibility of statements made by alleged sexual abuse victims. However, most of these assessment systems were not systematically developed using sound psychological principles, nor were they scientifically validated.

Current efforts in this area, led primarily by David Raskin (see, e.g., Raskin & Esplin, 1991) and Max Steller (see, e.g., Steller, 1989), represent significant improvements in the application of scientific principles of inquiry and validation. Together, these two researchers began the development of the SVA in 1985. There are three components to the SVA: (a) a structured interview with the witness, (b) a criterion-based content analysis (CBCA) of the interview data, and (c) integration of the CBCA with the information obtained from a set of questions that compose the Validity Checklist. It is important to note that the SVA does not assess the general credibility of a witness but rather assesses the validity of the statements produced by a witness.

It is beyond the scope of this chapter to detail the components of the SVA; however, Table 4.1 summarizes the 18 content criteria for the CBCA. There are no specific rules regarding how many of the criteria must be satisfied to support the conclusion that a particular account is true. As a general rule, however, to support the conclusion that an account is true, it is necessary that the three general characteristics specified at the top of Table 4.1 be satisfied. That is, the account must be logically coherent, have

TABLE 4.1
Content Criteria for Statement Analysis

General Characteristics

1. Logical structure—Is the statement coherent? Is the content logical? Do the different segments fit together? (Note: Peculiar or unique details or unexpected complications do not diminish logical structure.)
2. Unstructured production—Are the descriptions unconstrained? Is the report somewhat unorganized? Are there digressions or spontaneous shifts of focus? Are some elements distributed throughout? (Note: This criterion requires that the account be locally consistent.)
3. Quantity of details—Are there specific descriptions of place or time? Are persons, objects, and events specifically described? (Note: Repetitions do not count.)

Specific Contents

4. Contextual embedding—Are events placed in spatial and temporal context? Is the action connected to other incidental events, such as routine daily occurrences?
5. Interactions—Are there reports of actions and reactions or conversation composed of a minimum of three elements involving at least the accused and the witness?
6. Reproduction of speech—Is speech or conversation during the incident reported in its original form? (Note: Unfamiliar terms or quotes are especially strong indicators, even when attributed to only one participant.)
7. Unexpected complications—Was there an unplanned interruption or an unexpected complication or difficulty during the sexual incident?
8. Unusual details—Are there details of persons, objects, or events that are unusual, yet meaningful in this context? (Note: Unusual details must be realistic.)
9. Superfluous details—Are peripheral details described in connection with the alleged sexual events that are not essential and do not contribute directly to the specific allegations? (Note: If a passage satisfies any of the specific criteria 4–18, it probably is not superfluous.)
10. Accurately reported details misunderstood—Did the child correctly describe an object or event but interpret it incorrectly?
11. Related external associations—Is there reference to a sexually toned event or conversation of a sexual nature that is related in some way to the incident but is not part of the alleged sexual offenses?
12. Subjective experience—Did the child describe feelings or thoughts experienced at the time of the incident? (Note: This criterion is not satisfied when the witness responds to a direct question, unless the answer goes beyond the question.)
13. Attribution of accused's mental state—Is there reference to the alleged perpetrator's feelings or thoughts during the incident? (Note: Descriptions of overt behavior do not qualify.)

Motivation-Related Contents

14. Spontaneous corrections or additions—Were corrections offered or information added to material previously provided in the statement? (Note: Responses to direct questions do not qualify.)
15. Admitting lack of memory or knowledge—Did the child indicate lack of memory or knowledge of an aspect of the incident? (Note: In response to a direct question, the answer must go beyond "I don't know" or "I can't remember.")

Continued

TABLE 4.1 *(Continued)*

16. Raising doubts about one's own testimony—Did the child express concern that some part of the statement seems incorrect or unbelievable? (Note: Merely asserting that one is telling the truth does not qualify).
17. Self-depreciation—Did the child describe some aspect of his/her behavior related to the sexual incident as wrong or inappropriate?
18. Pardoning the accused—Did the child make excuses for or fail to blame the alleged perpetrator, or minimize the seriousness of the acts, or fail to add to the allegations when an opportunity occurred?

Note. Reprinted from *Behavioral Assessment, 13,* by D. C. Raskin and P. W. Esplin, "Statement Validity Assessment: Interview Procedures and Content Analysis of Children's Statements of Sexual Abuse," p. 279. Copyright © 1991, with permission from Elsevier Science.

a well-organized structure, and include a convincing quantity of specific details. *Logical coherence* refers to how well the different segments fit together and whether the statement makes logical sense. The *structure of the production* refers to whether the statement is well organized or whether there are digressions or shifts of focus. The *quantity of specific details* refers to whether descriptions include, for example, time, place, person, and objects. In a review of the literature on CBCA by Ruby and Brigham (1997), the criterion of wealth of details was reported to have the widest utility in differentiating between accounts of true and false events. It has not been determined, however, how many of the additional 15 criteria are sufficient to draw a conclusion regarding the truth value of an account.

The Validity Checklist was developed by Stellar (1989). The items in the Validity Checklist probe psychological characteristics of the interviewee, characteristics of the interview, the motivational context of the report, and the consistency of the report with other statements and lines of evidence. According to Steller (1989), although this portion of the SVA is "more subjective and less formalized" (p. 141) than the CBCA, it provides additional information that can be used to assess the truth value of a witness's statements by determining whether the statements are reasonable in light of what is known about the victim and the alleged acts.

The validity of the SVA has been tested in a number of studies. Landry and Brigham (1992) compared judges trained to use the CBCA with untrained judges in their ability to discriminate videotaped or transcribed accounts of adults describing a true or a false personally traumatic event. The CBCA-trained judges were significantly more accurate (55.3%) than untrained judges (46.9%). In a similar study, Tye, Henderson, and Honts (1995) reported that judges trained to use the CBCA could correctly classify 89% of the accounts of 28 children regarding a mock theft they observed. The children either reported the theft correctly, or they were encouraged to lie ⌐bout it. The level of accuracy for CBCA judges compared favorably with that of lay judges who were significantly better than chance but achieved only 56% (Experiment 1) and 65% (Experiment 2) accuracy. Several experimental studies have demonstrated that judges using the CBCA can discriminate between accounts of true events versus accounts of events that subjects were told to fabricate. Yuille (1988) had children tell a story about a true event or make up a story about a plausible but fabricated event. Using the CBCA, judges correctly classified 96% of the stories. In a similar study with adults, Zaparniuk, Yuille, and Taylor (1995) reported that CBCA-trained judges performed significantly better than chance at discriminating between accounts of subjects who saw a videotape of a crime and subjects who were read a description of the crime and were then asked to fabricate an account of the crime as if they had actually observed it. However, the results were significant for only 2 of the 3 judges who coded the accounts.

Tests of the validity of the SVA have come from field studies as well. For example, Esplin, Boychuk, and Raskin (1988) identified 20 children with documented histories of sexual abuse. They identified a different group of 20 children who had reported sexual abuse, but the cases were not confirmed and were strongly suspect; most of these cases involved custody disputes. Judges using the SVA criteria discriminated between these two groups at a highly significant level. In a similar study, Lamers-Winkelman, Buffing, and van der Zanden (1992) examined the accounts of 103 children who had reported having been sexually abused. Their claims of sexual abuse were independently classified as substantiated, highly probable, or unfounded. Judges using the CBCA criteria successfully discriminated among these three groups with older children but not with younger children. This result is not surprising given that the general characteristics of the CBCA are the most discriminating factors (i.e., the logical structure and amount of detail in the account), and preschoolers' narratives are less well structured than those of older children (Fivush & Slackman, 1986; Fivush, Kuebli, & Clubb, 1992).

The most comprehensive field study to date assessing the validity of the SVA was conducted by Lamb, Sternberg, Esplin, Hershkowitz, and Orbach (1997). Because questions have been raised regarding the representativeness of the cases used in a number of the previous studies assessing the SVA (see, e.g., Wells & Loftus, 1991), Lamb and his colleagues selected 98 active cases for which extensive interviews with youth investigators were available over an extended period of time. Using independent information such as medical reports, physical evidence, statements by other witnesses, and statements by the alleged perpetrator, the researchers classified each case as plausible or implausible. Significantly higher CBCA scores resulted for the plausible than the implausible cases. However, the differences in CBCA scores between the plausible and the implausible cases did not approach the high level reported by Raskin (see, e.g., Esplin et al., 1988), and the two groups could only be differentiated on 6 of the 14 CBCA criteria used. Lamb and his colleagues concluded that the precision of the CBCA is currently too poor to permit forensic application.

Similar results followed from a study by Ruby and Brigham (1998) designed to compare the effectiveness of the CBCA specifically for African American speakers. In this study, 6 African American and 6 White university students or staff members presented descriptions of two personal events, one true and one false. The speakers were given 1 or 2 days to prepare their presentations. They were instructed to describe incidents that they considered negative, emotional, and characterized by a loss of control. They were also instructed to be deceptively convincing when relaying the false story. Next, 143 White raters, trained to use the CBCA, then rated transcripts of the presentations. The raters were blind as to the ethnicity of the presenters. The results were that the raters were worse than chance at discriminating true from false accounts by White presenters; for African American presenters, there was no difference in the CBCA ratings for true and false events. In a discriminate analysis performed for the separate CBCA criteria, none of the criteria showed a significant positive correlation with truthfulness for both White and African American presenters. This study raises serious concerns about the utility of the CBCA for assessing the veracity of statements by African American and White individuals.

The results of a study by Steller, Wellershaus, and Wolf (1988) raise an interesting question about the validity of the SVA for discriminating between accounts of true versus false events. In this study, children were each asked to tell a story about a true event and one about an event that never really happened to them. The findings were that the SVA was more successful at discriminating accounts of true events from fabricated accounts of unfamiliar events (e.g., medical procedures such as having an operation) than from fabricated accounts of familiar events. If people generate accounts of true and false events on the basis of the schema-relevant information retained in their memory, and if people have more information in their schemata for familiar than unfamiliar events, it is not surprising that accounts of true and false familiar events would be more similar and thus less discriminable than accounts of true and false unfamiliar events. These results relate to the reports of Pezdek et al. (1997) and Pezdek and Hodge (1999) that it is easier to plant false memories for plausible than for implausible events. The interpretation of this result is that it is easier to plant a memory for an episode of an event about which one has a well-developed schema than for an event about which one does not have much schema-relevant knowledge.

The results of Steller et al. (1988) suggest that in real sexual abuse cases, the SVA may be effective at discriminating between true and fabricated accounts only for people without prior knowledge or experience with sexual acts. A similar concern has been expressed by Raskin and Esplin (1991): "A major limitation of CBCA is the difficulty in applying it to situations where the witness has other sources of information from which to invent an accusation that incorporates some or many of the content criteria" (p. 280). Similarly, Lamb et al. (1997) mentioned that the accounts of implausible cases that were most likely to be misclassified as plausible were those in which the central event—for example, an allegation of vaginal penetration—was described in the context of a familiar and more recent interaction with the alleged perpetrator. It may be possible that the SVA does not, in fact, discriminate between true versus false events; rather it discriminates between accounts of familiar versus unfamiliar events. After all, narrative accounts of familiar events would be expected to have a better logical structure and more detailed content than would the narrative accounts of unfamiliar events, and the familiarity of an event can come from direct personal experience or from indirect sources such as conversations with people and various forms of media.

REALITY MONITORING RESEARCH

Reality monitoring refers to the cognitive processes that are used to discriminate between perceived and imagined events (Johnson & Raye, 1981). Using a wide range of tasks, a number of researchers have demonstrated that memories for perceived events are phenomenologically different from memories for imagined events. This includes, for example, memories for perceived and imagined words (Foley, Johnson, & Raye, 1983), pictured objects (Johnson, Raye, Wang, & Taylor, 1979), actions (Foley & Johnson, 1985), and autobiographical events (Johnson et al., 1988).

The essential differences in the phenomenological characteristics of memories for perceived and imagined events were as follows: Whereas memories for perceived events contain more perceptual information (color and sound) and more contextual information (time and place), memories for imagined events contain more information about the cognitive processes that produced the memories. This concept is explained by the fact that memories for perceived events are retrieved from memory more automatically and thus involve fewer search and decision processes. These search and decision processes that can later serve as reality monitoring cues are thus less abundant for perceived than for imagined events.

In one of the most ecologically relevant studies on reality monitoring, Johnson et al. (1988) had participants think about three autobiographical events (a social occasion, a visit to a library, a trip to the dentist) and three imagined events (a dream, a fantasy, an unfulfilled intention). They then rated their own memories using the Memory Characteristics Questionnaire (MCQ) developed by Johnson et al. (1988). The MCQ, a copy of which is presented in Table 4.2, includes 39 questions that require the participant to rate the quality of a specific memory in terms of various aspects of the dimensions reported to distinguish between perceived and imagined events. Generally, the findings supported the idea that memories of perceived autobiographical events contained more contextual and perceptual information, and memories of imagined autobiographical events contained more information regarding the cognitive processes involved in activating the memory (e.g., "I remember that I did this because . . ."; "I know I didn't just imagine this because . . .")

Johnson et al. (1988) also compared MCQ ratings of perceived and imagined events for events that occurred recently or in childhood. Interestingly, although the MCQ ratings for perceived and imagined events were in the same direction for recent and childhood events, most of the differences between perceived and imagined events that were significant for recent events were not significant for childhood events. This finding suggests that perhaps the differences between the phenomenological characteristics of perceived and imagined events dissipate with time.

The MCQ ratings were developed to assess self-reported differences in the nature of memories for perceived and imagined events. Several investigators have tested whether the MCQ ratings can also be useful in discriminating between perceived and imagined events when applied by experimenters to judge the veracity of participants' memory accounts. Schooler, Gerhard, and Loftus (1986, Experiments 4 and 5) tested if judges trained to identify the reality monitoring criteria that discriminate between perceived and imagined events could discriminate between descriptions of perceived and suggested objects. The descriptions were obtained for objects perceived or suggested using the misinformation paradigm of Loftus, Miller, and Burns (1978). In both experiments, trained judges were significantly more accurate than untrained judges in classifying descriptions as originating from real or suggested events, but the difference in classification accuracy was significant only for suggested items and not for

TABLE 4.2
Memory Characteristics Questionnaire

My memory for this event:
1. is 1 = dim; 7 = sharp/clear.
2. is 1 = *black and white; 7 = entirely color.*
3. involves visual detail 1 = *little or none; 7 = a lot.*
4. involves sound 1 = *little or none; 7 = a lot.*
5. involves smell 1 = *little or none; 7 = a lot.*
6. involves touch 1 = *little or none; 7 = a lot.*
7. involves taste 1 = *little or none; 7 = a lot.*
8. Overall vividness is 1 = *vague; 7 = very vivid.*
9. My memory for the event is 1 = *sketchy; 7 = very detailed.*
10. Order of events is 1 = *confusing; 7 = comprehensible.*
11. Story line is 1 = *simple; 7 = complex.*
12. Story line is 1 = *bizarre; 7 = realistic.*
13. My memory for the location where the event takes place is 1 = *vague; 7 = clear/distinct.*
14. General setting is 1 = *unfamiliar; 7 = familiar.*
15. Relative spatial arrangement of objects in my memory for the event is 1 = *vague;* 7 = *clear/distinct.*
16. Relative spatial arrangement of people in my memory for the event is 1 = *vague;* 7 = *clear/distinct.*
17. My memory for the time when the event takes place is 1 = *vague; 7 = clear/distinct.*
18. for the year is 1 = *vague; 7 = clear/distinct.*
19. for the season is 1 = *vague; 7 = clear/distinct.*
20. for the day is 1 = *vague; 7 = clear/distinct.*
21. for the hour is 1 = *vague; 7 = clear/distinct.*
22. The event seems 1 = *short; 7 = long.*
23. The overall tone of the memory is 1 = *negative; 7 = positive.*
24. In this event I was 1 = *a spectator; 7 = a participant.*
25. At the time, the event seemed like it would have serious implications: 1 = *not at all;* 7 = *definitely.*
26. Looking back, this event did have serious implications: 1 = *not at all; 7 = definitely.*
27. I remember how I felt at the time when the event took place: 1 = *not at all; 7 = definitely.*
28. Feelings at the time were 1 = *negative; 7 = positive.*
29. were 1 = *not intense; 7 = very intense.*
30. As I am remembering now, my feelings are 1 = *not intense; 7 = very intense.*
31. I remember what I thought at the time: 1 = *not at all; 7 = clearly.*
32. This memory reveals or says about me: 1 = *not much; 7 = a lot.*
33. Overall, I remember this event: 1 = *hardly; 7 = very well.*
34. I remember events relating to this memory that took place in advance of the event: 1 = *not at all; 7 = yes, clearly.*
35. after the event: 1 = *not at all; 7 = yes, clearly.*
36. Do you have any doubts about the accuracy of your memory for this event? 1 = *a great deal of doubt; 7 = no doubt whatsoever.*
37. Since it happened, I have thought about this event: 1 = *not at all; 7 = many times.*
38. talked about it: 1 = *not at all; 7 = many times.*
39. About when did this event happen? Circle one: *just today   yesterday   few days ago   last week   few weeks ago   last month   few months ago   last year   longer* (if childhood, indicate age).

perceived items. Also, in both experiments, although the differences between trained and untrained judges on suggested items was significant, the difference was not a big one (20% improvement in Experiment 4 and 13% improvement in Experiment 5).

In a test of the extension of Johnson and Raye's (1981) model to children, Alonso-Quecuty, Hernandez-Fernaud, and Campos (1994) had 9-year-old children either view a film of a simple staged event (the perceived condition) or listen to a description of the film (the imagined condition). Experimenters then rated their accounts of these events. The accounts of the children in the perceived condition contained more sensory and contextual details than did the accounts of the children in the imagined condition. It is not clear, however, whether listening to a description of a film would qualify as an imagined event according to Johnson and Raye's framework. Perhaps the children in this condition simply remembered the verbal narration presented and did not actually generate the type of elaborative information that would be expected in Johnson and Raye's (1981) imagination conditions.

More recently, Roberts, Lamb, Zale, and Randall (1998) modified Johnson et al.'s (1988) MCQ so that the scale could be used by experimenters rating children's accounts of sexual abuse. A subset of the forensic interviews used by Raskin and Esplin (1991) was rated according to the MCQ criteria. These interviews were with children who had made reports of sexual abuse. The cases were independently classified as confirmed ($N = 10$) or unconfirmed ($N = 16$) on the basis of, for example, the availability of confessions, medical evidence, and physical evidence.

Overall, the total presence scores were significantly higher for the confirmed cases than for the unconfirmed cases. Separate t tests were conducted to compare scores for confirmed and unconfirmed cases on each of the 12 criteria of the MCQ. Significantly ($p < .05$) or marginally significantly ($p < .09$) higher scores for the confirmed cases occurred on ratings of perceptual features of people, actions, spatial information, temporal information, and self-reference. It appears, however, that the discriminating items on the MCQ were those that specifically predicted higher scores for perceived than for imagined events. Contrary to expectations, the unconfirmed cases did not receive higher self-reference scores nor higher thought and cognition scores than the confirmed cases; in fact, the trend was in the opposite direction. These findings are consistent with pilot results reported by Roberts, Lamb, and Randall (1997) that unconfirmed cases did not produce higher ratings of thoughts, rehearsals, and doubts than confirmed cases.

To date, findings regarding the effectiveness of the MCQ for discriminating between confirmed and unconfirmed cases of sexual abuse have not been impressive. The results of Roberts et al. (1998) and Roberts et al. (1997) are suggestive rather than conclusive because of the relatively small sample sizes in these studies. However, these results suggest that perhaps the MCQ is only effective at discriminating confirmed from unconfirmed cases of sexual abuse because the total amount of detail elicited by the MCQ differs between these two groups. If this is true, then there should be a significant correlation between the MCQ scores and the CBCA scores. Roberts et al. (1997) confirmed this prediction; the correlation between the two scales was $r = .76$ ($p < .03$). Additional research is clearly necessary to assess the utility of the MCQ for discriminating between true and false accounts of childhood sexual abuse.

MEMORIES FOR TRUE EVENTS VERSUS SUGGESTIVELY PLANTED FALSE EVENTS

There is a wealth of information available from which comparisons can be made of phenomenological characteristics of memories for true versus suggestively planted false events. This information has been published in the literature on planting false events in memory, in the suggestibility literature in which accounts of perceived versus suggested events have been compared, as well as the reality monitoring literature in which accounts of perceived versus imagined events have been compared. From the published research literature, we have selected the seven such studies that report recall data from which qualitative comparisons of accounts of true and false events have been made. The purpose of this section of the chapter is to summarize these seven studies and determine if their results suggest a consistent pattern of phenomenological characteristics that differentiate between accounts of true versus false events.

The first four studies are from the research literature on planting false events in memory. These include studies by Pezdek et al. (1997), Pezdek and Hodge (1999), Hyman and Pentland (1996), and Loftus and Pickrell (1995). The next two studies are from the suggestibility research literature. These include studies by Schooler, Clark, and Loftus (1988), and Schooler et al. (1988). The last study, by Johnson et al. (1988), is from the reality monitoring literature.

Pezdek et al. (1997) tested and confirmed the hypothesis that plausible false events are more easily planted in memory than implausible false events. In Experiment 1 of this study, 22 Jewish and 29 Catholic high school students were read descriptions of three true events (from mothers' reports) and two false events reported to have occurred when they were 8 years old. One false event described a Jewish ritual, and one described a Catholic ritual. After being read each description, each participant was asked what he or she remembered about the event. The results were that whereas 6 Catholics but 0 Jews remembered only the Catholic false event, 3 Jews but only 1 Catholic remembered only the Jewish false event. One person remembered both false events.

As part of this study, the researchers also compared various characteristics of the memories for the 13 participants who recalled at least one false event. In particular, it was predicted that compared to recalled false events, recalled true events would employ more words and receive higher ratings of clarity and confidence ("How confident are you that you could remember more about this event if given more time to think about it?"). These predictions were derived from a specific process model that describes how false events come to be planted in memory. According to this model, when a person is presented with a description of a specific instance of an activity and asked to verify whether this event happened to him or her, the person compares the instance described with his or her memory for related instances of that activity to determine whether there is a match. The more overlap there is between the information in the description and the information in memory, the more likely it is that a match will be indicated and the described event will be reported as true.

Once a false event is judged to be true, it is predicted that schema-relevant information in memory is activated and linked to the memory for the suggested false event. Memory for the false event thus includes information that was suggestively planted along with activated schema-relevant information. Furthermore, we predicted that when one retrieves a memory to determine whether there is a match between the memory and the described event presented, the schema-relevant information that was activated is less strongly associated with the constructed memory and is thus less clear and less confidently held than the information in memory that directly matched the presented experience. Consequently, because false events are likely to contain a higher proportion of activated schema-relevant information than are true events, memories for false events are predicted to be less clear and less confidently held than memories for true events.

In terms of the verbosity of the memory, memories for true events that are remembered contain the information presented in the described event as well as episodic memory for the event and activated information from schema relevant knowledge in memory. On the other hand, according to this model, memories for false events contain only the information presented in the description and activated information from schema-relevant knowledge in the memory. Because the false events did not actually occur, there is no episodic memory for the event. Thus, it was predicted that descriptions of false events would contain fewer words and fewer idea units than would descriptions of true events.

The results confirmed our hypotheses. Summarized in Table 4.3 are the findings from the seven studies to be reviewed in this section of the chapter. The findings are presented separately for the three phenomenological characteristics reported—confidence, verbosity, and clarity. As can be seen in Table 4.3, Pezdek et al. (1997) found that recall for false events (M = 15.64 words, 3.25 idea units) contained less information than recall for true events (M = 29.67 words, 5.57 idea units), and participants were less confident with false events (M = 4.79, on a 1 to 10 scale) than with true events (M = 6.80) that they could recall more information if given more time. In addition, memories for recalled false events (M = 4.00, on a 1 to 10 scale) were rated as less clear on average than were memories for recalled true events (M = 6.90).

In a similar study with children, Pezdek and Hodge (1999) read children descriptions of two true events and two false events, reported to have occurred when they were four years old. The children, ages 5 to 7 or 9 to 12 at the time of the study, were told what their mother remembered about each event. They were then asked what they remembered about the event. One false event described the child lost in a mall while shopping (the plausible false event); the other false event described the child receiving a rectal enema (the implausible false event). The major results were that whereas 14 children recalled the plausible but not the implausible false event, only 1 child recalled the implausible but not the plausible false event. Three additional children recalled both false events.

As part of this study, the researchers also assessed the verbosity of memories for true and false events. Consistent with the results of Pezdek et al. (1997), Pezdek and Hodge (1999) reported that of the 18 children who remembered at least one false event, significantly more idea units were recalled for true events (M = 4.86) than for false events (M = 3.06). Furthermore, of the 17 children who recalled the plausible false event, significantly more idea units were recalled for the true event (M = 5.06) than for the plausible false event (M = 3.24). Together these results suggest that the true events could be distinguished from the false events, even the plausible false event, by the number of details recalled.

In a study by Hyman and Pentland (1996), college-age participants were read descriptions of several true events (based on parent reports) and one false event reported to have occurred when the participant was a child. The false event described an event in which the participants attended a wedding and spilled a punch bowl on the parents of the bride. Participants were asked what they remembered about each event. If they could not recall an event they were asked either to form a mental image of the event and describe the image to the experimenter (the guided imagery condition), or they were simply asked to quietly think about the event (the control condition). This procedure was repeated on each of 3 consecutive days. The major result was that the guided imagery condition produced more confirmed false memories than did the control condition.

Participants in this study were also asked to rate the clarity of their mental image on a 1 (*low*) to 7 (*high*) scale, their confidence in the memory (on a 1 to 7 scale), the emotionality of the memory (on a 1 to 7 scale), and the positive–negative valence of the memory on a 1 (*negative*) to 7 (*positive*) scale. Although Hyman and Pentland (1996) did not specifically compare phenomenological characteristics of memories for true and false events, the relevant data can be abstracted from their study for this purpose, although significance tests on these comparisons are not available. In each case, comparisons are reported for the participants who always remembered the true events and those who reported that they did remember the false event.

In the control condition, true memories ($M = 5.35$) were rated as more confidently held than false memories ($M = 4.00$). The rated clarity was higher for true memories ($M = 4.87$) than for false memories ($M = 2.75$). Emotionality was rated higher for true memories ($M = 3.79$) than for false memories ($M = 1.75$), and true memories were rated as more positive in emotional tone ($M = 4.02$) than were false memories ($M = 3.25$). A similar pattern was reported in the imagery condition. True memories ($M = 5.57$) were rated as more confidently held than false memories ($M = 3.00$). The rated clarity was higher for true memories ($M = 5.00$) than for false memories ($M = 3.25$). The emotionality of true memories was rated higher for true ($M = 3.90$) than for false memories ($M = 2.17$), and true memories were rated as more positive in emotional tone ($M = 4.37$) than were false memories ($M = 3.58$). These results suggest that there is more information and more elaborated information in memory for true events than exist in memory for confirmed false events. True events are perceptually clearer and more confidently held, and they contain more positive information and more emotional information than do false events.

The fourth study from which phenomenological comparisons of true and false events can be compared is that of Loftus and Pickrell (1995). In this study, 24 volunteers suggested to an offspring or younger sibling that they had been lost in a shopping mall when they were about 5 years old. This false event was presented along with three true events. Each partici-

TABLE 4.3

Comparisons of Phenomenological Characteristics of True (Perceived or Watched) and False (Suggested or Imagined) Events in the Six Relevant Studies

Study	Measure	Perceived or Watched	Suggested or Imagined	Statistic	Significance
Confidence					
Pezdek et al. (1997)	Mean confidence for whether Ss could eventually report more details on a 1 (low) to 10 (high) scale	6.80	4.79	$t(13) = 3.50$	**
Schooler et al. (1986, Exp. 1)	Mean confidence rating on 1 (low) to 3 (high) scale	2.84	2.57	$t(87) = 2.33$	*
Schooler et al. (1988)	DNR	DNR	DNR	$t(12) = .75$	ns
Loftus & Pickrell (1995)	Mean confidence rating on a 1 (low) to 5 (high) scale	2.45	1.6	DNR	*
Johnson et al. (1988, Exp. 1)	Mean certainty rating for recent memories on a 1 (low) to 7 (high) scale	5.67	5.28	DNR	ns
Hyman & Pentland (1996)	Mean confidence rating on 1 (not) to 7 (very) scale in the control condition	5.35	4.00	DNR	DNR
	Mean rating of confidence in the memory from 1 (not) to 7 (very) imagery condition	5.57	3.00	DNR	DNR
Verbosity					
Pezdek et al. (1997)	Mean number of words	29.67	15.64	$t(13) = 4.65$	**
	Mean number of idea units	6.67	3.25	$t(13) = 4.63$	**
Pezdek & Hodge (1999)	Of the 18 children who remembered one false event, mean number of idea units	4.86	3.06	$t(17) = 2.36$	*
	Of the 17 children who recalled the plausible false event, mean number of idea units	5.06	3.24	$t(16) = 2.26$	*
Schooler et al. (1986, Exp. 1)	Mean number of words	18.34	25.14	$t(87) = 2.32$	*
Schooler et al. (1986, Exp. 2)	Mean number of words for real condition and both suggested conditions	7.04	12.69	$F(2,113) = 12.85$	**

Study	Measure	Perceived or Watched	Suggested or Imagined	Statistic	Significance
Schooler et al. (1988)	Mean number of words	22.12	23.74	$t(12) = .50$	ns
Loftus & Pickrell (1995)	Mean word length per description	138	49.9	DNR	*
Johnson et al. (1988, Exp. 2)	Mean number of idea units for recent events	2.02	1.53	DNR	ns
	Mean number of idea units for childhood events	1.98	1.49	DNR	ns
Sensory/Clarity					
Pezdek et al. (1997)	Mean clarity rating on 1 (low) to 10 (high) scale	6.90	4.00	$t(13) = 4.69$	**
Schooler et al. (1986, Exp. 1)	Percent of reports containing sensory information	41%	19%	$z = 1.76$	*
Schooler et al. (1986, Exp. 2)	Percent of reports containing sensory details collapsed across suggested conditions	82.5%	55%	$z = 2.98$	**
Schooler et al. (1988)	Mean frequency of sensory information included in reports	2.45	1.52	$t(12) = 2.96$	*
Loftus & Pickrell (1995)	Mean clarity ratings for the 5 people who recalled the false event, 1 (low) to 10 (high) scale	6.3	3.2	DNR	*
Hyman & Pentland (1996)	Mean clarity rating on 1 (not) to 7 (perfectly clear) scale for the control condition	4.87	2.75	DNR	DNR
	Mean clarity rating on 1 (not) to 7 (perfectly clear) scale for the imagery condition	5.00	3.25	DNR	DNR
Johnson et al. (1988, Exp. 1)	Mean rating on a 1 (vague) to 7 (clear) scale for vividness of childhood memories	4.97	4.78	DNR	ns
	Mean rating on a 1 (vague) to 7 (clear) scale for recent memories	5.69	5.06	DNR	ns
	Mean rating on a 1 (vague) to 7 (clear) scale for visual detail of recent memories	6.00	5.11	DNR	*
	Mean rating on a 1 (vague) to 7 (clear) scale for visual detail of childhood memories	5.22	4.56	DNR	ns

Note. Exp. = experiment; DNR = Data Not Reported; ns = not significant.
*p = .05.   **p = .01.

pant was asked what he or she remembered about each event. Six of the 24 participants reported either full or partial memory for the false event. The experimenters then examined the verbosity of the recalled descriptions of the true events and the remembered false events. Recalled true events contained more words ($M = 138$) than did recalled false events ($M = 50$). Also, mean clarity ratings in the second interview were higher for true events ($M = 6.3$) than for recalled false events ($M = 3.6$), and mean confidence ratings in the second interview were higher for true events ($M = 2.2$) than for recalled false events ($M = 1.4$). At the end of this study, participants were told that one of the events described had not really occurred. They were asked to pick which one this was, and 19 of the 24 subjects identified the false event correctly.

Schooler has conducted several experiments using the misinformation effect paradigm to compare phenomenological characteristics of memories for perceived and suggested events. Schooler et al. (1986, Experiments 1 and 2) had subjects view a sequence of slides. In the experimental condition, the sequence included a slide with a yield sign in it. In the suggested condition, the sequence did not include this critical target item. In a subsequent phase, a yield sign was suggested in the suggested condition but not in the experimental condition. In the experimental condition, 76% of the subjects reported having seen a yield sign (true), compared with 25% of the subjects in the suggested condition (false). To test the generalizability of the results, Experiment 2 was conducted with a stop sign as the critical item; similar findings were reported.

Phenomenological characteristics of the memories for perceived and suggested events were then examined. Compared with descriptions of perceived events, descriptions of suggested events less frequently included sensory properties of the sign (19% vs. 41%) but more often included functional information about the purpose of the sign (14% vs. 1%), first-person verbal hedges such as "I think" or "I believe" (38% vs. 12%), and descriptions of the cognitive processes associated with remembering or retrieving the event (29% vs. 3%). Similar results were obtained in Experiment 2, as well as in a separate study by Schooler et al. (1988) in which subjects were videotaped as they described the target items. The results of these three experiments are consistent with predictions of the reality monitoring model.

On the other hand, inconsistent with the results of the studies described above, in the Schooler et al. (1986) study, subjects who saw the yield sign used an average of 18.34 words to describe it, compared with 25.14 words for subjects for whom the yield sign was suggested. This finding was replicated in Experiment 2 of this study; the mean number of words used by subjects to describe the suggested stop sign was 12.69 (11.23 words in another suggested condition), compared with 7.04 words used by participants who saw the stop sign. However, in the study by Schooler et al. (1988), a range of objects less stereotypic than traffic signs (a robe, a shovel, a picture frame, a mailbox, etc.) were included in target slides, and no difference resulted between the verbosity of descriptions of perceived ($M = 22.12$ words) and suggested ($M = 23.74$ words) items. These findings are discrepant with the results of the other studies addressed in this section of the chapter, as well as with what might be predicted from the CBCA regarding the verbosity of true and false events.

One interpretation of the different results obtained by Schooler as compared with other researchers regarding the verbosity of descriptions of perceived and suggested items is that unlike the researchers in the other studies reported here, Schooler and his colleagues included in their word count all words provided. This included the words in statements such as, "I think it must have been there because . . . ," and "When I think about it, it seems to me that . . ." Because participants made more self-referencing statements in describing suggested items than perceived items, this would have inflated the word count for suggested items.

Another interpretation of why Schooler obtained higher verbosity ratings for suggested than perceived items is that perhaps the difference relates to whether participants were describing a simple object or a complex event. With a simple object, the verbal label captures a great deal of the information about the object (i.e., "stop sign," "yield sign"). If a person has seen a simple object, elaborative descriptive information is redundant with the simple verbal label. Thus, people who have seen a simple object are not likely to provide a great deal of descriptive information about the object. On the other hand, complex events such as getting lost in a mall and spilling punch at a wedding are not easily verbally labeled, and there are very few constraints on the range of elaborative details that might describe such events. It does appear, however, that with complex events, memories of perceived events will be described with significantly more words than will memories of suggestively planted events.

The seventh study to be reported in this section is the reality monitoring study by Johnson et al. (1988). In this study, people's reality monitoring ability for perceived and imagined autobiographical events was compared. Although this study was discussed previously in this chapter, some of the findings will also be reported here for comparison with the above studies on memory for perceived and suggested events. The findings were that perceived events were described using more idea units ($M = 2.02$ for recent events and 1.98 for childhood events) than were imagined events ($M = 1.53$

for recent events and 1.49 for childhood events). Perceived events ($M = 6.00$ for recent events and 5.22 for childhood events) were also rated higher in clarity of visual detail on a scale from 1 (*vague*) to 7 (*clear*) than imagined events ($M = 5.11$ for recent events and 4.56 for childhood events), although this difference was significant only for recent events. Differences in ratings of vividness of memories and confidence in the veracity of the memory did not significantly differ between the perceived and the imagined events in the Johnson et al. (1988) study (these means are presented in Table 4.2).

In summary, with the exception of the reports of verbosity in descriptions of perceived and suggested events by Schooler et al. (1986, 1988), these seven studies present a consistent pattern of results regarding phenomenological characteristics of memories for perceived and suggested or imagined events. Although people may erroneously report some false events as true, their descriptions of true events contain a greater clarity of perceptual details, they are more confidently held, and they are described with more words. These findings are consistent with the prediction that when one retrieves a memory to determine whether there is a match between the memory and the described event presented, schema-relevant information that is associated with the memory is less clear and less confidently held than information in the episodic memory that directly matches the presented experience. Furthermore, whereas memories for remembered true events contain the information presented in the described event as well as episodic memory for the event and schema-relevant information that is associated in memory, memories for false events contain only the information presented in the description and associated information from schema-relevant knowledge in memory.

CONCLUSION

Although accounts of memories for true and false events tend to differ in predictable and statistically significant ways, the tools available for determining the veracity of memory accounts are far less than perfect. Findings from the research on memory for true events versus suggestively planted false events dovetail nicely with findings from the reality monitoring research in suggesting that accounts of true events contain a greater clarity of perceptual details, they are more confidently held, and they are described with more words. This pattern is consistent for memory accounts of adults as well as children.

To the extent that the CBCA component of the SVA tool also assesses these qualities, it is not surprising that the CBCA facilitates the discrimination of accounts of true and false events. However, there is a need for additional research on the value added of the additional factors in the CBCA beyond the three general criteria. The relative importance of the 18 CBCA content criteria needs to be determined to provide a more precise interpretation of the score obtained in any case. Also, as we discussed earlier, it is not clear whether the organization and logical structure of a memory account are indicative of the veracity of the account, as is predicted by the CBCA, or whether these features simply correlate with the familiarity of the domain described. If accounts of familiar events received higher CBCA scores than accounts of unfamiliar events, this would be a serious limitation of the CBCA because the familiarity of an event can come from indirect sources such as conversations with people and various forms of media as well as from direct personal experience.

In the work reviewed in this chapter, the veracity of memory accounts has been determined by the relative quality of specific characteristics; the qualities of some event known to be false have been compared with the qualities of some event known to be true. This procedure has important applied implications. Social service agencies seek validity assessment tools to determine, for example, the veracity of reports of abuse in which the veracity of the alleged event is not known. The work reviewed in this chapter suggests that the veracity of an alleged event will be determined more accurately if blind raters can compare the qualities of the account of the reported event with the qualities of the account of some comparable event that is known to be true (a within-subject control condition). Because the qualities known to differentiate between accounts of true and false events also vary widely among individuals, we suggest that the predictive validity of any memory assessment tool would be enhanced if interviewers made within-subject comparisons of the account of the alleged event with the account of a comparable event known to be true.

REFERENCES

Alonso-Quecuty, M., Hernandez-Fernaud, E., & Campos, L. (1994, July). *Children's memory: Facts, fantasies, and lies.* Paper presented at the Fourth European Conference on Psychology and the Law, Barcelona, Spain.

Ceci, S. J., Loftus, E. F., Leichtman, M., & Bruck, M. (1994). The possible role of source misattributions in the creation of false beliefs among preschoolers. *International Journal of Clinical and Experimental Hypnosis, 42,* 304–320.

Esplin, P. W., Boychuk, T., & Raskin, D. C. (1988, June). *A field study of criteria-based content analysis of children's statement in sexual abuse cases.* Paper presented at the meeting of the NATO Advanced Study Institute on Credibility Assessment, Maratea, Italy.

Fivush, R., Kuebli, J., & Clubb, P. A. (1992). The structure of events and event representations: A developmental analysis. *Child Development, 63,* 188–201.

Fivush, R., & Slackman, E. (1986). The acquisition and development of scripts. In K. Nelson (Ed.), *Event knowledge: Structure and function in development* (pp. 71–96). Hillsdale, NJ: Lawrence Erlbaum Associates.

Foley, M. A., & Johnson, M. K. (1985). Confusions between memories for performed and imagined actions: A developmental comparison. *Child Development, 56,* 1145–1155.

Foley, M. A., Johnson, M. K., & Raye, C. L. (1983). Age-related changes in confusion between memories for thoughts and memories for speech. *Child Development, 54,* 51–60.

Hyman, I. E., & Pentland, J. (1996). The role of mental imagery in the creation of false childhood memories. *Journal of Memory & Language, 35,* 101–117.

Johnson, M. K., Foley, M. A., Suengas, A. G., & Raye, C. L. (1988). Phenomenal characteristics of memories for perceived and imagined autobiographical events. *Journal of Experimental Psychology: General, 117,* 371–376.

Johnson, M. K., & Raye, C. L. (1981). Reality monitoring. *Psychological Review, 88,* 67–85.

Johnson, M. K., Raye, C. L., Wang, A. Y., & Taylor, T. H. (1979). Fact and fantasy: The roles of accuracy and variability in confusing imaginations with perceptual experiences. *Journal of Experimental Psychology: Human Learning and Memory, 5,* 229–240.

Lamb, M. E., Sternberg, K. J., Esplin, D. C., Hershkowitz, I., & Orbach, Y. (1997). Assessing the credibility of children's allegations of sexual abuse: A survey of recent research. *Learning and Individual Differences, 9,* 175–194.

Lamers-Winkelman, F., Buffing, F., & van der Zanden, A. P. (1992, September). *Statement validity analysis in child sexual abuse cases: A field study.* Poster presented at the Third Conference of Law and Psychology, Oxford, England.

Landry, K. L., & Brigham, J. C. (1992). The effect of training in criteria-based content analysis on the ability to detect deception in adults. *Law and Human Behavior, 16,* 663–676.

Loftus, E. F., Miller, D. F., & Burns, H. J. (1978). Semantic integration of verbal information into a visual memory. *Journal of Experimental Psychology: Human Learning and Memory, 4,* 19–31.

Loftus, E. F., & Pickrell, J. E. (1995). The formation of false memories. *Psychiatric Annals, 25,* 720–725.

Pezdek, K., Finger, K., & Hodge, D. (1997). Planting false childhood memories: The role of event plausibility. *Psychological Science, 8,* 437–441.

Pezdek, K., & Hodge, D. (1999). Planting false childhood memories: The role of event plausibility. *Child Development, 70,* 887–895.

Pezdek, K., & Roe, C. (1994). Memory for childhood events: How suggestible is it? *Consciousness and Cognition, 3,* 374–387.

Pezdek, K., & Roe, C. (1997). The suggestibility of children's memory for being touched: Planting, erasing, and changing memories. *Law & Human Behavior, 21,* 95–106.

Raskin, D. C., & Esplin, P. W. (1991). Statement validity assessment: Interview procedures and content analysis of children's statements of sexual abuse. *Behavioral Assessment, 13,* 265–291.

Roberts, K. P., Lamb, M. E., & Randall, D. W. (1997, July). *Assessing the plausibility of allegations of sexual abuse from children's accounts.* Paper presented at the biennial meeting of the Society for Applied Research in Memory and Cognition, Toronto, Canada.

Roberts, K. P., Lamb, M. E., Zale, J. L. and Randall, D. W. (1998, March). *Qualitative differences in children's accounts of confirmed and unconfirmed incidents of sexual abuse.* Paper presented at the biennial meeting of the American Psychology-Law Society, Redondo Beach, CA.

Ruby, C. L., & Brigham, J. C. (1997). The usefulness of the criteria-based content analysis technique in distinguishing between truthful and fabricated allegations: A critical review. *Psychology, Public Policy, and Law, 3,* 705–737.

Ruby, C. L., & Brigham, J. C. (1998). Can criteria-based content analysis distinguish between true and false statements of African-American speakers? *Law and Human Behavior, 22,* 369–388.

Schooler, J., Clark, C. A., & Loftus, E. F. (1988). Knowing when memory is real. In M. M. Gruneberg, P. E. Morris, & R. N. Sykes (Eds.), *Practical aspects of memory: Current research and issues: Vol. 1. Memory in everyday life* (pp. 83–88). New York: Wiley.

Schooler, J., Gerhard, D., & Loftus, E. F. (1986). Qualities of the unreal. *Journal of Experimental Psychology: Learning, Memory, and Cognition, 12,* 171–181.

Steller, M. (1989). Recent developments in statement analysis. In J. C. Yuille (Ed.), *Credibility assessment* (pp. 135–154). Dordrecht, the Netherlands: Kluwer.

Steller, M., Wellershaus, P., & Wolf, T. (1988, June). *Empirical validation of criteria-based content analysis.* Paper presented at the meeting of the NATO Advanced Study Institute on Credibility Assessment, Maratea, Italy.

Tye, M. J. C., Henderson, S. A., & Honts, C. R. (1995, January). *Evaluating children's testimonies: CBCA and lay subjects.* Paper presented at the meeting of CRIMECON: International Internet Conference on Crime and Criminal Justice.

Undeutsch, U. (1989). The development of statement reality analysis. In J. C. Yuille (Ed.), *Credibility assessment* (pp. 101–119). Dordrecht, the Netherlands: Kluwer.

Wells, G. L., & Loftus, E. F. (1991). Is this child fabricating? Reactions to a new assessment technique. In J. Doris (Ed.), *The suggestibility of children's recollections* (pp. 168–171). Washington, DC: American Psychological Association.

Yuille, J. C. (1988, June). *A simulation study of criterion based content analysis.* Paper presented at the meeting of the NATO Advanced Study Institute on Credibility Assessment, Maratea, Italy.

Zaparniuk, J., Yuille, J. C., & Taylor, S. (1995). Assessing the credibility of true and false statements. *International Journal of Law Psychiatry, 18,* 343–352.

CHAPTER FIVE

Fuzzy-Trace Theory and False Memory

Memory Theory in the Courtroom

CHARLES J. BRAINERD
VALERIE F. REYNA
University of Arizona

DEBRA A. POOLE
Central Michigan University

In psychology, interesting empirical effects have a way of accumulating more rapidly than theoretical understanding. This gap can become very wide when a topic captures broad scientific attention, provoking simultaneous experimentation in many laboratories. The burgeoning literature on false memory is a case in point. At the moment, spontaneous and implanted false memories are being intensively studied, outside as well as inside the laboratory, new research paradigms are being developed, and variables are being identified that affect levels of false reporting (see other chapters in this volume). Although the clinical community is still vigorously debating the pervasiveness of potentially falsifying therapeutic techniques (e.g., Berwin, 1997; Pope, 1996), there is no longer any serious doubt about the pervasiveness of memory falsification in the scientific (e.g., Loftus, 1995) and legal (e.g., *State v. Hungerford*, 1995; *State v. Morahan*, 1995) communities.

However, our ability to account for false memories theoretically, to explain them as consequences of underlying processes that systematically distort recollection, is not what it should be. Consider, in this connection, a featured conclusion of the American Psychological Association's interim report on adults' false memories of childhood sexual abuse: "It is possible to construct convincing pseudo-memories for events that never occurred, although the mechanisms by which this occurs are not well understood" (Denton, 1994, p. 9). Consider, too, Ceci and Bruck's (1993) conclusion, in their review of studies of implanted false memories in children, that "the exact mechanisms involved in producing distortion in young children's reports are still being debated" (p. 432).

Why is theoretical explanation essential? The traditional scientific objectives of prediction and control are perhaps the first answers that come to mind. If researchers can spell out general theoretical principles that cut across experimental paradigms, they can predict new situations in which false memories will be present and, by manipulating the processes that are specified in those principles, they can control resulting levels of falsification. There is another, more practical, answer, however: forensic application.

As experimental demonstrations of false memory have multiplied, so has its use in prosecution and defense submissions in certain types of cases. Although false memory has figured most prominently in allegations of sexual abuse involving children or adults who were children at the time of the alleged abuse, it is cropping up in other types of cases, such as assault and personal injury (e.g., *Dosh v. Block Estate,* 1997). The typical false-memory case has three characteristics. First, there is little or no physical evidence that bears on the central allegations. Second, the relevant evidence therefore consists overwhelmingly of witness's recollections of events. Third, attorneys for plaintiffs, defendants, or both have some rationale for claiming that key witness recollections are based on false memories.

In such cases, memory researchers have been asked to provide expert testimony on this claim, often in pretrial evidentiary hearings. The researcher is confronted with the task of reviewing and explaining scientific findings that bear on the case, such as elucidating conditions that are associated with false memories (see Hembrooke & Ceci, 1998, for discussions of expert testimony). If the case ultimately goes to trial, that information may be entered as evidence during direct examination. Under the rules governing admission of expert testimony, experts must demonstrate that the conclusions they offer have achieved general acceptance within the community of experts (Frye test) or were derived from appropriate scientific methods (Daubert test).

What evidence does an expert supply to educate the trier of fact? In the absence of generally accepted theoretical principles, some specific experiment or group of experiments, will normally be cited, with analogies being drawn between its methodology and the details of the target case. Legal cases, however, present unique features that are not captured by individual experiments or groups of experiments. Cross-examining attorneys home in on this fact, identifying salient points of difference between the cited research and the details of the case. The objective is to convince the trier of fact that owing to numerous and fundamental points of difference, the expert's opinion is little more than a leap of faith.

If generally accepted theoretical principles are available, on the other hand, they provide grounds for the expert to select appropriate empirical findings and to argue their relevance to the issues at hand. Theoretical principles, referring as they do to underlying processes that are tapped by the designs of all experiments, are inherently transparadigmatic, constants in a sea of methodological flux. Scientific theories are predictive because they are, by their nature, applicable to new situations that differ in important respects from the research paradigms from which the principles evolved. Thus, when supplying scientific grounds for the types of conclusions that experts are asked to render in court, a good theory is a very practical thing.

In this chapter, therefore, we focus on theoretical explanations of false memory, with a view toward their forensic ramifications. The chapter is divided into three main sections. In the first, we describe phenomena that are experimental analogues of the false memories that are problematical in legal contexts. In the second, we review a series of theoretical principles that explain those phenomena and that also generate novel predictions that can be used to test the validity of the principles. In the third, we show how these same principles deliver the forensic goods. Predictions that the principles make on four topics of significant forensic interest are considered: age differences in memory falsification; the relative memorability of truth and fiction, including the phenomenon of false confession; the relative consistency of true and false reports; and the effects of nonsuggestive questioning. With each topic, we show how predictions made on theoretical grounds, predictions that have been confirmed empirically, are at odds with the law's view of memory.

CORE PHENOMENA

The scientific study of false memory deals with two broad classes of phenomena: *spontaneous false reports* and *implanted false reports* (Reyna, 1995). The former are products of endogenous distortion mechanisms that are part of the everyday functioning of memory (e.g., Wulf, 1922), whereas the latter have the additional feature that they correspond to exogenous misinformation that has been accidentally or deliberately implanted in individuals' memories (e.g., Loftus, 1979). Although many procedures have been used to study these phenomena (cf. other chapters in this volume), most experiments share three characteristics. First, the experimental participants, adults or children or both, are exposed to some memory targets. Depending on the experiment, they may be lists of words, pictures, sentences, statements that form a narrative, or staged events (live or filmed). Second, there is an interpolated activity of some sort. Third, the subjects respond to a memory test.

The first characteristic ensures that false-memory experiments inform forensic work. In legal cases, it is difficult to know which witness statements are based on false memories because there usually is no physical record (e.g., an audio or video recording) of events. In experiments, events are controlled by researchers, so that subsequent false reports can be identified reliably. The second characteristic determines whether an experiment deals with spontaneous or implanted false memories. If spontaneous false memories are the focus, the interpolated activity (e.g., solving arithmetic or spatial problems) is irrelevant to the memory targets (and to later tests). If implanted false memories are the focus, the activity (usually called the *misinformation phase*) presents information that conflicts with target events. The third characteristic supplies measures of true and false reporting. Although recall tests are sometimes administered (e.g., Cassel & Bjorklund, 1995; Cassel, Roebers, & Bjorklund, 1996), recognition tests are more common (e.g., Brainerd, Reyna, & Brandse, 1995; Ceci, Ross, & Toglia, 1987).

On recognition tests, participants are instructed to accept items that were presented as targets and to reject all other items. Such tests contain some or all of four types of items: targets, unpresented items that are irrelevant to the targets (*unrelated distractors*), unpresented items that overlap in meaning with targets and do not conflict with them (*consistent meaning-sharing distractors*), and unpresented items that conflict with the meaning of targets (*inconsistent meaning-sharing distractors*). For instance, suppose that the targets are statements comprising a narrative about an armed robbery in a store. The statements "The robber wore a mask" and "The robber demanded money from the clerk" appear in the narrative, but the statement "The robber carried a pistol" does not. "The robber demanded money from the clerk" and "The robber wore a mask" would be targets, "There was a shopping cart in the parking lot" would be an unrelated distractor, "The robber carried a pistol" would be a consistent meaning-sharing distractor, and "The clerk saw the robber's face" would be an inconsistent distractor. Unrelated distractors are administered to secure measures of response bias, which is the tendency to accept an item on some irrelevant basis (e.g., confusion, guessing, response sets).

In spontaneous false-memory experiments, three general findings are that (a) targets are accepted at higher rates than distractors, (b) consistent meaning-sharing distractors are accepted at higher rates than the other two types of distractors, and (c) inconsistent distractors are accepted at higher rates than unrelated distractors (for illustrative data, see Ackerman, 1994; Brainerd & Mojardin, 1998; Brainerd & Reyna, 1996; Reyna & Kiernan, 1994, 1995). The extent to which false alarms to meaning-sharing distractors exceed baseline responses (false alarms to unrelated or inconsistent distractors) is a measure of spontaneous memory falsification (called *the false-recognition effect*). Finding B shows that spontaneous memory falsification responds to variations in the degree of overlap between presented and unpresented material.

In implantation experiments, the misinformation that is presented before memory is tested typically consists of suggestions about unpresented but related material that either conflicts with specific targets (e.g., "Do you remember that the clerk saw the robber's face?") or does not conflict with specific targets (e.g., "Do you remember that the robber carried a pistol?"). Two general findings are that (a) hit rates are lower for targets when conflicting information has been presented than when it has not been, and (b) false-alarm rates for distractors are higher when they have been presented as misinformation than when they have not (e.g., Belli, 1989; Mojardin, 1998; Pezdek & Roe, 1995, 1997; Tversky & Tuchin, 1989). Although both results have been called *misinformation effects,* we distinguish them by referring to the former as *hit suppression* and the latter as *false-alarm elevation.*

EXPLAINING FALSE MEMORIES

The preliminary criteria of generality that a theory of false memory should meet are (a) Its principles should cut across the standard paradigms in which false memories have been studied; (b) those principles should explain both spontaneous and implanted false memories; (c) those principles should explain developmental variability in false memories; and, crucially, (d) those principles should make novel predictions, including ones about everyday memory phenomena that may have forensic implications. In the present section, we summarize a candidate theory, fuzzy-trace theory (FTT), to show how its principles account for the basic effects in standard paradigms and show how they explain developmental variability. In the next section, we explore predictions about selected forensic questions and summarize recent findings on those predictions.

Principles of FTT

Parallel Verbatim–Gist Storage. The first principle deals with the types of memories that participants store about targets and about interpolated misinformation. Many findings suggest that adults and children deposit verbatim traces of targets' surface forms and other item-specific information ("The robber demanded money from the clerk"), plus gist traces of targets' semantic, relational, and elaborative properties ("armed robbery story"; for a review of FTT, see Reyna & Brainerd, 1995). Although verbatim and gist traces are stored for the same inputs (indeed, they are alternative representations of inputs), gist traces do not seem to be extracted from verbatim traces, but, rather, verbatim and gist traces appear to be stored in a parallel manner. Key experimental results that favor parallel storage are ones in which targets' meanings are deposited before the targets themselves have been fully processed (for a review, see Brainerd & Reyna, 1993). The missing-letter effect (Moravcski & Healy, 1995) provides an example: Participants can often fail to recognize the constituent letters of familiar words, even though they have processed and stored the words' meanings. Other examples come from problem-solving tasks in which participants identify global relations among targets after encoding only a few of them (e.g., Brainerd & Reyna, 1995; Reyna & Brainerd, 1990).

Dissociated Verbatim–Gist Retrieval. The second principle is concerned with functional relations between verbatim and gist traces. Prior research on the accessibility of these memories (for reviews, see Brainerd & Poole, 1997; Reyna & Titcomb, 1996) points to two factors as being especially important in determining whether verbatim or gist traces are retrieved on a memory test: (a) the retrieval cues that are supplied by the test and (b) the rates at which verbatim and gist traces are forgotten. Regarding the first factor, when targets are presented as test items ("The robber demanded money from the clerk"), they are usually better retrieval cues for verbatim than for gist traces, assuming that both types of memories are still accessible (Brainerd, Reyna, & Kneer, 1995). When meaning-sharing distractors are presented ("The robber carried a pistol"), they are usually better retrieval cues for gist traces than for verbatim traces (Reyna & Kiernan, 1994). Consequently, target hits are predominately verbatim

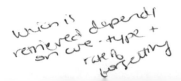

which is retrieved depend
on cue-type +
rate of forgetting

based, whereas distractor false alarms are predominantly gist based. Although this idea is consistent with modern theories of retrieval (e.g., Tulving & Thomson, 1971), empirical support comes from studies of on-line relations between the retrieval of verbatim and gist memories on memory tests (Ackerman, 1992, 1994; Brainerd & Gordon, 1994; Brainerd & Reyna, 1995; Marx & Henderson, 1996; Reyna, 1996a; Reyna & Kiernan, 1994, 1995). In such studies, it has been found that hits and false-alarms to meaning-sharing distractors often are independent, that some manipulations affect hit rates but not false-alarm rates, that other manipulations affect false-alarm rates but not hit rates, and that still other manipulations have opposite effects on hit and false-alarm rates.

Regarding the second factor, forgetting rates, there is a research tradition that favors the view that verbatim traces become inaccessible more rapidly than gist traces (e.g., Gernsbacher, 1985; Murphy & Shapiro, 1994). As time passes, then, the putative memorial basis for initial hits fails more rapidly than that for false alarms. The memories that are accessed by targets therefore will tend to switch from verbatim traces ("The robber demanded money from the clerk") to gist traces ("armed robbery story"), whereas the gist traces that are accessed by distractors ("armed robbery story") will be more stable (Brainerd, Reyna, & Brandse, 1995; Reyna & Kiernan, 1994).

remember-know

Experiences of Remembrance. The third principle is concerned with the types of subjective impressions that are provoked by the information that participants retrieve on a memory test. Since the appearance of an influential paper by Mandler (1980), a test item has been thought to provoke at least two distinct subjective reactions. One, which has been variously called *recollection* or *feeling of remembering* or *explicit memory*, involves remembrance of having encountered specific items earlier in the experiment. The other, which has been variously called *familiarity* or *feeling of* *graded* *knowing* or *implicit memory*, involves global impressions of having experienced certain meanings or relations earlier in the experiment, impressions that are not grounded in recollection of specific items. One line of evidence that bears on this distinction consists of data showing that the two types of remembrance can have opposite effects on false-alarm rates (Horton, Pavlick, & Moulin-Julian, 1993). Another line of evidence comes from research on Jacoby's (1991) process-dissociation model. This model contains separate parameters for item-specific recollection and nonspecific familiarity, and manipulations have been identified (e.g., dividing attention at study or at test) that affect one parameter but not the other (for a review, see Brainerd, Reyna, & Mojardin, 1999).

In FTT, retrieval of verbatim traces supports feelings of item-specific recollection, whereas feelings of nonspecific familiarity are supported by retrieval of gist memories (Brainerd & Reyna, 1998a). Retrieval of verbatim traces produces access to representations of particularized surface structures, leading to feelings of reexperiencing those surface structures (e.g., the exact wording of "The robber demanded money from the clerk" is seen in the mind's eye or heard in the mind's ear). On the other hand, retrieval of gist memories produces access to semantic information, which can lead to feelings of reexperiencing familiar meanings ("armed robbery story") that are not accompanied by recollection of specific target events but are consistent with many possible events (e.g., robbers usually wear masks and carry weapons).

Although retrieval of gist memories can support nonspecific impressions of having experienced certain meanings or relations, recent studies suggest that, under some conditions, it can also support feelings of item-specific recollection (for a review, see Reyna & Lloyd, 1997). So far, the two experimental conditions that seem to induce gist-based feelings of item-specific recollection are (a) retrieved gist memories represent meanings that have been repeatedly cued at study and therefore are very strong (e.g., "armed robbery story" is cued by multiple statements in the narrative), and (b) meaning-consistent test items provide privileged access to those meanings, as when statements involving the word "crime" provide privileged access to meanings that were stored during a robbery story (Brainerd & Reyna, 1998b; Reyna, 1996a, 1996b). Although it appears that gist memories can sometimes support feelings of item-specific recollection, it is clear, empirically, that those feelings have a different origin than those that accompany the retrieval of verbatim traces because they can occur for meaning-sharing distractors that were never experienced (cf. Payne, Elie, Blackwell, & Neuschatz, 1996; Reyna, 1996b; Reyna & Kiernan, 1994; Robinson & Roediger, 1997).

Identity, Nonidentity, and Similarity.   The final principle is concerned with the types of judgments about test items that are supported by item-specific recollection and nonspecific familiarity. Experimental findings (e.g., Brainerd, Reyna, & Kneer, 1995; Hintzman & Curran, 1994) have suggested that feelings of item-specific recollection support all-or-none judgments of identity–nonidentity about test items, whereas feelings of nonspecific familiarity support graded similarity judgments. When a verbatim memory is retrieved, comparison to the surface form of the test item will support a categorical judgment of identity or nonidentity of surface forms (Brainerd, Reyna, & Kneer, 1995). When a gist memory is retrieved, the memory produces feelings of nonspecific familiarity; comparison to the gist representation of the test item will support a judgment of degree of similarity between the contents of the representations (Schacter, Verfaellie, & Anes, 1997; Tun, Wingfield, Rosen, & Blanchard, 1998). But when a retrieved gist memory is strong, it can provoke feelings of item-specific recollection (Brainerd & Reyna, 1998a; Reyna, 1996b).

Behaviorally, verbatim retrieval supports target hits (identity judgments) and correct rejections of meaning-sharing distractors (nonidentity judgments; Brainerd et al., 1999; Brainerd, Stein, & Reyna, 1998). For instance, retrieval of the verbatim trace of "The robber wore a mask" supports acceptance of that test item, but it also supports rejection of "The clerk saw the robber's face." Verbatim retrieval leads to across-the-board rejection of distractors such as the latter, as well as meaning-consistent distractors such as the "The robber carried a pistol," because no matter how much meaning overlap there is, a demonstrable mismatch exists between the remembered surface forms of the presented statements and the surface forms of the test items (Brainerd, Reyna, & Kneer, 1995; Clark & Gronlund, 1996). Thus, verbatim retrieval can provoke either judgments of identity of surface forms (e.g., when the probe is the target that produced that trace) or judgments of nonidentity of surface forms (e.g., when the probe is a meaning-sharing distractor or some other target).

Gist retrieval also will support target hits. If the accompanying subjective experience is nonspecific familiarity, hits result when the judged level of meaning overlap is great enough to exceed some subjective threshold. Unlike verbatim retrieval, gist retrieval will also support false alarms to meaning-sharing distractors—again, from similarity judgment if the accompanying experience is familiarity or if the accompanying experience is item-specific recollection.

Explaining Spontaneous and Implanted False Reports

The four principles that we have just summarized are used in the following way to explain the two basic types of false-memory reports. First, to account for spontaneous false memories, false alarms to meaning-sharing distractors ("The robber carried a pistol") can occur for two main reasons: retrieval of gist memories of targets and reliance on various nonmemorial processes (e.g., response bias). When gist memories are retrieved, false alarms can be inferences that are based on familiarity of meaning ("It was an armed robbery story and robbers usually carry guns") or illusions of item-specific recollection. The false-recognition effect (i.e., higher false-alarm rates for meaning-sharing distractors than for unrelated distractors) then falls out of the fact that one of the bases for false alarms (gist retrieval) necessarily is more frequent with meaning-sharing distractors. Higher false-alarm rates for consistent meaning-sharing distractors ("The robber carried a pistol") than for inconsistent distractors ("The clerk saw the robber's face") follows from the fact that the latter can produce retrieval of conflicting verbatim traces (the statement "The robber wore a mask" appeared in the story) but the former cannot (there were no statements about weapons in the narrative).

Second, to account for implanted false memories, both false-alarm elevation and hit suppression must be explained. As with the false-recognition effect, gist retrieval is one basis for false-alarm elevation: Gist memories of inconsistent distractors will be more accessible if those distractors are presented during the misinformation phase. Unlike the false-recognition effect, verbatim retrieval is another basis for false-alarm elevation: Verbatim traces of inconsistent distractors may be retrieved because those distractors were presented during the misinformation phase. If they are retrieved when such distractors are tested, they can support false identity judgments, assuming that the conflict between these distractors and earlier targets was not detected during the misinformation phase (Reyna & Titcomb, 1996).

Concerning hit suppression, unlike false recognition and false-alarm elevation, retrieval of gist traces should not be the basis for this effect because gist traces support hits (e.g., "armed robbery story" supports acceptance, not rejection, of "The robber wore a mask" and "The robber demanded money from the clerk"). If a target ("The robber wore a mask") is subsequently misinformed ("The clerk saw the robber's face"), although the misinformation implants incorrect memories of a surface detail, it also supplies additional practice at retrieving gist memories ("armed robbery story") that will support acceptance of that target. Thus, gist memories may be more accessible for misinformed targets than for control targets that are not presented during the misinformation phase (Reyna, 1996b). The principal reason for hit suppression should therefore be verbatim rather than gist retrieval: The misinformation phase makes additional verbatim traces available ("The clerk saw the robber's face") that conflict with previously stored verbatim traces ("The robber wore a mask"). When the former are retrieved on memory tests, they can support false nonidentity judgments about targets (i.e., hit suppression), again assuming that the conflict between targets and misinformation was not detected during the misinformation phase.

Summing up, in FTT's analysis of implanted false memories, retrieval of verbatim traces of misinformation can lower hit rates (through false nonidentity judgments) and raise false-alarm rates (through false identity judgments). Furthermore, retrieval of gist traces of misinformation can increase false-alarm rates (through similarity judgments or false identity judgments). This analysis leads to a straightforward prediction on which data are available. Other things being equal, false-alarm elevation should exceed hit suppression. Misinformation implants verbatim memories that conflict with surface details of target material and that will therefore support false alarms to misinformation-embodying distractors and incorrect rejections of targets. Data that are consistent with this scenario have been reported by Tversky and Tuchin (1989) and by Pezdek and Roe (1995). Tversky and Tuchin found that false-alarm elevation was roughly one third greater than hit suppression, and in Pezdek and Roe's (1995) experiment, false-alarm elevation was roughly five times greater than hit suppression.

THEORETICAL PREDICTIONS AND THE LAW'S VIEW OF MEMORY

It is not widely understood that prediction is the litmus test of theory. Although theories must, of necessity, explain known effects, that is only the first step. Explanations of known effects are postdictions, and the history of psychology teaches that there are many ways of postdicting any set of findings. Explanations should therefore be regarded as promissory notes that need to be tested by assessing their power to forecast new effects, especially ones that are not anticipated by competing theories or that seem counterintuitive on their face. Such predictions have been emphasized in research on FTT (Miller & Bjorklund, 1998).

Our aim in this section is not to undertake a comprehensive review of those predictions but to address a related forensic question: Does FTT make any novel or counterintuitive predictions in the forensic sphere? Experience has shown that it does (e.g., Poole, 1995). Moreover, some of its predictions challenge well-known assumptions that the law makes about the memory reports of witnesses (Reyna, 1998; Reyna & Brainerd, 1997; Wohlmuth, 1997). We examine predictions and data that challenge four assumptions: (a) that false memories are more common in children than adults; (b) that truth is more memorable than fiction; (c) that reports of true events are more consistent than reports of false events; and (d) that neutral, nonsuggestive questioning does not falsify memory. Although these assumptions are cornerstones of the law's view of memory, FTT predicts that each will be violated under conditions that the theory specifies.

False Memories Are More Common in Children than Adults

As previously noted, the possibility of false-memory reports is a central concern in cases involving children or adults who were children at the time of alleged events because the law has long held that children's memories are more malleable and prone to falsification than adults'. The prevalence of this assumption is demonstrated in the competency voir dire for children under a specified age (McGough, 1994). Although there has been a trend in recent years to eliminate statutes that require children to demonstrate competency (Ceci & Bruck, 1995), nonetheless many child witnesses still participate in voir dire, and investigative protocols often include preliminary assessments of children's competency (Poole & Lamb, 1998). These practices have been reinforced by recent literature reviews, which have concluded that preschoolers are more susceptible to misinformation than older children (Ceci & Bruck, 1993; McAuliff, Kovera, & Viswesvaran, 1998).

Contrary to the law's assumption, FTT predicts that there that there is no single, monolithic developmental trend in memory falsification and that, instead, different trends (i.e., age increases, decreases, invariances) can be observed under different conditions. This prediction follows because FTT contains *opponent processes* that (a) have opposite effects on memory falsification but that (b) vary in the same direction with age (Brainerd & Reyna, 1998a). Insofar as spontaneous false memories are concerned, one process supports false alarms to meaning-consistent distractors (gist-based judgments of similarity or false identity), but the other process supports correct rejections (verbatim-based nonidentity judgments). Because both processes improve with age between early childhood and young adulthood, the false-recognition effect ought to exhibit developmental decreases within this age range when experimental conditions (e.g., instructions, materials) favor verbatim retrieval, developmental increases when conditions favor gist retrieval, and age invariance when conditions provoke comparable rates of verbatim and gist retrieval.

Insofar as implanted false memories are concerned, we saw that hit suppression is attributed to the retrieval of verbatim traces of misinformation, whereas false-alarm elevation is attributed to this mechanism and to the retrieval of gist traces of targets and of misinformation. As with the false-recognition effect, then, memory processes that make performance more accurate and memory processes that make it less accurate both are improving with age (between early childhood and young adulthood). Concerning age variability in hit suppression, the accessibility of verbatim and gist traces of targets improves with age, all of which increase hit rates, but so does the accessibility of verbatim traces of misinformation, which decreases hit rates. Concerning age variability in false-alarm elevation, accessibility of verbatim traces of targets improves with age, which decreases false alarms, but so does accessibility of verbatim and gist traces of misinformation and gist traces of targets, which increases false alarms. Hence, inconsistencies in observed developmental trends in misinformation effects can be expected because the opponent memory processes that contribute most to acceptance rates for targets and distractors will vary from study to study as a function of design factors (Reyna, 1996a).

Recent literature reviews have been more consistent with FTT's analysis of developmental change than the law's. Concerning spontaneous false memories, Reyna and Kiernan (1994) reviewed developmental studies of false recognition of meaning-sharing sentences. As predicted, they found that developmental trends varied from study to study. For instance, findings of no age change were obtained in some studies (e.g., Paris & Carter, 1973), whereas other studies obtained contrasting age trends in different conditions (e.g., Brown, Smiley, Day, Townsend, & Lawton, 1977; Paris & Mahoney, 1974). Brainerd and Reyna (1998b) and Tun et al. (1998) reviewed the parallel child and aging literatures, respectively, on false recognition of meaning-sharing words. They, too, noted between-study variations in reported trends.

Developmental variability in implanted false memories also has been the subject of inconsistent findings (Doris, 1991). In their influential literature review, Ceci and Bruck (1993) reported that age declines in misinformation effects had been obtained in most studies. However, they also observed that age declines have usually not been detected after the preschool years and that some studies that included preschoolers failed to detect age declines (e.g., Howe, 1991; Poole & Lindsay, 1996). Recently, developmental increases in misinformation effects have also been reported (Pezdek & Roe, 1995, 1997). In their first study, Pezdek and Roe observed increases in both hit suppression and false-alarm elevation between preschool and age 10. In one of their conditions, there was a 300% increase in hit suppression and a 157% increase in false-alarm elevation. In a second condition, hit suppression was age invariant, but false-alarm elevation increased by 57%.

Truth Is More Memorable Than Fiction

Relative Memorability of Actual Events Versus Nonevents. The most self-evident of all tenets about memory, whether in the courtroom or everyday life, is that events that actually happened to us are more likely to be remembered than events that did not. Naturally, common sense acknowledges that recollection is fallible. But common sense is equally firm in its conviction that, overwhelmingly, events that are part of individuals' personal histories are more likely to be remembered than events that are not. This conviction is so deeply embedded in individuals' sense of self that it is both difficult and troubling to imagine that it could be wrong. Consistent with this notion, hits to targets ordinarily exceed false alarms to meaning-sharing distractors by a wide margin in studies of both spontaneous and implanted false memories (e.g., Cassel & Bjorklund, 1995; Reyna & Kiernan, 1994; Tussing & Greene, 1998). Nevertheless, FTT identifies circumstances in which things that were never experienced could be just as likely to be remembered as things that were, and circumstances in which things that were never experienced could be more likely to be affirmed.

Such predictions fall out because, according to FTT, verbatim traces simultaneously support identity judgments about actual events (hits) and nonidentity judgments about nonevents with similar meaning (correct rejections) and therefore provide the basis for distinguishing events that were actually experienced from those that could have been experienced. Gist traces support similarity judgments about actual events (hits), but they also support similarity judgments about nonevents with similar meaning (false alarms). Although gist traces may be more likely to support similarity and identity judgments about actual events than about nonevents with similar meaning (because the meaning overlap will be greater for actual events), reliance on such traces will increase false-alarm rates, as compared with reliance on verbatim traces. Thus, shifting the general basis for memory performance toward gist ought to increase the subjective memorability of events that were never experienced, relative to those that were. There are many possible methods of accomplishing this, such as (a) instructing subjects to concentrate on meaning at study (e.g., Toglia, Neuschatz, & Goodwin, 1998); (b) instructing them to do likewise at test (e.g., Reyna & Kiernan, 1995); (c) presenting several targets at study that converge on a single meaning (e.g., Underwood, 1965); (d) testing memory after a retention interval (e.g., Reyna & Kiernan, 1994); and (e) administering meaning-sharing distractors that are especially good examples of the gist of experience (e.g., Reyna, 1996b).

Reyna and Kiernan (1994, Experiment 1) demonstrated that Method D can make it difficult to discriminate targets from meaning-sharing distractors, even when retention intervals are short in comparison with those in legal cases. They presented sentence triads to children in which the first two stated a familiar relation between common objects (e.g., "The cocoa is hotter than the tea. The tea is hotter than the coffee."), and the third stated a property of one of the objects (e.g., "The cocoa is very sweet."). Participants were instructed to remember these sentences for later memory tests, and they were given a test immediately after. Discrimination of targets from meaning-sharing distractors (e.g., "The coffee was cooler than the tea. The cocoa was hotter than the coffee.") was excellent, with hit rates averaging 76% and false-alarm rates averaging 38%. A week later, however, false-alarm rates for meaning-sharing distractors were the same as hit rates for targets. In a second experiment, Reyna and Kiernan (1994) found that combining Methods A and B made certain types of meaning-sharing distractors just as memorable as targets on immediate tests. They instructed participants to concentrate on meaning and ignore exact wording as statements were presented and to do likewise on memory tests. On tests that were administered only a few seconds after target presentation, the acceptance rate for targets (80%) and did not differ significantly from the acceptance rate for certain types of meaning-sharing distractors (78%).

Roediger and McDermott (1995) and several other investigators have recently demonstrated that Methods C and E can make meaning-sharing distractors seem just as memorable as targets immediately after study. Participants studied a series of short word lists (cf. Table 5.1), with the targets on each list instantiating a certain theme (e.g., furniture and medical themes in Table 5.1). A word that is an especially good example of a list theme was omitted from each study list (*chair* and *doctor* in Table 5.1), but it was included in test lists. On immediate memory tests, false-alarm rates for these distractors did not differ significantly from hit rates.

Other experiments have established that combinations of the methods listed previously can make events that never happened seem even more memorable than events that did. For instance, Payne et al. (1996) and McDermott (1996) reported experiments in which they combined the procedures of Roediger and McDermott (1995) with a long-term retention interval (Method D). Payne et al. found that after a 1-day delay, hit rates for targets such as *hospital* and *sofa* averaged 56%, but false-alarm rates

TABLE 5.1
Lists of Targets That Converge on Shared Meanings

Shared Meanings	Targets
Furniture words	*Table, sit, legs, seat, couch, desk, recliner, sofa, wood, cushion, swivel, stool, sitting, rocking, bench* (critical missing word: *chair*)
Medical words	*Nurse, sick, lawyer, medicine, health, hospital, dentist, physician, ill, patient, office, stethoscope, surgeon, clinic, cure* (critical missing word: *doctor*)

for distractors such as *doctor* and *furniture* averaged 67%. McDermott, using free recall tests, found that after a 2-day delay, correct recall of targets averaged 17%, but incorrect recall of meaning-sharing distractors averaged 24%.

In the same vein, Brainerd and Reyna (1998b), using materials that combined Methods C and E, found that meaning-sharing distractors were accepted at higher rates than targets immediately after presentation when participants were urged to focus on the substance of their experience while responding to memory tests (Method B). Research on such instructions is highly relevant to the memory reports that figure in legal cases, and in psychotherapy as well because, in both instances, practices are used that encourage people to rely on the substance of experience. Brainerd and Reyna (1998b) noted that during the evidence-gathering phase of criminal investigations, police interviewers are trained to use interrogation procedures that coax witnesses to assent to things that they cannot clearly remember (e.g., "Was the robber carrying a pistol?") because those things are consistent with the gist of events that witnesses do clearly remember, or with the gist of witnesses' previous statements, or with the gist of statements made by others. Concerning psychotherapy, they noted that several practices are in routine use (e.g., bibliotherapy, guided imagery, memory regression, memory work, and self-hypnosis) that encourage patients to go beyond what they explicitly remember and recollect things that could or should have happened to them on the basis of beliefs or feelings about their lives. The targets to which the participants in Brainerd and Reyna's (1998b) experiments were exposed consisted either of materials like those in Table 5.1 or of word lists containing multiple exemplars (e.g., *collie, poodle, spaniel; Boston, Chicago, New York*) of familiar categories (*dog, city*). When participants were instructed to rely on the substance of their experience, distractors whose meanings had been repeatedly cued (e.g., *dog, city*) were accepted at higher rates than targets (e.g., *collie, Boston*) on immediate memory tests.

Summing up, as predicted, the memorability of events that were not experienced has been found to increase relative to the memorability of actual events when retrieval of gist traces is facilitated. Moreover, also as predicted, evidence has accumulated that under certain conditions, the memorability of nonevents equals or exceeds that of actual events. Such evidence bears on the assumption that witnesses are more likely to remember true events than false ones because, as several writers have commented (e.g., Ceci & Bruck, 1995; Poole & Lindsay, 1995), there are inherent factors that favor reliance on gist in interviews and in sworn testimony, factors that parallel laboratory methods of stimulating gist processing.

More rely on gist -
more believe false
mmys

Three factors that are invariably present are that witnesses concentrated on the gist of events as they experienced them (Method A), that gist memories that have been repeatedly cued are operative during interviews and testimony (Method C), and that long intervals elapse between events and witnesses' memory reports (Method D). Concerning the first factor, it is well known that unless instructions to the contrary are received, people's natural tendency is to focus on the meaning of experience rather than on exact surface details (Bransford & Franks, 1971). Concerning the second factor, the crimes (e.g., armed robbery) with which defendants are charged constitute strong uniting themes that have been exemplified by many events of which witnesses are aware. Concerning the third factor, although witness interviews sometimes occur shortly after events, delays of days or weeks are normally involved, and sworn testimony is not taken until weeks, months, or years have passed.

A fourth factor, which parallels Method E, is present in many cases. The key events about which witnesses are questioned are often very good examples of the operative theme (e.g., "Did the robber carry a pistol? Did the robber demand money?"). Unlike the first three factors, this one is not always present in legal cases because the events on which many cases turn are incidental to the operative theme. A fifth factor, which parallels Method B, is the one discussed by Brainerd and Reyna (1998b): Police investigative interviews incorporate procedures that urge witnesses to assent to things that they cannot clearly remember but that are consistent with the gist of events.

A Theory of False Confession. The presence in legal cases of a confluence of gist-facilitating factors means that, as a matter of course, some types of false reports may, for purely memorial reasons, be just as likely or even more likely than some types of true reports to be introduced in evidence and accepted as credible by triers of fact. Another particularly interesting implication is that these gist-facilitating factors may supply a memorial explanation of the puzzling but well-established phenomenon of false confession. Triers of fact regard confessions as singularly credible evidence of guilt (Gudjonsson, 1992), and police interrogation techniques (e.g., Inbau, Reid, & Buckley, 1986) are expressly designed to maximize the chances of obtaining confessions from suspects. False confessions traditionally have been viewed as aberrations resulting from either extreme coercion (e.g., the widely discussed Michael Pardue case in Alabama) or psychopathology. In the decade and half since the advent of DNA testing, however, a number of more prosaic examples have come to light of defendants who confessed to crimes, were convicted and imprisoned but were

Interview/interrogation pusher post

subsequently exonerated by DNA evidence. Newspapers continue to report cases in which, although neither extreme coercion nor psychopathology was evident, suspects confessed to crimes during interrogation but were exonerated by DNA evidence before trial.

According to FTT, confessing to crimes that were not committed can have a firm basis in suspects' natural memory processes. Because strong gists are operative in criminal investigations, gist-based similarity judgments may make it seem as though events that cannot be remembered must have happened, to suspects as well as to investigators (Reyna, 1998). Furthermore, the fact that strong gists can support illusions of item-specific recollection means that suspects may have clear (but illusory) memories of physical details of crimes that they did not commit (Reyna, 1996b). These principles, that the processing of strong gist memories may support both feelings of familiarity and illusions of item-specific recollection by suspects about events in which they did not participate, leads to predictions about the content of confessions that are known or suspected to be false.

First, statements in which suspects acknowledge that certain things must have happened even though they cannot specifically recollect those things as having happened should be common features of such confessions. According to FTT, these are the sorts of subjective experiences that accompany similarity judgments. In this connection, Ceci and Bruck (1995) provide examples of such statements in questionable confessions that were obtained in child abuse cases. Other examples can be found in the transcript of a confession in a recent California case (State v. Henderson, 1997). The defendant, William Martin Henderson, allegedly confessed to a count of child sexual abuse during an interview in which he was moderately intoxicated. However, a review of the transcript reveals that the statements made by Mr. Henderson, which the prosecution represented to the jury as a confession, consisted of instances in which he agreed with assertions by the police interrogator, Detective Martin Eberling, that he must have improperly touched two children. Such instances were accompanied by assertions by Mr. Henderson that although he believed improper touches must have occurred for reasons provided to him by Detective Eberling, he had no recollection of having touched the two children in the alleged manner. Even Detective Eberling's report of the interrogation acknowledged that Mr. Henderson "denies being able to recall the incident, but believes that if his sons saw it, and told him it was true, that it must be." Nevertheless, Mr. Henderson was convicted of sexual abuse, and in post-trial interviews, jury members cited his confession as the principal basis for conviction.

The second prediction that FTT makes is that even when confessions are demonstrably false, they may contain clear recollections by suspects of having participated in events in which they could not possibly have participated. This, of course, is one of the most bewildering features of cases in which competent defendants confessed to crimes, were convicted and imprisoned, but were later exonerated by unimpeachable physical evidence. In some of those cases, the confessions contained vivid recollections of specific events and physical details of crimes that must have been confabulations. According to FTT, suspects can have illusory recollections of specific experiences, even when those experiences have not been suggested to them by interviewers because of reliance on strong gist memories.

The prediction that false confessions routinely contain statements that certain events must have happened but cannot be remembered seems sensible, but the prediction that, in the absence of extreme coercion and psychopathology, false confessions may also be supported by illusory recollections of specific events and physical details vexes our intuition. Prospective evidence from experiments in which the events that suspects experienced are fully known to researchers, rather than retrospective evidence from legal cases, therefore is crucial. Such evidence can be found in a recent study by Kassin and Kiechel (1996). Participants performed a computer reaction-time task and were told that if they deliberately or accidentally pressed a certain key, serious damage to the computer system would result. The computer crashed while subjects were performing the task, and the experimenter accused them of having pressed the key. Computer logs showed that none had actually pressed the key. Following interrogations by a confederate and by the experimenter, however, 69% of the subjects falsely confessed to pressing the key and signed a false confession. Of these subjects, 13% confabulated specific events or details to support their confessions (e.g., "I hit it with the side of my right hand right after you called out the 'A'"). Of special theoretical interest, false confessions were obtained from 100% of the participants in a condition that made it difficult to process verbatim details during the reaction-time task (Method A above), and 35% of these participants confabulated specific events.

True Reports Are More Consistent Than False Ones

It is commonplace for witnesses' statements to contradict each other. Mutually contradictory statements cannot both be true, and, without physical records of events, it is impossible to be certain where the truth lies. However, triers of fact must assign degrees of credibility to conflicting statements in rendering verdicts, and attorneys must decide which statements to challenge in court. What criteria should be used? Here, a basic tenet of the law's view of memory is that, over time, true reports will be more consistent than false ones. Indeed, consistency is the most commonly cited criterion for judging statement credibility in surveys of attorneys and judges (Fisher & Cutler, 1992). This criterion is predicated on the following line of reasoning (Brainerd & Poole, 1997). As long as the information in false reports has not been suggested to witnesses by others, it is outside the scope of their experience and, hence, is not founded on stored memories of experience. Whatever the bases for false reports are (e.g., momentary confusion, bias, lying), those bases are inherently ephemeral, as compared with the memories that support true reports, which means that false reports should not exhibit much consistency over time and that such consistency as they do exhibit should be less than that displayed by true reports.

Although this reasoning may seem convincing, FTT makes two predictions that challenge it (Reyna, 1998). First, spontaneous false reports can be quite consistent over time, and under specific conditions, their consistency can equal or exceed that of true reports. Second, the consistency of spontaneous false reports is apt to exceed that of implanted false reports. We sketch the grounds for each prediction and summarize relevant experimental findings.

Consistency of Spontaneous False Reports.   The flaw in the above line of reasoning is the claim that spontaneous false reports are not based on stored memories of experience. It has been shown that such reports are not necessarily rooted in momentary confusion, bias, or lying but instead can be based on stored memories of the gist of experience. When they are, false reports should display considerable consistency over time (Brainerd, Reyna, & Brandse, 1995), with levels of consistency depending on the stability of the relevant memories. According to FTT, when false reports are memory based, the memories will tend to be gist traces, whereas when true reports are memory based, the memories will tend to be verbatim traces, at least during early interviews. This fact leads to the first prediction about consistency. Research suggests that, over time, memories of the gist of experience become inaccessible more slowly than verbatim traces. Therefore, the predominate memorial basis for false reports fails more slowly than that for early true reports, and false reports could be quite consistent over time, even more consistent than true reports. The key proviso is that this prediction holds only when false reports are based on gist memories rather than on confusion, bias, lying, or other transient factors.

[Handwritten annotation:] Initially report based on verbatim + gist — not consistent b/c verbatim is lost

Initial support for this prediction came from three experiments by Brainerd, Reyna, and Brandse (1995). In the first experiment, children listened to a list of familiar nouns (e.g., *clock, star*). Following a 5-minute buffer activity, they received a recognition test consisting of targets and equally familiar but unrelated distractors, and this test was repeated a week later. The consistency of initial hits and false alarms over the 1-week interval was measured. There were two findings. First, both hits and false alarms displayed statistically significant consistency. Second, the level of consistency for false alarms (69% overall) was slightly, though not significantly, greater than that for hits (63% overall). In a second experiment, Brainerd, Reyna, and Brandse hypothesized that if distractors were semantically related to targets (e.g., *dog* and *furniture* when *collie* and *table* were targets), false alarms would be more likely to be based on gist memories and should show increased consistency over time. As in the first experiment, both hits and false alarms to semantically related distractors displayed statistically significant consistency. However, false alarms to semantically related distractors were significantly more consistent than hits (92% vs. 72%).

In a final experiment, Brainerd, Reyna, and Bransde (1995) evaluated the hypothesis that the high levels of consistency for false alarms were due to reliance on semantic gist by making it unavailable. The design was the same as Experiment 2, except that children listened to lists of familiar nouns and nonsense words (e.g., *kef, cej, mivig, tijly*). On the immediate and 1-week tests, the crucial items for which consistency was measured were nonsense targets and distractors that were rhymes of nonsense targets (e.g., *tef* if *kef* was a target or *tivig* if *mivig* was a target). Both nonsense targets and rhyming nonsense distractors displayed significant consistency over the 1-week retention interval. However, relative consistency was the reverse of Experiment 2 (56% for targets and 45% for distractors).

These consistency findings for word lists were replicated with adults in Payne et al.'s (1996) and McDermott's (1996) experiments, the designs of which were described earlier. In Payne et al.'s experiment, relative consistency of hits and false alarms was measured by comparing hit and false alarm rates for participants who received an immediate recognition test with those for participants who received a 1-day delayed test. It was found that the hit rate fell from 68% to 56%, but the false-alarm rate for meaning-sharing distractors only fell from 70% to 67%. In McDermott's experiments, consistency was also measured by comparing target and distractor performance on immediate and delayed tests. In her first experiment, participants responded to immediate recall tests and 2-day delayed tests. True recall of targets fell by 37%, but false recall of meaning-sharing distractors fell by only 21%. In a second experiment, true recall again declined much more than false recall.

Findings that parallel those for word lists have been reported for statements about everyday events by Poole (1995) and by Brainerd and Mojardin (1998). Poole and White (1991) reported an experiment in which children and adults observed a series of staged events, followed by an immediate recall test and a 1-week delayed test. Rates of false reporting were low on the immediate test; most things that children recalled were true. When Poole calculated the consistency of true and false reports for these data, the level for false reports (76%) was slightly, though not significantly, higher than that for true reports (72%). Brainerd and Mojardin reported research in which the consistency of children's true and false reports was measured across 1-week and 1-month intervals (Experiment 1) and across a 1-week interval in adults (Experiment 2). The targets and distractors in their experiments were sentences about everyday objects and relations that had been adapted from the materials in Reyna and Kiernan's (1994) experiments. With children, they found that false-alarm consistency always equaled or exceeded hit consistency over both the 1-week and the 1-month delays. With adults, they found that false-alarm consistency also equaled or exceeded hit consistency over the 1-week delay.

Consistency of Implanted False Reports.   If one accepts the common-sense reasoning that justifies the consistency criterion, implanted false reports differ from spontaneous ones in that they can be based on memories of actual experience, albeit experience of misinformation. It follows from such reasoning that, over time, implanted false reports should be more consistent than spontaneous ones. FTT's analysis of false memory suggests a different possibility. Because spontaneous and implanted false reports can both be based on memories of experience, an important factor determining their relative consistency is the stability of the respective memories. As noted earlier, gist is the predominate memorial basis for spontaneous false reports, whereas implanted false reports can be based on either verbatim traces of misinformation or on gist. The discrepancy in verbatim and gist forgetting rates then leads one to predict that when spontaneous and implanted false reports are both memory based, spontaneous ones will be more consistent.

This prediction is difficult to evaluate with extant data because misinformation experiments with adults, which account for the great bulk of the literature, have rarely included long-term retention sessions. Most experiments that included such sessions have been conducted with children, but the memory measures in those studies have usually been recall tests (e.g., Cassel & Bjorklund, 1995; Salmon & Pipe, 1997). With recall tests, children's rates of spontaneous false reporting are often near zero in misinformation studies, so comparisons of consistency levels for spontaneous versus implanted false reports are impractical. However, Brainerd and Poole (1997) noted that it is possible to test a related prediction about the relative consistency of implanted false reports versus true reports (rather than spontaneous false reports) that is of considerable forensic interest.

Work has recently been reported in which mathematical models were used to factor the respective contributions of verbatim and gist memories to implanted false reports (Brainerd & Reyna, 1998a). That work suggested that initial false reports of misinformation-embodying distractors are based on verbatim traces (of misinformation) even more often than initial true reports are based on verbatim traces (of target presentations). This disparity in verbatim reliance should be most pronounced in experiments in which targets are presented in one session, and misinformation and initial memory tests are presented in a later session (e.g., Poole & Lindsay, 1995), owing to the different forgetting rates for verbatim and gist traces. If verbatim reliance is greater for false reports of misinformation-embodying distractors than for true reports, FTT predicts that the latter will be more consistent over time.

To evaluate this possibility, Brainerd and Poole (1997) reviewed studies of childhood misinformation effects that included both immediate and delayed memory tests (e.g., Ceci, Huffman, Smith, & Loftus, 1994; Ceci, Loftus, Leichtman, & Bruck, 1994; Huffman, Crossman, & Ceci, 1996). After their review, they made the following conclusion:

> On the basis of FTT's distinction between verbatim and gist bases for true and false reports, the designs of most childhood misinformation studies favor long-term survival of both types of reports, coupled with higher survival rates for true reports. Available data, though not extensive, are consistent with these predictions. The predictions were borne out for retention intervals ranging from one month to two years, and they were borne out for memory tests that focused on complete mini-events as well as for tests that focused on smaller units of experience. Although, so far, children's false reports in misinformation studies have displayed less stability than their true reports, the absolute levels of stability for false reports have been high. Consequently, the bottom line is that persistence of a report—even over a period as long as 2 years—is no guarantee that it is a true report. (p. 144)

Lest these findings be taken as showing that implanted false reports are inherently less consistent over time than true reports, it should be added that according to FTT, the opposite result could be obtained if verbatim traces of misinformation are especially strong. For instance, in an analogy to legal cases in which witnesses have been repeatedly misinformed about events (cf. Ceci & Bruck, 1995), this result might be accomplished by presenting targets once but presenting misinformation several times. A relevant experiment has already been reported by Zaragoza and Mitchell (1996; see also, Reyna, 1996b). Adults viewed a film depicting a burglary and a police car chase and then answered a questionnaire about the film. Some questions misinformed events in the film, with some events being misinformed once and others being misinformed three times. Recognition tests were administered immediately after misinformation for some participants, after 2 days for other participants, and after one week for other participants. For events that had been misinformed three times, the hit rate declined from 89% on the immediate test to 71% after 2 days and to 60% on the 1-week test. In contrast, the false-alarm rate for misinformation-embodying distractors did not decline between the immediate and 2-day tests and declined by only 8% between the 2-day and 1-week tests.

Reminiscence and Consistency.   Another factor increases the inconsistency of true reports relative to false ones: *reminiscence*—the reporting of information on later recall tests that was not reported earlier. This phenomenon has been extensively investigated in both the adult memory literature (for a review, see Payne, 1987) and the memory development literature (for a review, see Brainerd, Reyna, Howe, & Kingma, 1990). Some work in forensic contexts has also been conducted (e.g., Bornstein, Leibel, & Scarberry, 1998). The standard result in both laboratory and forensic settings is that reminisced information is much more likely to be true than false. For instance, Bornstein et al. reported that witnesses to a violent scene recalled 24% more information after three follow-up tests than they had on an initial test and that more than 90% of the newly recalled information was true.

The fact that reminisced information is overwhelmingly true information has been interpreted as showing that reminiscence improves the overall accuracy of testimony (Brainerd & Ornstein, 1991). Note, however, that it has negative consequences for the consistency criterion. Witnesses' statements can manifest two general types of inconsistency: (a) Event A is reported at Time 1 but not at Time 2 or (b) Event A is reported at Time 2 but not at Time 1. Up to this point, researchers have been concerned primarily with the Type A inconsistencies, emphasizing that FTT's memory distinctions specify conditions under which such inconsistencies will be no more frequent for false reports than for true ones (or will be more frequent for true reports). However, consideration of research on Type B

Reminiscence more likely to be true than false

inconsistencies suggests that the baseline situation is that they are far more common when Event A is true than when it is false. Ironically, although research has suggested that new information recollected at Time 2 is overwhelmingly true, testimony that contains Type B inconsistencies is especially apt to be challenged in court. Attorneys regard Type B inconsistencies as inherently suspicious because they violate the basic rule that information is forgotten with time. In court, attorneys argue that Type B inconsistencies are due to factors such as contamination of witnesses through communication with interested parties and witnesses "getting their stories straight" (e.g., *Dosh v. Block Estate,* 1997).

Neutral Questions Do Not Falsify Witnesses' Memories

During the past decade, the power of suggestive questioning to falsify the contents of children's and adults' memories has been much discussed in the scientific literature (e.g., Ceci & Bruck, 1995; Loftus, Feldman, & Dashiell, 1995), in court opinions (e.g., *State v. Hungerford,* 1995; *State v. Morahan,* 1995), and in the popular press. There is now wide consensus that such questioning can increase witnesses' levels of false reporting and decrease their levels of true reporting. What about questioning that is not explicitly suggestive, that neither misinforms nor misleads but simply attempts to diagnose the contents of memory? We refer to this as *mere memory testing* to distinguish it from explicitly suggestive questioning. (As discussed in Reyna and Lloyd's, 1997, review, we also acknowledge that there are intermediate cases in which questions are not explicitly suggestive but are implicitly leading, e.g., Bjorklund, Bjorklund, Brown, & Cassel, 1998.)

Brainerd and Ornstein (1991) pointed out that the standard view of mere memory testing is that, first, it does not falsify the contents of memory by adding recollections of events that witnesses did not experience and that, second, it inoculates true memories against forgetting. Taken together, these two ideas imply that mere memory testing enhances the accuracy of later testimony: "Testimony would be expected to be facilitated as a consequence of . . . repeated questioning" (Brainerd & Ornstein, 1991, p. 18). Poole and White (1995), in a review of relevant studies of eyewitness memory, concluded that available evidence supported this interpretation:

> Laboratory simulations of eyewitness testimony offer strong corroborating evidence that multiple testing sessions preserve memories over time. . . . We are aware of no studies in which multiple interviews with nonsuggestive questions were associated with increases in the amount of inaccurate information recalled. (p. 34)

Experiments by Dent and Stephenson (1979) and by Hudson (1990) are illustrative. In the former, participants viewed a film of a theft and were administered recall tests (a) immediately, and after 1 day, 2 days, 2 weeks, and 2 months; or (b) after 2 weeks and 2 months only; or (c) after 2 months only. On the 2-month test, subjects in Condition A recalled more correct information and the same amount of incorrect information as those in Conditions B and C. In Hudson's study, children participated in four creative movement workshops and recalled the first workshop 4 weeks later. Half of the children also participated in practice interviews immediately after each workshop. Children in the practice group recalled more activities, without increasing the number of errors reported.

Despite the uniformity of the data reviewed by Poole and White (1995), Brainerd and Reyna (1996) argued that they cannot be accepted at face value for two reasons. First, that mere memory testing does not increase levels of false reporting is suspicious because memory tests provide practice at retrieving the gist traces that support false reports as well as the verbatim traces that support true ones. Second, in all studies, recall tests were used to measure the effects of mere memory tests. Such tests are less sensitive to the contents of memory than recognition tests are (Baddeley, 1976) and are not typical of practices in investigative interviewing, which tend to include high proportions of recognition probes (Warren, Woodall, Hunt, & Perry, 1996). Hence, mere testing effects must be investigated with recognition tests. The effects of mere recognition tests can be assessed by comparing performance on a terminal recognition test for material that has or has not received a prior recognition test, and the effects of mere recall tests can be assessed by comparing performance on a terminal recognition test for material that has or has not received a prior recall test. Both types of studies have now been reported and, in both instances, mere memory tests have elevated false reporting on terminal recognition tests.

Experiments of the first type have been reported by Brainerd and Reyna (1996) and by Brainerd and Mojardin (1998). Brainerd and Reyna's (1996) participants studied a list of common nouns, participated in an irrelevant buffer activity, and then either (a) responded to an immediate recognition test followed by a 1-week delayed test (Experiment 1) or (b) responded to a 1-week delayed test followed by a 2-week delayed test (Experiment 2). Both tests contained targets, meaning-sharing distractors (e.g., *dog* and *furniture* if *collie* and *table* were studied), and unrelated distractors. However, on Test 2 half of the items had been presented on Test 1 and half had not. Contrary to the notion that mere memory testing does not create false memories, it was found in both experiments that false-alarm rates for meaning-sharing distractors were higher if they had been previously tested than if they had not been. Contrary to the notion that mere memory testing improves overall accuracy, the elevation in false-alarm rates as a function of prior testing was greater than the elevation in hit rates. Brainerd and Mojardin (1998) reported the same general pattern for sentences about everyday objects and relations. Their participants studied a series of sentences, participated in a buffer activity, responded to an immediate recognition test, then either (a) responded to 1-week and 1-month delayed tests (Experiment 1) or (b) responded to a 1-week delayed test (Experiment 2). As in Brainerd and Reyna's (1996) experiments, the delayed tests always included mixtures of previously tested and previously untested targets and distractors. On both 1-week and 1-month delayed tests, false alarms to meaning-sharing distractors were higher for previously tested items, and prior tests reduced overall accuracy because they elevated false alarm rates more than hit rates.

An experiment in which the effects of prior recall tests on terminal recognition tests were assessed has been reported by Payne et al. (1996, Experiment 1). Participants studied lists such as those in Table 5.1. Half of the lists were followed by a recall test and half were not. After the lists had been presented, half of the participants received an immediate recognition test and half received a 1-day delayed recognition test. Concerning false-memory creation, mere recall tests had the same effect on delayed (but not immediate) recognition as mere recognition tests had in the Brainerd and Reyna (1996) and Brainerd and Mojardin (1998) studies: On the delayed test, the false-alarm rate for meaning-sharing distractors was 71% if a prior recall test had been administered and 62% if it had not been. Unlike mere recognition testing, however, mere recall testing produced neither net losses nor net gains in accuracy on the delayed test, and it actually improved overall accuracy on the immediate test. To determine whether the latter findings represent fundamental differences in the effects of mere recall testing versus mere recognition testing, we conducted a study that replicated Payne et al.'s (1996) design, except that our delayed test occurred after 1 week. Data from the immediate test showed that the elevation in false alarms produced by a prior recall test was nearly twice as great as the elevation in hits (19% vs. 10%). On the 1-week delayed test, false-alarm elevation was slightly greater than hit elevation (12% vs. 9%).

Summing up, contrary to the principle that questions that are not explicitly misleading do not falsify the contents of memory, it has now been reported that false-alarm rates on terminal recognition tests are elevated when prior memory testing consists of either recognition or recall. In addition, when prior memory testing involves recognition, it has been found that overall accuracy is lowered because prior testing increases false alarms more than it increases hits. This latter finding has not been consistently obtained, however, when prior testing involves recall.

Beyond the test sensitivity motivation for using recognition measures to assess the effects of mere memory testing, such measures are forensically appropriate because most witness interviews and sworn testimony are heavily laced with questions involving either yes–no recognition ("Did A happen?") or forced-choice recognition ("Which happened, A or B?") Attorneys and police interviewers regard such questions as essential because the rules of evidence demand that witnesses' recollections of key events be reliable. With children, it is not uncommon for the great preponderance of questions to consist of yes–no or forced-choice recognition because children, particularly preschoolers, provide very limited information on recall tests (Cassel & Bjorklund, 1995). For instance, in a recent case of suspected child abuse in Arizona (*Casey v. La Petite et al.*, 1994), 60% of the questions posed in a police interview of a preschool child involved recognition, and the only recall questions to which the child responded were ones that inquired about the child's age. Even when children respond adequately to recall questions, interviews may still be dominated by recognition questions, as in the aforementioned California case (*State v. Henderson*, 1997).

SUMMARY

We have proposed that the use of memory theories can enhance the reliability of expert testimony and make it more robust against the standard criticism that the designs of individual experiments cannot be generalized to the unique features of legal cases. To illustrate this proposal, we described a theory that explains the types of false-memory reports about which researchers often are asked to provide expert testimony. The theory uses three memory processes (identity judgments, nonidentity judgments, and similarity judgments) to account for both spontaneous and implanted false reports and for the basic patterns of findings that are associated with these phenomena. Importantly, the theory makes novel predictions that qualify four key assumptions that the law makes about memory—namely, that false memories are more common in children than adults; that truth is more memorable than fiction; that reports of true events are more consistent than reports of false events; and that neutral, nonsuggestive questioning does not falsify memory. We reviewed research showing that, in each instance, available data are more consistent with theoretical predictions than with the law's view of memory. We also showed that the theory provides an account of the memorial processes that may be responsible for some types of false confessions.

To conclude, it is interesting to conjecture about why memory theory has not figured prominently in expert testimony. A likely reason is the rules of evidence that govern the admission of expert testimony. Those rules focus on whether expert testimony either reflects the consensus of the expert community (Frye test) or whether it involves well-established experimental findings generated by scientifically reliable procedures that have been subjected to peer review (Daubert test). From this perspective, the key features of memory theories, that they explain otherwise disconnected findings and make novel predictions, may seem irrelevant in the courtroom. Another likely reason for the dearth of memory theory in expert testimony is that, to many people, the term *theory* is synonymous with speculative opinions and untested assumptions of the sort that underlie dubious types of expert testimony that have recently been ruled admissible, especially so-called syndrome testimony in child abuse cases. In syndrome testimony, an expert, usually a clinical psychologist, social worker, or psychiatrist, may offer the opinion that a child was abused, even though there is no physical evidence of abuse, because the child exhibits certain behaviors (e.g., eating disorders, insomnia, nightmares, phobias) that the expert claims to have observed in confirmed cases of abuse (see Ceci & Bruck, 1995). Some recent legal developments, such as the Daubert test, are designed to correct this tendency to admit testimony that relies on subjective belief and speculation that is not supported by empirical findings (McGough, 1994; Poole & Lindsay, 1998).

As has been noted, however, a good theory is explanatory and predictive, not speculative. Furthermore, it would be misguided to believe that the reliability of expert testimony requires that a distinction be maintained between experimental findings and the theories that explain them, or to believe that a sharp distinction is even possible. The fact that the designs of experiments and the features of legal cases are never completely parallel ensures that experts must exercise judgment in the selection of experiments to cite. Such judgments reflect experts' implicit theories of how individual variables affect memory performance and how those variables interact with each other. For instance, it is not theory-free to assume, for purposes of testimony, that data from a study in which recall tests were administered 2 hours after an event and data from a study in which recognition tests were administered 2 weeks after an event are equally applicable to a case in which the plaintiffs are preschool children. That judgment is based on an implicit theory of the relative sensitivity of recall and recognition tests at this age level following different amounts of delay. Would it not be better to make such implicit theories explicit and open to examination?

Although the courts must try to restrict themselves to well-established scientific data on memory to assist triers of fact in evaluating the credibility of evidence, theory serves two enduring functions in expert testimony. First, whether experts acknowledge it or not, theory guides their choice of research findings and therefore the conclusions that they offer. Second, because of a theory's ability to predict counterintuitive phenomena, it provides experts with tools to explain facts of individual cases that appear incomprehensible and to anticipate circumstances in individual cases wherein the intuitively appealing assumptions that the law makes about memory are apt to be wrong.

ACKNOWLEDGMENTS

This work was supported by grants from the National Science Foundation to C. J. Brainerd and V. F. Reyna (SBR-9730143) and to D. A. Poole (SBR-9409231). We thank Maggie Bruck and Robert Rosenthal for their helpful advice on an early version of this chapter.

REFERENCES

Ackerman, B. P. (1992). The sources of children's errors in judging causal inferences. *Journal of Experimental Child Psychology, 54,* 90–119.

Ackerman, B. P. (1994). Children's source errors in referential communication. *Journal of Experimental Child Psychology, 58,* 432–464.

Baddeley, A. D. (1976). *The psychology of memory.* New York: Basic Books.

Belli, R. F. (1989). Influences of misleading postevent information: Misinformation interference and acceptance. *Journal of Experimental Psychology: General, 118,* 72–85.

Berwin, C. R. (1997). Commentary on dispatch from (un)civil memory wars. In J. D. Read & D. S. Lindsay (Eds.), *Recollections of trauma: Scientific evidence and clinical practice* (pp. 194–196). New York: Plenum.

Bjorklund, D. F., Bjorklund, B. R., Brown, R. D., & Cassel, W. S. (1998). Children's susceptibility to repeated questions: How misinformation changes children's answers and their minds. *Applied Developmental Psychology, 2,* 101–113.

Bornstein, B. H., Leibel, L. H., & Scarberry, N. C. (1998). Repeated testing in eyewitness memory: A means to improve recall of a negative emotional event. *Applied Cognitive Psychology, 12,* 119–132.

Brainerd, C. J., & Gordon, L. L. (1994). Development of verbatim and gist memory for numbers. *Developmental Psychology, 30,* 163–177.

Brainerd, C. J., & Mojardin, A. H. (1998). Children's and adults' spontaneous false memories: Long-term persistence and mere-testing effects. *Child Development, 69,* 1361–1377.

Brainerd, C. J., & Ornstein, P. A. (1991). Children's memory for witnessed events: The developmental backdrop. In J. Doris (Ed.), *The suggestibility of children's recollections* (pp. 10–20). Washington, DC: American Psychological Association.

Brainerd, C. J., & Poole, D. A. (1997). Long-term survival of children's false memories: A review. *Learning and Individual Differences, 9,* 125–152.

Brainerd, C. J., & Reyna, V. F. (1993). Memory independence and memory interference in cognitive development. *Psychological Review, 100,* 42–67.

Brainerd, C. J., & Reyna, V. F. (1995). Autosuggestibility in memory development. *Cognitive Psychology, 28,* 65–101.

Brainerd, C. J., & Reyna, V. F. (1996). Mere memory testing creates false memories in children. *Developmental Psychology, 32,* 467–478.

Brainerd, C. J., & Reyna, V. F. (1998a). Fuzzy-trace theory and children's false memories. *Journal of Experimental Child Psychology, 71,* 81–129.

Brainerd, C. J., & Reyna, V. F. (1998b). When events that were never experienced are easier to remember than events that were. *Psychological Science, 6,* 484–489.

Brainerd, C. J., Reyna, V. F., & Brandse, E. (1995). Are children's false memories more persistent than their true memories? *Psychological Science, 6,* 359–364.

Brainerd, C. J., Reyna, V. F., Howe, M. L., & Kingma, J. (1990). The development of forgetting and reminiscence. *Monographs of the Society for Research in Child Development, 53*(2–3, Whole No. 222).

Brainerd, C. J., Reyna, V. F., & Kneer, R. (1995). False-recognition reversal: When similarity is distinctive. *Journal of Memory and Language, 34,* 157–185.

Brainerd, C. J., Reyna, V. F., & Mojardin, A. H. (1999). Conjoint recognition. *Psychological Review, 106,* 160–179.

Brainerd, C. J., Stein, L., & Reyna, V. F. (1998). On the development of conscious and unconscious memory. *Developmental Psychology, 34,* 342–357.

Bransford, J. D., & Franks, J. J. (1971). The abstraction of linguistic ideas. *Cognitive Psychology, 2,* 231–380.

Brown, A. L., Smiley, S. S., Day, J. D., Townsend, M. A. R., & Lawton, S. C. (1977). Intrusion of a thematic idea in children's comprehension and retention of stories. *Child Development, 48,* 1454–1466.

Casey v. La Petite et al., Superior Court, Pima County, Arizona, 1994.

Cassel, W. S., & Bjorklund, D. F. (1995). Developmental patterns of eyewitness memory and suggestibility: An ecologically-based short-term longitudinal study. *Law and Human Behavior, 19,* 507–532.

Cassel, W. W., Roebers, C. E. M., & Bjorklund, D. F. (1996). Developmental patterns of eyewitness responses to repeated and increasingly suggestive questions. *Journal of Experimental Child Psychology, 61,* 116–133.

Ceci, S. J., & Bruck, M. (1993). Suggestibility of the child witness: A historical review and synthesis. *Psychological Bulletin, 113,* 403–439.

Ceci, S. J., & Bruck, M. (1995). *Jeopardy in the courtroom.* Washington, DC: American Psychological Association.

Ceci, S. J., Huffman, M. L., Smith, E., & Loftus, E. F. (1994). Repeatedly thinking about a non-event: Source misattributions among preschoolers. *Consciousness and Cognition, 3,* 388–407.

Ceci, S. J., Loftus, E. F., Leichtman, M. D., & Bruck, M. (1994). The possible role of source misattributions in the creation of false beliefs among preschoolers. *International Journal of Clinical and Experimental Hypnosis, 42,* 304–320.

Ceci, S. J., Ross, D. F., & Toglia, M. P. (1987). Suggestibility in children's memory: Psycholegal implications. *Journal of Experimental Psychology: General, 116,* 38–49.

Clark, S. E., & Gronlund, S. D. (1996). Global matching models of recognition memory: How the models match the data. *Psychonomic Bulletin & Review, 3,* 37–60.

Dent, H. R., & Stephenson, G. M. (1979). An experimental study of the effectiveness of different techniques of questioning child witnesses. *British Journal of Social and Clinical Psychology, 18,* 41–51.

Denton, L. (1994, December). Interim report spells out five conclusions. *APA Monitor,* p. 9.

Doris, J. L. (Ed.). (1991). *The suggestibility of children's recollections.* Washington, DC: American Psychological Association.

Dosh v. Block Estate, Superior Court, Clark County, Nevada, 1997.

Fisher, R. P., & Cutler, B. L. (1992, September). *The relation between consistency and accuracy of witness testimony.* Paper presented at the Third European Conference on Law and Psychology, Oxford, England.

Gernsbacher, M. A. (1985). Surface information loss in comprehension. *Cognitive Psychology, 17,* 324–363.

Gudjonsson, G. (1992). *The psychology of interrogations, confessions, and testimony.* London: Wiley.

Hembrooke, H., & Ceci, S. J. (1998). *Expert witnesses in child abuse cases: What can and should be said in court.* Washington, DC: American Psychological Association.

Hintzman, D. L., & Curran, T. (1994). Retrieval dynamics of recognition and frequency judgments: Evidence for separate processes of familiarity and recall. *Journal of Memory and Language, 33,* 1–18.

Horton, D. L., Pavlick, T. J., & Moulin-Julian, M. W. (1993). Retrieval-based and familiarity-based recognition and the quality of information in episodic memory. *Journal of Memory and Language, 32,* 39–55.

Howe, M. L. (1991). Misleading children's story recall: Forgetting and reminiscence of the facts. *Developmental Psychology, 27,* 746–762.

Hudson, J. A. (1990). Constructive processing in children's event memory. *Developmental Psychology, 26,* 180–187.

Huffman, M. L., Crossman, A., & Ceci, S. (1996, March). *An investigation of the long-term effects of source misattribution error: Are false memories permanent?* Poster session presented at the meeting of the American Psychology-Law Society, Hilton Head, SC.

Inbau, F. E., Reid, J. E., & Buckley, J. P. (1986). *Criminal interrogation and confessions* (3rd ed.). Baltimore: Williams & Wilkins.

Jacoby, L. L. (1991). A process dissociation framework: Separating automatic from intentional uses of memory. *Journal of Memory and Language, 30,* 513–541.

Kassin, S. M., & Kiechel, K. L. (1996). The social psychology of false confessions: Compliance, internalization, and confabulation. *Psychological Science, 7,* 125–128.

Loftus, E. F. (1979). *Eyewitness testimony.* Cambridge, MA: Harvard University Press.

Loftus, E. F. (1995). Memory malleability: Constructivist and fuzzy-trace explanations. *Learning and Individual Differences, 7,* 133–138.

Loftus, E. F., Feldman, J., & Dashiell, R. (1995). The reality of illusory memories. In D. L. Schacter, J. T. Coyle, G. D. Fischbach, M. M. Mesulam, & L. E. Sullivan (Eds.), *Memory distortion: How minds, brains, and societies reconstruct the past* (pp. 47–68). Cambridge, MA: Harvard University Press.

Mandler, G. (1980). Recognizing: The judgment of previous occurrence. *Psychological Review, 87,* 252–271.

Marx, M. H., & Henderson, B. (1996). A fuzzy trace analysis of categorical inferences and instantial associations as a function of retention interval. *Cognitive Development, 11,* 551–569.

McAuliff, B., Kovera, M., & Viswesvaran, C. (1998, March). *Methodological issues in child suggestibility research: A meta-analysis.* Paper presented at the meeting of the American Psychology-Law Society, Redondo Beach, CA.

McDermott, K. B. (1996). The persistence of false memories in list recall. *Journal of Memory and Language, 35,* 212–230.

McGough, L. S. (1994). *Child witnesses: Fragile voices in the American legal system.* New Haven, CT: Yale University Press.

Miller, P. H., & Bjorklund, D. F. (1998). Contemplating fuzzy-trace theory: The gist of it. *Journal of Experimental Child Psychology, 71,* 184–193.

Mojardin, A. H. (1998). *The underlying memory processes of adult's spontaneous and implanted false memories.* Unpublished doctoral dissertation, University of Arizona, Tucson.

Moravcski, J. E., & Healy, A. F. (1995). Effect of meaning on letter detection. *Journal of Experimental Psychology: Learning, Memory, and Cognition, 21,* 82–95

Murphy, G. L., & Shapiro, A. M. (1994). Forgetting of verbatim information in discourse. *Memory & Cognition, 22,* 85–94.

Paris, S. G., & Carter, A. Y. (1973). Semantic and constructive aspects of sentence memory in children. *Developmental Psychology, 9,* 109–113.

Paris, S. G., & Mahoney, G. J. (1974). Cognitive integration in children's memory for sentences and pictures. *Child Development, 45,* 633–643.

Payne, D. G. (1987). Hypermnesia and reminiscence in recall: A historical and empirical review. *Psychological Bulletin, 101,* 5–27.

Payne, D. G., Elie, C. J., Blackwell, J. M., & Neuschatz, J. S. (1996). Memory illusions: Recalling, recognizing, and recollecting events that never occurred. *Journal of Memory and Language, 35,* 261–285.

Pezdek, K., & Roe, C. (1995). The effect of memory trace strength on suggestibility. *Journal of Experimental Child Psychology, 60,* 116–128.

Pezdek, K., & Roe, C. (1997). The suggestibility of children's memory for being touched: Planting, erasing, and changing memories. *Law & Human Behavior, 21,* 95–106.

Poole, D. A. (1995). Strolling fuzzy-trace theory through eyewitness testimony (or vice versa). *Learning and Individual Differences, 7,* 87–94.

Poole, D. A., & Lamb, M. E. (1998). *Investigative interviews of children.* Washington, DC: American Psychological Association.

Poole, D. A., & Lindsay, D. S. (1995). Interviewing preschoolers: Effects of nonsuggestive techniques, parental coaching, and leading questions on reports of nonexperienced events. *Journal of Experimental Child Psychology, 60,* 129–154.

Poole, D. A., & Lindsay, D. S. (1996, June). *Effects of parental suggestions, interviewing techniques, and age on young children's event reports.* Paper presented at the meeting of the NATO Advanced Study Institute, Recollections of Trauma: Scientific Research and Clinical Practice, Port de Bourgenay, France.

Poole, D. A., & Lindsay, D. S. (1998). Assessing the accuracy of young children's reports: Lessons from the investigation of child sexual abuse. *Applied and Preventive Psychology, 7,* 1–26.

Poole, D. A., & White, L. T. (1991). Effects of question repetition on the eyewitness testimony of children and adults. *Developmental Psychology, 27,* 975–986.

Poole, D. A., & White, L. T. (1995). Tell me again and again: Stability and change in the repeated testimonies of children and adults. In M. S. Zaragoza, J. R. Graham, C. N. Gordon, R. Hall, R. Hirschman, & Y. S. Ben-Porath (Eds.), *Memory and testimony in the child witness* (pp. 24–43) New York: Harper & Row.

Pope, K. S. (1996). Memory, abuse, and science: Questioning claims about the false memory syndrome epidemic. *American Psychologist, 51,* 957–974.

Reyna, V. F. (1995). Interference effects in memory and reasoning: A fuzzy-trace theory analysis. In F. N. Dempster & C. J. Brainerd (Eds.), *New perspectives on interference and inhibition in cognition* (pp. 29–61). New York: Academic Press.

Reyna, V. F. (1996a). Meaning, memory and the interpretation of metaphors. In J. Mio and A. Katz (Eds.), *Metaphor: Pragmatics and applications.* Mahwah, NJ: Lawrence Erlbaum Associates.

Reyna, V. F. (1996b, November). *Repetition dissociates verbatim and gist memory for narratives.* Paper presented at the meeting of the Psychonomic Society, Chicago, IL.

Reyna, V. F. (1998). Fuzzy-trace theory and false memory. In M. Intons-Peterson & D. Best (Eds.), *Challenges and controversies: Memory distortions and their prevention* (pp. 15–27). Mahwah, NJ: Lawrence Erlbaum Associates.

Reyna, V. F., & Brainerd, C. J. (1990). Fuzzy processing in transitivity development. *Annals of Operations Research, 23,* 37–63.

Reyna, V. F., & Brainerd, C. J. (1995). Fuzzy-trace theory: An interim synthesis. *Learning and Individual Differences, 7,* 1–75.

Reyna, V. F., & Brainerd, C. J. (1997). Commentary on article by Professor Wohlmuth. *Journal of Contemporary Legal Issues, 8,* 287–298.

Reyna, V. F., & Kiernan, B. (1994). The development of gist versus verbatim memory in sentence recognition: Effects of lexical familiarity, semantic content, encoding instructions, and retention interval. *Developmental Psychology, 30,* 178–191.

Reyna, V. F., & Kiernan, B. (1995). Meaning, memory, and the development of metaphor. *Metaphor & Symbolic Activity, 10,* 309–331.

Reyna, V. F., & Lloyd, F. (1997). Theories of false memory in children and adults. *Learning and Individual Differences, 9,* 95–124.

Reyna, V. F., & Titcomb, A. L. (1996). Constraints on the suggestibility of eyewitness testimony: A fuzzy-trace theory analysis. In D. G. Payne & F. G. Conrad (Eds.), *A synthesis of basic and applied approaches to human memory.* Mahway, NJ: Lawrence Erlbaum Associates.

Robinson, K. J., & Roediger, H. L. (1997). Associative processes in false recall and false recognition. *Psychological Science, 8,* 231–237.

Roediger, H. L., III, & McDermott, K. B. (1995). Creating false memories: Remembering words not presented on lists. *Journal of Experimental Psychology: Learning, Memory, and Cognition, 21,* 803–814.

Salmon, K., & Pipe, M.-E. (1997). Props and children's event reports: The impact of a 1-year delay. *Journal of Experimental Child Psychology, 65,* 261–292.

Schacter, D. L., Verfaellie, M., & Anes, M. D. (1997). Illusory memories in amnesic patients: Conceptual and perceptual false recognition. *Neuropsychology, 35,* 319–334.

State v. Henderson, Superior Court, Santa Barbara County, California, 1997.

State v. Hungerford, Supreme Court, New Hampshire, 94-S-045 thru 94-S-047 (1995).

State v. Morahan, Supreme Court, New Hampshire, 93-S-1734 thru 93-S-1936 (1995).

Toglia, M. P., Neuschatz, J. S., & Goodwin, K. A. (1998). Recall accuracy and illusory memories: When more is less. *Memory, 2,* 233–256.

Tulving, E., & Thomson, D. M. (1971). Retrieval processes in recognition memory: Effects of associative context. *Journal of Experimental Psychology, 87,* 116–124.

Tun, P. A., Wingfield, A., Rosen, M. J., & Blanchard, L. (1998). Response latencies for false memories: Gist-based processes in normal aging. *Psychology and Aging, 13,* 230–241.

Tussing, A. A., & Greene, R. L. (1998). *Differential effects of repetition on true and false recognition.* Manuscript submitted for publication.

Tversky, B., & Tuchin, M. (1989). A reconciliation of evidence on eyewitness testimony: Comments on McCloskey and Zaragoza. *Journal of Experimental Psychology: General, 118,* 86–91.

Underwood, B. J. (1965). False recognition produced by implicit verbal responses. *Journal of Experimental Psychology, 70,* 122–129.

Warren, A. R., Woodall, C. E., Hunt, J. S., & Perry, N. W. (1996). "It sounds good in theory, but . . .": Do investigative interviewers follow guidelines based on memory research? *Child Maltreatment, 1,* 231–245.

Wohlmuth, P. C. (1997). Jurisprudence and memory research. *Journal of Contemporary Legal Issues, 8,* 249–286.

Wulf, F. (1922). Beitrage zur psychologie der gestalt: IV. Uber die veranderung von vorstellungen. *Psychologische Forschung, 1,* 333–375.

Zaragoza, M. S., & Mitchell, K. J. (1996). Repeated exposure to suggestion and the creation of false memories. *Psychological Science, 7,* 294–300.

CHAPTER SIX

The Cognitive Neuroscience of Constructive Memory

DANIEL L. SCHACTER
KENNETH A. NORMAN
WILMA KOUTSTAAL
Harvard University

False memories have been studied by cognitive psychologists for decades, dating at least to the pioneering studies of Bartlett (1932). False memories are important theoretically because they emphasize that memory is not a literal reproduction of the past but instead depends on constructive processes that are sometimes prone to errors, distortions, and illusions (for recent reviews, see Estes, 1997; Johnson, Hashtroudi, & Lindsay, 1993; Roediger, 1996; Schacter, 1995, 1996). As highlighted by the other contributions to this volume, contemporary cognitive psychologists have been intensively concerned with false memories and constructive aspects of remembering, in part as a result of real-world controversies concerning the suggestibility of children's memory (e.g., Ceci & Bruck, 1995; Schacter, Kagan, & Leichtman, 1995) and the accuracy of memories recovered in psychotherapy (e.g., Lindsay & Read, 1996; Loftus, 1993; Schacter, Koutstaal, & Norman, 1997).

In contrast, neuropsychologists and neuroscientists who have focused on brain substrates of remembering and learning have tended to pay less attention to memory errors, distortions, and related phenomena. During the past several years, however, cognitive neuroscientists have exhibited signs of increasing interest in phenomena that illuminate constructive aspects of remembering, such as false recognition and confabulation (cf.

Moscovitch, 1995; Schacter & Curran, 1995; Squire, 1995). In this chapter, we attempt to integrate diverse empirical and theoretical observations concerning constructive memory phenomena from four different areas of research: cognitive studies of young adults, neuropsychological investigations of brain-damaged patients, studies of cognitive aging, and research using brain-imaging techniques.

We will begin by sketching a general framework that places the study of constructive memory phenomena in a broader conceptual context. We then examine observations from relevant research domains concerning two major types of memory distortions: (a) false recognition, and (b) intrusions and confabulations. Finally, we consider several recent studies concerned with whether false memories can be reduced or suppressed.

CONSTRUCTIVE MEMORY: A GENERAL FRAMEWORK

Our conceptualization of constructive memory functions, which we will refer to as the *constructive memory framework* (CMF), draws on notions put forward previously by Johnson et al. (1993), McClelland, McNaughton, and O'Reilly (1995), Moscovitch (1994), Norman and Schacter (1996), and Squire (1992), among others. We begin by noting that representations of new experiences can be conceptualized as patterns of features, with different features representing different facets of the experience: the outputs of perceptual modules that analyze specific physical attributes of incoming information, interpretation of these physical attributes by conceptual or semantic modules, and actions undertaken in response to incoming information (cf. Johnson & Chalfonte, 1994; Metcalfe, 1990; Moscovitch, 1994; Schacter, 1989). Constituent features of a memory representation are distributed widely across different parts of the brain, such that no single location contains a complete record of the trace or engram of a specific experience (Damasio, 1989; Squire, 1992). Retrieval of a past experience involves a process of pattern completion (McClelland et al., 1995) in which a subset of the features composing a particular past experience are reactivated, and activation spreads to the rest of the constituent features of that experience.

A memory system that operates in such a manner must solve a number of problems if it is to produce mainly accurate representations of past experience. Features composing an episode must be linked together at encoding to form a bound or coherent representation (Moscovitch, 1994; Schacter, 1989). Inadequate feature binding can result in source memory failure, in which people retrieve fragments of an episode but are unable to recollect how or when the fragments were acquired (Johnson et al., 1993; Schacter, Harbluk, & McLachlan, 1984; Squire, 1995). As we discuss later in this chapter, source memory failure is an important contributor to various memory illusions and distortions. Source memory failures may also occur when binding processes are unimpaired, but not enough information that is diagnostic of the item's source is included in the bound representation. A closely related encoding process, sometimes referred to as *pattern separation* (McClelland et al., 1995), is required to keep bound episodes separate from one another in memory. If episodes overlap extensively with one another, individuals may recall the general similarities (Hintzman & Curran, 1994) or gist (Reyna & Brainerd, 1995) common to many episodes but fail to remember distinctive, item-specific information that distinguishes one episode from another.

Similar kinds of problems arise when retrieving information from memory. Retrieval cues can potentially match stored experiences other than the sought-after episode (Nystrom & McClelland, 1992). Thus, retrieval often involves a preliminary stage in which the rememberer forms a more refined description of the characteristics of the episode to be retrieved (Burgess & Shallice, 1996; Norman & Bobrow, 1979). This process has been called *focusing* (Norman & Schacter, 1996). Poor retrieval focus can result in recollection of information that does not pertain to the target episode or may produce impaired recall of an episode's details, insofar as activated information from nontarget episodes interferes with recall of target information. When the pattern completion process produces a match, a decision must be made as to whether the information that is delivered to conscious awareness constitutes an episodic memory, as opposed to a generic image, fantasy, or thought. This phase of retrieval involves a criterion-setting process in which the rememberer needs to consider the diagnostic value of perceptual vividness, semantic detail, and other kinds of information for determining the origin of the retrieved pattern (Johnson et al., 1993). As Johnson et al. point out, the use of lax source-monitoring criteria increases the probability of accepting images, fantasies, or other internally generated information as evidence of external events that never happened. If retrieved information is accepted as an episodic memory, the rememberer must also determine whether the memory pertains to the sought-after episode or to some other stored episode.

A wide variety of brain regions are likely implicated in these and other aspects of constructive memory functions. For example, recent brain imaging studies, using such techniques as positron emission tomography (PET) and functional magnetic resonance imaging (fMRI), indicate that distributed networks of structures are involved in both episodic encoding and retrieval (for reviews, see Buckner & Tulving, 1995; Ungerleider, 1995). Nonetheless, two brain regions are especially relevant to phenomena of constructive memory: the medial temporal area, including the hippocampal formation, and the prefrontal cortex. It has long been known that the medial temporal region is implicated in memory functions because damage to this area produces severe impairment of episodic memory for recent events (Mayes, 1988; Squire, 1992). Recent neuroimaging data indicate that the medial temporal area is involved in encoding novel events into episodic memory (Brewer, Zhao, Glover, & Gabrieli, 1998; Stern et al., 1996; Tulving, Markowitsch, et al., 1994; Wagner et al., 1998; see also Schacter & Wagner, 1999). Indeed, a consensus account has begun to emerge regarding how exactly the hippocampus implements feature binding and pattern separation (most recently expressed by McClelland et al., 1995; see also Squire & Alvarez, 1995; Treves & Rolls, 1994). According to this account, distributed patterns of activity in the neocortex (corresponding to individual episodes) are linked to sparse neuronal representations in Region CA3 of the hippocampus; essentially, each episode is assigned its own hippocampal "index." Pattern separation is achieved to the extent that the hippocampus is able to assign nonoverlapping CA3 representations to different episodes; some minimal amount of difference needs to exist between episodes, or else the pattern separation process will fail (O'Reilly & McClelland, 1994). The hippocampal index corresponding to a particular episode may only need to last until the neocortex consolidates the episode (by directly linking all of the constituent features of the episode to one another), at which point the index can be assigned to a new episode (Squire & Alvarez, 1995; but see Nadel & Moscovitch, 1997).

The medial temporal region is also thought to play a role in pattern completion at retrieval (cf. Moscovitch, 1994). In the account of McClelland et al. (1995), during retrieval of recent episodes (for which there is still a hippocampal index corresponding to the episode), cues activate the episode's index in Region CA3 of the hippocampus, and activation spreads from the index to all of the features composing that episode. Once an episode has been consolidated in the neocortex, however, activation can spread directly between the episode's features, and the hippocampus no longer plays a crucial role in pattern completion. Although the neuroimaging data on medial temporal contributions to episodic retrieval are not entirely clear cut—many studies have failed to observe medial temporal activity during retrieval (for discussion, see Buckner et al., 1995; Shallice et al., 1994; Ungerleider, 1995)—a number of brain imaging studies have implicated the medial temporal area in the successful recollection of recently acquired information (Nyberg, McIntosh, et al., 1996; Schacter, Reiman, et al., 1995; Schacter, Alpert, Savage, Rauch, & Albert, 1996; Schacter, Savage, Alpert, Rauch, & Alpert, 1996; Squire et al., 1992).

The prefrontal cortex has also been implicated in episodic memory retrieval. Neuroimaging studies have consistently revealed evidence of prefrontal activity during episodic retrieval, especially in the right hemisphere (for reviews, see Buckner, 1996; Nyberg, Cabeza, & Tulving, 1996; Tulving, Kapur, Markowitsch, Craik, Habib, & Houle, 1994), and recent data from electrophysiological studies using event-related potentials have provided converging evidence (Wilding & Rugg, 1996; Johnson, Kounios, & Nolde, 1997). Although the exact nature of the functions indexed by these activations remains to be determined, they appear to tap effortful aspects of retrieval (Schacter, Alpert, et al., 1996) related to focusing or entering the retrieval mode (Nyberg et al., 1995), postretrieval monitoring and criterion setting (Johnson, Kounios, & Nolde, 1997; Rugg et al., 1996), or both (Norman & Schacter, 1996).

In summary, CMF emphasizes encoding processes of feature binding and pattern separation and retrieval processes of focusing, pattern completion, and criterion setting. We have suggested further that medial temporal and prefrontal regions play important roles in various aspects of these component processes. We next consider phenomena of constructive memory in light of this general framework.

PHENOMENA OF CONSTRUCTIVE MEMORY

We have organized our review of recent studies by considering two major phenomena that are central to CMF: *false recognition*, in which people claim that a novel word, object, or event is familiar; and *intrusions* and *confabulations*, in which people produce nonstudied information in memory experiments (intrusions) or narrative descriptions of events that never happened (confabulations). We subdivide relevant research into four domains of investigation: cognitive experiments with intact individuals, neuropsychological studies of brain-damaged patients, research on aging memory, and brain imaging experiments.

False Recognition: Illusory Familiarity and Recollection

Cognitive Studies of Normal Subjects.   One of the most extensively studied examples of false recognition arises in investigations of the effects of misleading postevent suggestions, pioneered by Loftus and her colleagues (for a recent review, see Loftus, Feldman, & Dashiell, 1995). Such studies typically have involved two phases. Participants first viewed slides or a videotape depicting a sequence of events and then were asked questions about the events; some questions contained suggestions of incidents that never occurred. Loftus and her colleagues have shown that people falsely claim to have seen, or to recognize as "old," some of the suggested events. Although Loftus' early claim that suggested information replaces or over-writes the initial event has been challenged (McCloskey & Zaragoza, 1985), more recent studies have indicated that false recognition in the mis-leading information paradigm is largely attributable to source-monitoring confusions, with people failing to recollect whether the suggested infor-mation was originally presented in the videotape or slides or occurred only in the postevent narrative (e.g., Belli, Lindsay, Gales, & McCarthy, 1994; Johnson et al., 1993; Lindsay, 1990; Zaragoza & Lane, 1994). Insofar as thinking about an event frequently involves mentally picturing the event, mere contemplation of a suggested event can result in a vivid and detailed representation that is difficult to distinguish from stored repre-sentations of events that were actually perceived. This process could some-times lead individuals to mistakenly ascribe their recollections of an event to the original videotape even though they are also aware that references to the event occurred during postretrieval questioning (Zaragoza & Mit-chell, 1996; see also Fiedler, Walther, Armbruster, Fay, & Naumann, 1996). Also, participants may not always recognize the need for or consis-tently implement adequate source monitoring. Dodson and Johnson (1993) have shown that false recognition can be reduced by requiring par-ticipants to adopt strict source-monitoring criteria: College students were less likely to claim that they had seen a picture of an object they had only read about when they were probed about the source than when they were given a forced-choice recognition test.

Although studies of misleading suggestions provide a prominent exam-ple of false recognition, recent interest in the phenomenon is partly attrib-utable to a demonstration of exceptionally high levels of false recognition by Roediger and McDermott (1995; see also Read, 1996). They revived and modified a procedure originally described by Deese (1959) for produc-ing large numbers of intrusions on a free-recall test. College students studied a list of semantic associates (presented auditorily), all of which converged on a single nonpresented theme word; later, at test, partici-pants frequently incorrectly claimed the nonpresented word was part of the list (e.g., participants who studied *drowsy, bed, tired, pillow, rest, paja-mas,* and other associated words later claimed to remember having been exposed to the nonpresented theme word, *sleep*). False-alarm rates exceeded 70% in some conditions and were nearly as high as the hit rates. Participants expressed as much confidence in these false recognitions as they did in accurate recognitions of previously studied words. Moreover, when asked whether they possessed a specific recollection of having encountered the word (a *remember* response; cf. Gardiner & Java, 1993; Tulving, 1985) or whether it just seemed familiar (a *know* response), participants provided as many remember responses to nonstudied theme words as they did to studied words. (For an example of false remembering in the domain of autobiographical memory, see Conway, Collins, Gathercole, & Anderson, 1996.) Finally, the strength of the false-recognition effect is a direct function of the number of associates presented during study (Robinson & Roediger, 1997).

CMF provides two potential explanations for this false-recognition effect. One possibility is that false recognition in the Deese–Roediger-McDermott paradigm resulted from a failure of pattern separation: Studying numerous semantically related words might result in unacceptably high levels of overlap between item representations. Pattern separation failure (i.e., assigning multiple similar items to the same hippocampal index) leads to excellent memory for what the items have in common (gist information) but impaired recall of distinctive, item-specific information. Because they lack specific recollection, participants are forced to rely on memory for gist, which does not discriminate well between studied items and nonstudied theme words. This idea is consistent with data from Mather, Henkel, and Johnson (1997) and Norman and Schacter (1997), who examined the qualitative characteristics of participants' memories and found that both true and false recognition were driven by retrieval of semantic associations (i.e., participants typically claimed to remember nonpresented lures because they recalled associated items) and also that participants retrieved little item-specific information overall.

It is also possible to explain false recognition of semantically related lures by appealing to the notion of *implicit associative responses*—the idea that people overtly or covertly generate a nonpresented lure word at the time of study in response to an associate (Underwood, 1965). From this perspective, false recognition is viewed as a kind of source confusion, where people fail to recollect whether they actually saw or heard a word at study or generated it themselves. Both of these ideas are consistent with the finding reported by Mather et al. (1997) that false-recognition effects were larger when semantic associates related to a particular theme word were all presented consecutively (in blocks) than when associates of different theme words were intermixed. Insofar as blocking increases the salience of list themes, it should result in increased generation of theme words, and it sho᾽ ld also increase the likelihood that people will notice and encode commonalities between same-theme items, thereby decreasing pattern separation.

Both Mather et al. (1997) and Norman and Schacter (1997) found that although participants recalled little specific information overall, veridical recognition of previously presented words was accompanied by recollection of more auditory detail from the study phase (i.e., what the word sounded like when it was initially presented) and related contextual information (e.g., reactions triggered by the item at study) than was false recognition. Importantly, however, people were not able to make use of these small qualitative differences to reject theme words; both studies found that requiring participants to carefully scrutinize their memories during the recognition test by asking them to indicate whether they could recollect various qualitative details of the items they designated as *old* did not reduce the magnitude of the false-recognition effect after blocked study (although increased scrutiny did result in diminished false recognition following randomly intermixed study in the Mather et al. experiment).

Mather et al. (1997) also found that, in a situation where different speakers read different study lists, participants were willing to assign a source to a majority of their false recognitions (see also Payne, Elie, Blackwell, & Neuschatz, 1996). Furthermore, participants were better than chance at choosing the "correct" source for the lures they falsely recognized (i.e., the speaker who read words semantically related to the lure). However, Mather et al. found that participants reported no greater vividness of auditory detail for correct than for incorrect source identifications.

In the Deese–Roediger-McDermott paradigm, it is extremely difficult to tease apart the implicit associative response and pattern separation failure accounts of false recognition. In other situations, however, interpretation is less ambiguous. The idea that false alarms can be driven by implicit associative responses is supported by studies by Wallace and colleagues (Wallace, Stewart, & Malone, 1995; Wallace, Stewart, Sherman, & Mellor, 1995) on false recognition of spoken words. Participants heard a series of spoken sound stimuli in which a nonpresented target word (e.g., *January*) was disqualified as a candidate early in a nonword (e.g., *Jatuary*) or late (e.g., *Januaty*). On a subsequent test, false-recognition rates were considerably higher for lure words that had been disqualified late during initial exposure than for those that had been disqualified early. Wallace, Stewart, Sherman, and Mellor (1995) argued that increased false recognition of late-disqualified words could be attributed to the increased probability that participants internally generated the lure word as part of an activated cohort of physically similar words (Marslen-Wilson & Zwitserlood, 1989).

Evidence consistent with false recognition driven by pattern separation failure is provided by Koutstaal and Schacter (1997), who showed people pictures from various categories (e.g., cars, footwear), intermixed with unrelated pictures that did not belong to any of the categories. After a 3-day delay, they tested recognition of previously studied pictures, nonstudied pictures that were perceptually and conceptually similar to those previously studied, and new unrelated pictures. Despite the fact that recognition memory for pictures usually yields high hit rates and low false-alarm rates, participants showed robust false recognition to similar pictures, particularly when many instances of a category had been presented during study. Koutstaal and Schacter reasoned that it is highly unlikely that participants generated the related picture during the study phase of the experiment, in the same sense that they might generate *sweet* when hearing a list of associates. Rather, false recognition in this experiment appears to be caused by high levels of similarity between items, resulting in robust memory for gist information about perceptual or conceptual features of studied pictures but poor memory for picture-specific details.

False recognition also occurs when people miscombine elements of words or other stimuli they have recently studied (e.g., Underwood, Kapelak, & Malmi, 1976). Drawing on previous work concerning similar kinds of miscombinations in perception (Treisman & Schmidt, 1982), Reinitz, Lammers, and Cochran (1992) labeled such distortions *memory conjunction errors*. Reinitz et al. (1992) found significant numbers of memory conjunction errors with stimuli comprised of nonsense syllables; people claimed to have seen conjunction stimuli in which syllables from two previously studied stimuli were recombined. They also demonstrated similar conjunction errors during recognition of faces, when features from separate previously studied faces were conjoined in a single face. Furthermore, Reinitz, Morrissey, and Demb (1994) found that requiring participants to divide their attention between tasks while they studied faces reduced the hit rate for actually studied faces to the same level as the false-alarm rate for conjunction faces. Taken together, these results suggest that focal attention during encoding is critically important for binding facial features into a unified representation, and less important for encoding individual facial features.

Neuropsychological Studies of Brain-Damaged Patients. Although neuropsychological studies of memory disorders have long been concerned with the status of recognition memory after brain damage, it is only recently that systematic investigations of false recognition in patients with brain lesions have appeared. Delbecq-Derouesné, Beauvois, and Shallice

(1990) described a patient (R. W.) who, after an operation to repair a ruptured anterior communicating artery aneurysm, made an abnormally large number of confident false recognitions. R. W. showed relatively more preserved free recall of studied items, although he did make large numbers of recall intrusions. A computerized tomography (CT) scan revealed bilateral areas of hypodensity in the medial aspects of the frontal lobes, as well as in the right temporal pole and the fusiform and parahippocampal gyri. Delbecq-Derouesné et al. suggested that R. W. suffered from an impairment in a postretrieval verification or criterion-setting process.

Parkin, Bindschaedler, Harsent, and Metzler (1997) have recently described another patient (J. B.) who suffered a ruptured anterior communicating artery aneurysm; CT scans showed atrophy in the left frontal lobe. Like R. W., J. B. made a large number of false recognitions that were accompanied by high confidence—he often said that he was "sure" that he had been exposed to target materials that had never been shown to him previously. When asked to make remember–know judgments about previously studied and nonstudied words, all of J. B.'s false alarms to nonstudied words were accompanied by "know" responses—that is, J. B. felt that these items were familiar and thus was certain that they had appeared in the study list, but he did not have a specific recollection of having encountered them. When J. B. studied and was tested on various kinds of visual patterns, Parkin et al. found that J. B. did not make excessive numbers of false alarms when distractor items on a recognition test were perceptually dissimilar from studied items.

Schacter and Curran and their colleagues (Curran, Schacter, Norman & Galluccio, 1997; Schacter, Curran, Galluccio, Milberg, & Bates, 1996) have described a patient (B. G.) with an infarction of the posterior aspects of the right frontal lobe who in some respects resembles patients R. W. and J. B. Patient B. G. shows pathologically high rates of false recognition to a wide variety of experimental materials, including words, sounds, pictures, and pseudowords. This phenomenon is not limited to lures that are semantically related to studied items; for example, when B. G. studied a list of unrelated words, he false alarmed excessively to nonstudied unrelated words. However, as with patient J. B., Schacter, Curran, et al. found that B. G.'s pathological false recognition could be sharply reduced by testing him with items that differed substantially from those he had studied earlier (e.g., after studying pictures of inanimate objects from various categories, B. G. almost never made false-recognition responses to pictures of animals). Unlike J. B., when asked to make remember–know judgments about test items, most of B. G.'s false alarms were accompanied by "remember" responses.

Schacter, Curran, et al. (1996) suggested that B. G.'s false-recognition deficit stems from use of inappropriate decision criteria at test. According to this account, B. G. claimed to remember an item when that item matched the general characteristics of the study episode, whereas control participants claimed to remember that a word or picture had appeared on a study list only when they retrieved specific information about that item's presentation at study. This criterion-setting deficit might stem from an inability to form an appropriately focused description of the study episode. It is also possible that, in addition to (or instead of) faulty criterion setting, B. G.'s susceptibility to false recognition results from failure to encode distinctive item attributes at study. From the perspective of CMF, this encoding failure would result in excessive feelings of familiarity for attributes common to multiple items at study (including new occurrences of those attributes in lure items), and poor memory for item-specific details.

Using signal detection analyses, Curran et al. (1997) found that B. G. consistently used excessively liberal response criteria compared with matched controls, but there was also evidence of impaired sensitivity. When Curran et al. increased B. G.'s ability to recollect specific details about presented words by providing a semantic encoding task, B. G. assigned remember responses to more than 80% of studied items, but all of his false alarms were know responses. These observations suggest that B. G. can discriminate well between studied and nonstudied items when he has access to high-quality recollective information about specific studied items; otherwise, he relies on a signal that reflects the general similarity between study and test items.

Finally, Curran et al. (1997) analyzed exactly what B. G. claimed to recall when he made a remember false alarm and found that he tended to provide associations to other words or sometimes to events in his life—specific information from an inappropriate context. In light of other evidence that frontal lobe damage is associated with impaired memory for source information (Butters, Kasniak, Glisky, Eslinger, & Schacter, 1994; Janowsky, Shimamura, & Squire, 1989; Milner, Corsi, & Leonard, 1991; Schacter et al., 1984), it seems likely that deficient source monitoring (inability to assess whether an association triggered by an item at test is a memory from the study phase, is derived from some other episode, or is being generated for the first time at test) contributes to the character of B. G.'s false recollections.

Excessive levels of false recognition of related lures have also been reported in studies of patients whose cerebral hemispheres have been surgically separated. Phelps and Gazzaniga (1992) showed two split-brain patients, J. W. and V. P., slide sequences depicting everyday scenes (making

cookies, bowling) and then tested yes–no recognition of previously studied slides, schema-consistent lures that had not been studied but that fit
with the studied scene, and schema-inconsistent lures that were unrelated
to the studied scene. Hits and false-alarm rates to studied slides and unrelated lures did not differ as a function of hemisphere, but left-hemisphere
responses were associated with more false alarms to schema-consistent
lures than right-hemisphere responses. Metcalfe, Funnell, and Gazzaniga
(1995) tested another split-brain patient, J. W., and found that J. W.'s left
hemisphere made more false alarms than the right hemisphere to related
words, faces, and visual patterns. The authors of both studies explained
their findings in terms of hemispheric differences in encoding: The left
hemisphere is thought to be biased toward schematic (categorical, gist)
information, whereas the right hemisphere encodes more item-specific
details and hence is better positioned to discriminate between studied and
nonstudied schema-consistent items.

The foregoing studies indicate that increased susceptibility to false recognition is associated with ventromedial and posterior frontal lobe damage and with left hemisphere functioning in split-brain patients. More research is needed to pinpoint the exact kinds of frontal lobe damage that
trigger increased false recognition. In any case, none of these patients exhibited the severe and pervasive memory loss observed in amnesic syndromes associated with damage to the medial temporal lobes, which have
been the focus of extensive neuropsychological study (e.g., Mayes, 1988;
Parkin & Leng, 1993; Squire, 1992). Several recent studies have begun to
explore false recognition in amnesic patients, with sharply contrasting results emerging from different types of false-recognition paradigms.

Two recent studies have examined memory conjunction errors using
variants of the procedures introduced by Reinitz et al. (1992). Reinitz, Verfaellie, and Milberg (1996) found that normal controls made more *old* responses to studied compound words (e.g., *handstand* and *shotgun*) than to
conjunction lures in which features of studied words were recombined
(e.g., *handgun*), but amnesic patients failed to discriminate between studied words and conjunction lures (primarily because they made fewer *old*
responses to studied words than controls). Kroll, Knight, Metcalfe, Wolf,
and Tulving (1996) reported increased memory conjunction errors to recombined words in patients with left but not right hippocampal lesions
and increased conjunction errors to combined faces for both types of
patients. Conjunction errors were more pronounced when items from
which features were combined were separated by only a single item during the study phase than when they were separated by five items. Kroll
et al. suggested that hippocampal lesions produce disinhibited binding,

such that the damaged system binds features from different stimuli across an excessively broad temporal window.

In contrast to the aforementioned findings of normal or even increased levels of false recognition to conjunction lures in patients with medial temporal lobe damage, two recent experiments have revealed reduced levels of false recognition in these patients. Schacter, Verfaellie, and Pradere (1996), using a procedure similar to that of Roediger and McDermott (1995), found that amnesic patients showed reduced levels of false recognition to semantic associates of previously studied words. These findings imply that encoding, retention, and/or retrieval of the information that drives false recognition in this paradigm depend on the medial temporal and/or diencephalic brain regions that are damaged in amnesic patients. Schacter, Verfaellie, and Anes (1997) replicated the Schacter, Verfaellie, and Pradere (1996) results with a different set of semantically related words (Shiffrin, Huber, & Marinelli, 1995) and extended them to the domain of perceptual false recognition: Amnesic patients made fewer false alarms than did matched controls to nonstudied words (e.g., *fate*) that were orthographically and phonologically similar to previously studied words (e.g., *lake, fake*). Conceptual false recognition in the control group was associated primarily with remember responses, whereas perceptual false recognition was associated primarily with know responses. The fact that amnesic patients showed similarly reduced levels of false recognition for both types of responses implies that structures that are damaged in amnesic patients are relevant to both of these forms of explicit memory (cf. Knowlton & Squire, 1995; also see Koutstaal, Schacter, Verfaellie, Brenner, & Jackson, 1999).

In all of the foregoing neuropsychological investigations, false recognition occurred in the context of an episodic memory test: Participants were asked to make their old and new judgments with respect to a specific episode (the study phase). Rapcsak and colleagues (Rapcsak, Polster, Comer, & Rubens, 1994; Rapcsak, Polster, Glisky, & Comer, 1996) have recently described a different kind of false recognition in which patients, asked whether they have ever seen a particular face, claim that unfamiliar faces are familiar to them. These patients are characterized by damage to posterior regions of the right hemisphere and, in some instances, damage to the right frontal lobe. Rapcsak et al. (1996) argued that in most patients, false recognition is attributable to impaired face perception; patients tend to rely on isolated facial features when making recognition decisions. However, one of these patients (with a right frontal lesion) did not suffer from obvious perceptual deficits. Rapcsak et al. (1996) argued that this patient's false-recognition problem stems from an inability to engage strategic-monitoring and criterion-setting processes. Although the relationship between false recognition of this sort and false recognition on episodic memory tests (e.g., Curran et al., 1997; Parkin et al., 1997; Schacter, Curran, et al., 1996) remains to be elucidated, the fact that both kinds of impairment can occur after right frontal lobe damage suggests that the relation between the two merits closer examination in future studies.

Aging Memory.   Early studies of aging memory reported that elderly adults show increased false recognition of semantically related distractors in paradigms in which young adults show relatively small false-recognition effects (Hess, 1984; Rankin & Kausler, 1979; Smith, 1975). More recent studies have replicated these findings (Isingrini, Fontaine, Taconnat, & Duportal, 1995) and extended them to paradigms that produce high levels of false recognition even in younger adults.

Norman and Schacter (1997) reported that older adults show increased susceptibility to false recognition of semantic associates in the Deese–Roediger-McDermott converging associates paradigm (discussed earlier). Like younger adults, elderly individuals expressed high confidence in their false memories, frequently claimed to remember nonpresented words, and when asked to rate various qualitative features of their memories, indicated that false recognitions were based primarily on recollection of semantically associated items. However, memory for auditory details of the initial presentation discriminated less well between true and false recollections in older than in younger adults, suggesting that failure to retrieve specific sensory details is related to age-related increases in false recognition (although it is unclear whether sensory details are not encoded in the first place or whether they are encoded but not recalled because of interference from similar studied items). Because older adults showed increased susceptibility to false recognition even when they were instructed to rate the qualitative characteristics of their memories (Experiment 2) or to provide explanations of what they remembered (Experiment 1), the age effect is probably not attributable to a failure to consider relevant memorial attributes (cf. Multhaup, 1995). Tun, Wingfield, Rosen, and Blanchard (1998) have reported additional evidence of age-related increases in false recognition with a similar paradigm, using both accuracy and latency measures.

Although the foregoing experiments all used verbal materials, two recent studies examined whether older adults show increased false recognition after studying scenes or pictures. Schacter, Koustaal, Johnson, Gross, and Angell (1997) exposed participants to videotaped scenes of everyday events and later showed them photographs of some previously viewed actions, together with actions that had not been seen previously. On a subsequent recognition test, participants were given brief verbal descriptions of individual objects or actions and instructed to respond "old" only when they specifically remembered seeing the object or action in the videotape; participants were explicitly warned that some of the items on the recognition test occurred only in photographs. Older adults showed greater false recognition of objects and actions that had appeared only in photographs than did younger adults.

The false-recognition effect observed by Schacter, Koutstaal, Johnson, et al. (1997) is clearly attributable to source confusion on the part of elderly adults; participants had actually seen photographs of the falsely recognized actions earlier. This observation fits with other evidence indicating that older adults often exhibit disproportionately impaired source memory compared with younger adults (e.g., Brown, Jones, & Davis, 1995; Johnson, DeLeonardis, Hashtroudi, & Ferguson, 1995; Schacter, Osowiecki, Kaszniak, Kihlstrom, & Valdiserri, 1994). Additional analyses conducted by Schacter, Koutstaal, Johnson, et al. (on data from their Experiment 2) showed that, as with the results described earlier from the Deese converging associates paradigm, the elderly were not successful at retrieving perceptual and contextual details that could be used to differentiate sources. Therefore, in this paradigm, source confusions are not simply a matter of recollecting useful contextual information and then failing to make use of it.

Koutstaal and Schacter (1997) compared older and younger adults using their picture recognition paradigm (discussed earlier) in which participants study exemplars of pictures from various categories intermixed with unrelated pictures and later make old–new recognition judgments about previously studied pictures, related lure pictures, and unrelated lure pictures. Older adults consistently exhibited higher levels of false recognition of related pictures than did younger adults; also, older adults showed normal hit rates to studied pictures from large categories and impaired hit rates to unrelated pictures. Overall, this pattern of results indicates age-related preservation of access to general similarity information (driving both hits and false alarms to items from studied categories) together with age-related impairment of access to item-specific, distinctive information (thereby explaining impaired hit rates to unrelated pictures).

Although the exact mechanisms remain to be elucidated, within CMF such effects could be attributable to impaired pattern separation in older adults, caused either by generally indistinct encoding or by specific impairment of the hippocampal mechanisms involved in pattern separation and binding (see also Schacter, Koutstaal, & Norman, 1997). This latter idea is consistent with PET evidence indicating decreased hippocampal activation during encoding of novel faces in the elderly (Grady et al., 1995). Alternatively, the effects described previously could be attributable to a failure to engage in effortful focusing processes that facilitate retrieval of item-specific information. This idea is consistent with PET evidence showing abnormal frontal lobe activations in the elderly in test conditions that require effortful retrieval (Schacter, Savage, et al., 1996). One final possibility is that elderly adults do successfully recollect item-specific information but fail to use this information when making their recognition decisions (i.e., a criterion-setting deficit).

Brain Imaging Studies.   Despite the recent surge of brain imaging studies of memory noted earlier, only a handful of recent studies have examined false recognition. In a PET study, Schacter, Reiman, et al. (1996) adapted procedures from Deese (1959) and Roediger and McDermott (1995) to examine brain activity of healthy young individuals during true versus false recognition. Compared with a control condition in which participants fixated on a crosshair, a variety of brain regions showed significant blood flow increases for both true and false recognition, including several areas previously implicated in episodic retrieval: the anterior prefrontal cortex, medial parietal cortex, left middle temporal gyrus, cerebellum, and left parahippocampal gyrus. Although direct comparison between true and false recognition yielded little evidence of significant blood flow differences, two suggestive trends were evident in this comparison. First, there was evidence of increased left superior temporal activity during veridical recognition; the activity may reflect memory for auditory rehearsal at study, which presumably occurred more for studied items than nonstudied associates. Second, there was a trend toward increased right anterior prefrontal activity during false recognition. This trend was replicated and extended in an fMRI study conducted by Schacter, Buckner, Koutstaal, Dale, and Rosen (1997). In addition, using new fMRI procedures that allow analysis of the time course of blood flow increases (Buckner et al., 1996), they documented a late onset of anterior prefrontal activations relative to other brain areas. This latter finding suggests that anterior prefrontal activations during false recognition reflect processes that operate on the output of the memory system, such as postretrieval monitoring or criterion setting (cf. Rugg et al., 1996; Schacter, Reiman, et al., 1996).

Johnson, Nolde, et al. (1997) used event-related potentials (ERPs, which measure averaged electrophysiological activity that is time locked to a specific stimulus) to investigate true and false recognition of semantically related words. They found that when studied words, nonstudied semantic associates, and nonstudied unrelated words were tested for recognition in separate blocks (as required by PET), ERP differences between true and false recognition were observed at frontal and left parietal electrode sites, providing a good fit with the PET data. However, when the word types were randomly intermixed during recognition testing (as is usually done in purely cognitive experiments), differences were greatly attenuated (cf. Düzel, Yonelinas, Mangun, Heinze, & Tulving, 1997). Johnson, Nolde, et al. (1997) noted that in the randomly intermixed testing condition, participants could do reasonably well by relying on semantic similarity information alone (i.e., they could reject nonstudied unrelated items). However, with blocked testing, semantic similarity information does not discriminate well between items of a particular type, and hence participants may have used stricter criteria (e.g., trying to recall perceptual details) in this condition.

Intrusions and Confabulations

Evidence concerning false recognition leaves open the question of whether people recall on their own nonpresented items or events that never happened. This question is addressed by research concerning *recall intrusions,* in which nonstudied information is produced together with previously studied information, and *confabulation,* in which people provide narrative accounts of events that did not occur.

Cognitive Studies of Normal Subjects. It is known that people sometimes produce incorrect items on free-recall tests, but such recall intrusions are usually infrequent. In contrast, using the lists of semantic associates described earlier with respect to false recognition, Deese (1959) demonstrated that participants often intrude nonpresented false targets that are strong associates of previously presented words. A large number of recent studies, beginning with Roediger and McDermott (1995), have explored the parameters of this false-recall effect. In general, manipulations that affect false recognition of semantic associates in the Deese paradigm affect false recall in a similar fashion. For example, McDermott (1996) found that false recall occurs more frequently when semantic associates of a particular theme word are studied in a block, as opposed to being randomly intermixed with associates of other theme words.

An important observation is that false recall appears to be more enduring than recall of studied items: McDermott (1996) found that when participants were tested 2 days after study, false recall of critical lures exceeded correct recall of studied words (see Payne et al., 1996, for a similar finding with false recognition). Moreover, Robinson and Roediger (1997) found that, while veridical recall is reduced by adding unrelated filler items to the study list, false recall is unaffected by this manipulation. McDermott (1996) also found that false recall persisted even when associate lists were repeatedly presented and tested, thereby providing multiple opportunities for participants to notice that lure words were not actually presented. There was some reduction of false recall across repeated trials, implying that people could make use of increasingly available item-specific information to suppress false recalls (cf. Brainerd, Reyna, & Kneer, 1995; Hintzman, Curran, & Oppy, 1992), but even after five trials participants still produced over 30% of the critical lure words.

Although it may seem paradoxical for false recall to be more robust than accurate recall, this idea follows from the fact that semantic features of the nonpresented theme word occur multiple times at study (insofar as they are shared and activated by several individual list items), whereas the features that distinguish a specific list item from other items occur only once (unless study lists are presented repeatedly). Payne et al. (1996) found that providing repeated recall tests (without any intervening study trials) resulted in consistent but small increases in false recall across trials, whereas veridical recall showed little evidence of across-test increases; this result may occur because list items cue the critical lure but do not cue each other.

False recall in the Deese–Roediger-McDermott paradigm (like false recognition in this paradigm) could result from participants having generated the lure at study (and then making a source-monitoring error), or simply from the semantic features of the lure having been strongly activated at study. As such, false recall belongs to a large class of intrusion phenomena in which the intruding information was either activated or generated earlier in the experiment. Along these lines, Roediger, Jacoby, and McDermott (1996) reported that participants in postevent misinformation experiments will intrude misleading postevent suggestions on free-recall tests. Another relevant example is the memory distortion known as *boundary extension*: After having viewed a partial photograph of a scene, people tend to recall having seen a larger expanse of the scene than they actually did; the boundaries of the scene are extended in memory (Intraub, Bender, & Mangels, 1992; Intraub, Gottesman, Willey, & Zuk, 1996). Intraub et al. (1996) argued that boundary extension reflects the fact that during scene perception, information about the expected layout of a scene is automatically activated.

From the perspective of CMF, recall distortion can also occur when people fail to construct a retrieval cue that is fully consistent with information in the target trace; insofar as recall is a pattern-completion process that seamlessly merges the retrieval cue with retrieved information, any inaccuracies in the cue might be carried over to the output of the pattern-completion process. For example, during the phase of retrieval we have called *focusing,* people may use schematic knowledge (information that is easily accessed because it has been encountered on multiple occasions) and information that is present in the test environment to construct cues, which in turn are used to access specific past episodes. Normally, this process produces reasonably accurate memory, but distortions of recall can arise when schematic knowledge or physical retrieval cues fail to accurately describe a particular episode. For example, Bahrick, Hall, and Berger (1996) found that students with high grade-point averages tended to inflate their grades in classes where they did not get As, in keeping with the general idea that they received As most of the time (for another example of schema-driven recall errors, see Vicente & Brewer, 1993). Also relevant here are studies of retrospective bias: distorted recollection of past perceptions and attitudes that is driven by present knowledge and beliefs (cf. Dawes, 1988; Ross, 1989). For example, when supporters of Ross Perot recalled after the November 1992 election how they felt when Perot temporarily dropped out of the race in July 1992, their recollections were systematically biased by their present feelings toward Perot (Levine, 1997). Retrospective bias can be thought of as a special case of the general principle that recall distortion will occur when the retrieval target (e.g., what one thought of Ross Perot in June 1992) is inconsistent with presently available knowledge (e.g., what one thinks of Ross Perot now).

Ochsner, Schacter, and Edwards (1997) have reported a somewhat different but related type of recall bias. College students studied faces while listening to a corresponding voice speaking in an angry or happy tone. Ochsner et al. reported that participants later tended to recall that faces with slightly positive expressions had been accompanied by a happier tone of voice than faces with slightly negative expressions, even though there was no relation between facial expression and tone of voice. This is yet another situation in which information present in the retrieval cue overshadows information present in the target trace. Although contemporary models allow for such effects (e.g., McClelland, 1995), there has been little attempt thus far to consider them from a cognitive neuroscience perspective.

The studies of intrusions and retrospective biases reviewed thus far do not address whether normal adults can be induced to recall entire events that never happened. In a well-known study by Loftus (1993), young adults were asked by their relatives to try to remember a childhood event that had never occurred—being lost in a shopping mall. After repeated questioning, 4 of 5 participants in an initial study developed detailed recollections of the false event. Studying a larger sample, Loftus and Pickrell (1995) reported that approximately 25% of participants developed detailed false recollections. One limitation of such a procedure is that the experimenter has no way of knowing whether the suggested event did in fact occur. Because most people presumably have been lost at least sometime in their lives, it is possible that such veridical experiences may provide the basis for the false recollection. Using a slightly different procedure, Hyman and colleagues queried college students about actual events from their childhood as well as fabricated but exceedingly improbable events, such as causing an accident by releasing a parking brake when left alone in a car. Hyman, Husband, and Billings (1995) reported that none of their sample provided false memories when initially queried about such events, but after being repeatedly questioned, about 25% falsely recalled at least one of the fabricated events. In follow-up studies, Hyman and Pentland (1996) found that the probability of false-event recall was increased significantly by instructions to imagine the suggested event. Imagery has also been implicated in the related phenomenon of imagination inflation, in which simply imagining an event leads to increases in subjective estimates of the likelihood that the event actually occurred (cf. Garry, Manning, Loftus, & Sherman, 1996).

Although the mechanisms of these "confabulatory" false-recall effects remain poorly understood, source confusions may play a role: As people repeatedly think about or imagine an event, they may retrieve fragments of other actual events, without recognizing them as such. Furthermore, the more that a person thinks about an event, the easier it becomes to retrieve details pertaining to that event; numerous studies have shown that retrieval fluency is a key determinant of whether a particular conscious experience is interpreted as a memory (cf. Jacoby, Kelley, & Dywan, 1989; Lindsay & Kelley, 1996; see also Rankin & O'Carroll, 1995). Also, a PET study conducted by Kosslyn et al. (1993) found that visual imagery activated some of the same brain regions as visual perception. These results suggest that visual imagery may enhance the subjective reality of falsely recalled events because it draws on some of the same neural circuitry as does veridical perception (see also Silbersweig et al., 1995).

Neuropsychological Studies of Brain-Damaged Patients. Confabulatory responses—spontaneous narrative reports of events that never happened—in brain-damaged patients have been known to neurologists and neuropsychologists for decades (for reviews, see Johnson, 1991; Moscovitch,

1995). In addition, more recent experimental studies have examined intrusions on free-recall tests in various patient populations. Although confabulations and intrusions are sometimes treated synonymously (e.g., Kern, Van Gorp, Cummings, Brown, & Osato, 1992), we prefer to examine them separately and leave open questions about the nature of their relations. We first summarize recent studies of intrusions and then consider confabulatory phenomena.

Schacter, Verfaellie, and Pradere (1996) examined false recall of semantically related lures in amnesic patients using the previously described procedures developed by Deese (1959) and Roediger and McDermott (1995). They found that although both veridical and false recall were impaired in amnesics, false recall was relatively more preserved. The robustness of false recall can be explained in terms of the fact, discussed earlier, that the constituent semantic features of nonpresented theme words were activated multiple times at study (presumably resulting in increased trace strength). Overall, the results from this experiment suggest that amnesics' free recall consists entirely of degraded semantic gist information, whereas normal controls recall both gist information and specific information about individual items.

Dalla Barba and Wong (1995) found that both amnesic patients and patients with memory deficits attributable to Alzheimer's disease (AD) made an abnormally large number of intrusions when they studied items from various categories and were cued with category names; neither patient group showed an excessive number of intrusions on a free-recall test. From this result, we can conclude that intrusions are likely to occur when participants are faced with strong retrieval cues ("strong" in the sense that it is easy to think of specific fruits in response to the category cue *fruit*) but memory traces are degraded. Studying items along with category names helped alleviate cued-recall intrusions in patients with intact semantic memory but not in patients with impaired semantic memory.

A major focus in recent studies of intrusion errors concerns whether and to what extent the tendency to make intrusion errors is related to frontal lobe damage. Two of the frontally lesioned patients discussed earlier who showed robust false recognition (J. B., studied by Parkin et al., 1997, and R. W., described by Delbecq-Derouesné et al., 1990) also made an abnormally high number of intrusion errors on free-recall tests. These patients both suffered damage to the ventromedial regions of the frontal lobes (and possibly adjoining brain regions) brought on by ruptured anterior communicating artery aneurysms. Interestingly, Patient B. G. (Curran et al., 1997; Schacter, Curran, et al., 1996), whose lesion was limited to the posterior lateral frontal lobe (and did not include ventromedial frontal cortex), was extremely susceptible to false-recognition errors but did not show abnormally high levels of intrusion errors on free-recall tests (Norman, Koutstaal, Schacter, & Galluccio, 1997).

Group studies of recall intrusions in frontal-damaged patients have found mixed results, which is not surprising in light of the heterogeneity of lesion sites and etiologies in these patients (as well as the heterogeneity of recall paradigms used in these studies). Stuss et al. (1994) failed to find abnormally high intrusion rates in patients with unilateral and bilateral frontal lobe damage on immediate free recall of categorized and unrelated word lists. By contrast, Daum, Mayes, Schwarz, and Lutgehetman (1999) found that patients with unilateral frontal lobe lesions made more intrusion errors than patients with posterior cortical lesions and normal controls on delayed recall of stories, categorized word lists, and dot patterns. Kern et al. (1992) found that intrusion errors on tests of story recall, design recall, and object recall were slightly (nonsignificantly) greater in AD patients with relatively impaired frontal functioning than in AD patients with relatively intact frontal functioning. However, it is unclear whether this association is specifically related to frontal lobe dysfunction or whether it simply reflects global severity of deficit.

Following up on Dalla Barba and Wong's (1995) findings, Dalla Barba, Parlato, Iavarones, and Boller (1995) also used a category-cued recall test to examine the relation between intrusion errors, performance on neuropsychological tests of frontal lobe dysfunction, and awareness of memory deficit (anosognosia; McGlynn & Schacter, 1989) in AD patients. Dalla Barba, Parlato, et al. (1995) found a strong relationship between intrusion errors and degree of anosognosia, such that patients who were unaware of their memory deficits made more intrusion errors than those who exhibited awareness of deficit. Because anosognosia is often associated with frontal lobe impairment (McGlynn & Schacter, 1989; Stuss, 1991), this relationship indirectly suggests a link between intrusion errors and frontal impairment. The only measure of frontal functions that correlated with intrusion errors and awareness of deficit was verbal fluency; intrusion errors and awareness of deficit were uncorrelated with performance on tests thought to tap (primarily dorsolateral) frontal functioning, including card sorting, sequencing, and cognitive estimation.

Questions concerning the role of frontal lobe damage have also assumed paramount importance in discussions of confabulation. The general features of confabulation are well summarized by Johnson (1991), Moscovitch (1995), and Burgess and Shallice (1996). Confabulations are typically false narrative accounts of personal experiences, although under some conditions patients may confabulate about factual knowledge (cf.

Dalla Barba, 1993; Moscovitch, 1995). Confabulations usually draw on bits and pieces of the patient's actual past experiences, with episodes confused in time and place, but confabulated autobiographical memories may sometimes incorporate knowledge acquired from other sources. Confabulations are typically not intentionally produced and do not appear to be measured attempts to attract attention or compensate for memory loss (though also see Conway & Tacchi, 1996). Patients typically present confabulations without awareness that their memories are false and are more generally unaware of their own memory deficits (e.g., McGlynn & Schacter, 1989). Confabulation usually occurs together with anterograde amnesia (i.e., poor memory for recent events). Finally, confabulations may sometimes contain bizarre or fantastic content (Kopelman, 1987; Talland, 1965) that patients nonetheless accept as veridical.

A number of early case reports of confabulation described patients with damage to the ventromedial aspects of the frontal lobes (e.g., Stuss, Alexander, Lieberman, & Levine, 1978), particularly on the right (e.g., Joseph, 1986). Damage limited to dorsolateral frontal regions does not appear to produce confabulation; conversely, confabulating patients frequently perform well on tasks that are sensitive to dorsolateral frontal damage, such as cognitive estimation and card sorting (Dalla Barba, 1993; Dalla Barba, Cipolotti, & Denes, 1990). More recently, Benson et al. (1996) described a case of alcohol-induced Korsakoff amnesia in which the patient exhibited spontaneous confabulation together with severe memory loss during the early phases of the disorder. Single photon emission (SPECT) scanning at this time revealed hypoperfusion (low blood flow) in the medial diencephalic brain region typically associated with memory loss in Korsakoff patients, as well as hypoperfusion in the orbitomedial frontal lobe. When the patient was assessed again 4 months later, the amnesia persisted but confabulation had disappeared. Repeated SPECT scanning revealed continuing hypoperfusion in the medial diencephalic region but normal perfusion in the frontal regions that had previously shown abnormal blood flow (see also Conway & Tacchi, 1996).

Importantly, observations of patients with ruptured aneurysms of the anterior communicating artery (ACoA) suggest that ventromedial frontal lesions are not sufficient to produce confabulation. Ruptured ACoA aneurysms can result in damage to a wide range of structures in the general region of the ventromedial frontal lobes, including (but not limited to) the basal forebrain and the head of the caudate nucleus. The basal forebrain is closely linked to the hippocampus, and ACoA patients with basal forebrain damage show a form of amnesia (for a review of the neuropsychological consequences of ACoA damage, see DeLuca & Diamond,

1995). Confabulation is reasonably common following ruptured ACoA aneurysms (especially during the acute phase that immediately follows rupture), and a number of recent studies have examined groups of ACoA patients with the goal of relating confabulatory symptoms to underlying neuroanatomical damage. These studies have established that both ventromedial frontal lobe damage and amnesia subsequent to basal forebrain damage must be present for lasting confabulation to occur; neither kind of damage on its own seems to suffice (DeLuca, 1993).

Although some progress has been made in understanding the brain regions associated with confabulation, and the domains of confabulation are beginning to be specified (e.g., episodic vs. semantic memory; cf. Dalla Barba, 1993; Moscovitch, 1995), there has been relatively little experimental work that allows firm conclusions about the nature of the memory processes that are compromised in patients who confabulate and/or show robust free recall intrusions. In general, theoretical attention has focused on impaired criterion-setting and monitoring processes (e.g., Burgess & Shallice, 1996; Conway & Tacchi, 1996; Johnson, 1991; Moscovitch, 1995). Norman and Schacter (1996) pointed out that theories of confabulation need to explain why incorrect information comes to mind in the first place (in addition to why participants fail to reject this incorrect information). From the perspective of CMF, one possibility is that focusing processes are impaired in confabulating patients (i.e., they submit vague cues to memory or cues that are inordinately biased by the individual's present internal and external environment); another possibility is that the process of pattern completion is itself dysfunctional. Regarding this latter possibility, the basal forebrain (which is damaged in ACoA patients who confabulate) is a major source of the neurotransmitter acetylcholine, and Hasselmo (1995) has argued that acetylcholine plays a key role in regulating the dynamics of pattern-completion processes in the hippocampus and other brain structures.

One final unresolved issue is the relationship between intrusions, confabulation, and false recognition. Neuroanatomically, all three deficits appear to require damage to either the posterior or ventromedial prefrontal cortex. Functionally, this damage probably relates to monitoring and criterion-setting deficits that are present, to some extent, in all three syndromes (if these processes were unimpaired, patients would be able to reject nontarget information). On the basis of data from Patient B. G. (whose lesion was limited to the posterior prefrontal cortex), it appears that frontal damage by itself is sufficient to cause false recognition. However, at least in ACoA patients, both ventromedial frontal and basal forebrain damage must be present for confabulations or robust free-recall intrusions to occur. The fact that the critical lesion for intrusions and confabulations extends outside of the prefrontal cortex is consistent with the claim that poor monitoring (resulting from frontal lobe damage) in and of itself is not sufficient to explain retrieval of incorrect information; some other functional deficit has to be present. Finally, it appears that free-recall intrusions can occur in the absence of confabulation (e.g., Parkin, Bind-schaedler, et al.'s, 1996, patient J. B. showed a strong tendency to make free-recall intrusions despite the fact that he no longer confabulated spon-taneously), suggesting that confabulation involves additional functional deficits or that confabulation is a more extreme manifestation of the same functional deficits that are responsible for free-recall intrusions.

Aging Memory. There has been comparatively little systematic investi-gation of false recall in normal aging. Two recent studies have shown that older adults are more susceptible to false recall of semantic associates in the Deese (1959) paradigm than are younger adults. In each of two exper-iments, Norman and Schacter (1997) found that older adults recalled fewer previously studied items and intruded more related false targets than did younger adults. In Norman and Schacter's (1997) experiments, associate lists were presented together in blocks, as in Roediger and Mc-Dermott (1995). Tun et al. (1998) randomly intermixed the associate lists during presentation and found that whereas older adults recalled fewer studied items than younger adults, they produced just as many semanti-cally related lures. As with false recognition, these age-related increases in false recall (relative to correct recall) could be attributable to source con-fusions, overreliance on gist information, or both.

SUPPRESSING FALSE MEMORIES:
PERSPECTIVES FROM CMF

In the preceding sections, we considered experimental situations in which young adults, elderly adults, and brain-damaged patients exhibited high rates of false recall and false recognition. In this section, we discuss recent studies that have examined whether and to what extent high levels of false recall and recognition can be reduced or suppressed. For example, several studies using the Deese–Roediger-McDermott paradigm have revealed that warning participants about the presence of semantically related lure words in the recognition test can produce modest reductions in the level of false recognition (Gallo, Roberts, & Seamon, 1997; McDermott & Roediger, 1998).

A number of studies have taken a different approach to the issue of false-memory suppression, which follows directly from the CMF analysis of robust false recall and recognition. As discussed previously, in CMF high levels of false recognition tend to be observed following encoding conditions that minimize recollection of distinctive, item-specific details (i.e., when there is poor pattern separation). In these situations, participants are forced to rely on memory for semantic gist, which does not discriminate well between studied items and similar lures. Conversely, under conditions in which studied items trigger rich recollections of item-specific details, participants can reject related lures on the grounds that they do not trigger similarly detailed recollections. One way to increase recollection of item-specific details is to make stimuli more distinctive (i.e., enhance pattern separation). Another way to increase rich recollection is to provide multiple presentations of target stimuli.

Several studies have found that healthy young adults are able to suppress false recognition in situations that are designed to promote recollection of item-specific details. Schacter, Israel, and Racine (1999; see also Israel & Schacter, 1997) compared false recognition of Deese–Roediger-McDermott lists in an encoding condition in which participants both heard and saw study list words (the words-only condition) with an encoding condition in which participants heard the study list words and saw a picture corresponding to each word (the words-plus-pictures condition). They reasoned that the presentation of pictures with study list words would increase pattern separation and hence would provide a basis for reducing false-recognition responses. Consistent with this idea, Schacter, Israel, and Racine reported that participants who studied associate lists accompanied by pictures showed considerably lower levels of false recognition to related lure words than did participants who studied only words. Koutstaal, Schacter, Galluccio, and Stofer (1999) took a conceptually similar approach in an experiment with the categorized pictures paradigm that, as discussed previously, produces large age-related increases in false recognition of novel pictures (Koutstaal & Schacter, 1997). Koutstaal et al. (1999) reported that false recognition was reduced significantly when participants were given, at the time of study, distinctive verbal elaborators that emphasized unique aspects of each picture.

Importantly, in both of the experiments just described, encoding distinctiveness was manipulated on a between-groups basis (i.e., one group was given either pictures or verbal elaborators at encoding and another group was not). Schacter, Israel, and Racine (1999) found that when the presence of pictures at encoding was manipulated on a within-groups basis (i.e., some word lists were studied with pictures and others were not), participants failed to show suppression of false recognition after picture encoding. Schacter, Israel, and Racine suggest that, in the between-subjects paradigm, participants in the picture-encoding condition used a "distinctiveness heuristic" to suppress false recognition. Participants in this condition expected that studied items would be reliably accompanied by recollection of distinctive pictorial details and thus refrained from saying "old" unless an item triggered recollection of pictorial information. Because related lures tend not to trigger recollection of pictorial information (at least, not to the same extent as studied items), this constraint helped participants reduce false recognition. By contrast, when encoding distinctiveness was manipulated within groups, use of a global distinctiveness heuristic (i.e., demanding recollection of pictorial information for all test items, regardless of whether items were or were not accompanied by pictures at study) did not yield differential rates of false recognition for lists that were studied with pictures compared with lists that were not studied with pictures. In principle, if participants could remember which lists were studied in the picture condition, they could selectively demand pictorial recall for these lists—but not for lists that were studied without pictures—thereby yielding suppression in the picture-encoding condition. However, under the experimental conditions examined by Schacter, Israel, and Racine, participants were apparently unable to recall such list-specific information and thus relied on a more global distinctiveness heuristic.

Presenting study list items multiple times also leads to suppression of false recall and recognition in young adults. In an experiment that used repeated presentations of the Deese–Roediger-McDermott semantic associate lists, McDermott (1996) found that college students showed increased veridical recall rates and decreased false-recall rates across five study and test trials. The proportion of items that were correctly recalled nearly doubled across trials, and the proportion of items falsely recalled was reduced by a comparable amount. Also, in an experiment comparing true and false recognition of semantic associates, Schacter, Verfaellie, Anes, and Racine (1998) observed across-trial patterns in middle-aged participants that were similar to those reported by McDermott (1996), with true recognition increasing and false recognition decreasing across trials. In a similar experiment, Kensinger and Schacter (1999) found that college students showed significant across-trial reductions in false recall and false recognition.

One possible explanation of this suppression effect is that, as with the pictorial and verbal elaboration studies discussed earlier, participants are using a global distinctiveness heuristic. With increasing repetitions, participants may come to demand access to increasingly elaborated and distinctive representations of the study list items, and this process could allow them to reject related lure items that do not possess these distinctive features. Another potential explanation for reduced false recognition in this paradigm is that, when the study lists are repeated, participants actively look for the nonpresented theme words during the repeated presentations; when they fail to encounter these words, they make a "mental note" that the word was not presented. Participants may be encouraged to adopt such a strategy because nonpresented lure words do appear on recognition tests that are given after each list presentation. Participants may thus compare which items are present on the recognition test and on the study list, noting the presence of the related lure word on the former and its absence on the latter.

Elderly adults have shown normal suppression of false recognition compared with younger adults in situations where encoding distinctiveness is manipulated on a between-groups basis. Schacter, Israel, and Racine (1999) found that elderly subjects showed normal suppression of false recognition when semantic associate lists were accompanied by pictures compared with a word-only encoding condition. Koutstaal et al. (1999) found that elderly adults showed normal suppression of false recognition when pictures were studied with distinctive verbal descriptions compared with a control condition. In both of these paradigms, suppression can be explained by the hypothesis that participants in the more distinctive condition applied a distinctiveness heuristic.

Kensinger and Schacter (1999) also examined suppression of false recall and false recognition in older adults across multiple study and test trials. Whereas younger adults showed significant across-trial reductions in false recall and false recognition, older adults showed no across-trial reduction of either false recall or recognition. One possibility is that the failure of elderly adults to show false memory suppression in this paradigm is attributable to an age-related failure to develop increasingly detailed memory traces with list repetition. Another explanation is that, with repetition, young but not elderly adults actively note that related lure words appear on recognition tests but not on study lists. A related possibility is that because related lure words were tested repeatedly, elderly adults failed to show suppression because they were disproportionately prone to source memory confusions, that is, an inability to remember whether a critical lure had been previously studied or whether it had only appeared on a recognition test.

To understand why older adults failed to show false-recognition suppression in Kensinger and Schacter's (1999) repeated-presentation paradigm yet showed normal false-recognition suppression in the paradigms of Koutstaal et al. (1999) and Schacter, Israel, and Racine (1999), one needs to consider differences between the paradigms. Perhaps most important, source confusions may be operative in the repeated-list procedure that are not operative in the paradigms of Koutstaal et al. and Schacter, Israel, and Racine, which used only a single recognition test. As noted above, test-induced source confusions likely affect older adults more than younger adults. It would be possible to eliminate such source confusions by testing recognition only once. In view of the evidence that elderly participants are just as likely as young adults to apply a global distinctiveness heuristic (Schacter, Israel, & Racine, 1999; Koutstaal et al., 1999), elderly individuals should show false-recognition suppression when list repetition is manipulated between subjects (thereby creating conditions in which a distinctiveness heuristic can successfully reduce false recognition), and only a single recognition test is given (thus eliminating possible contributions of source confusions). By this view, elderly adults in the multiple presentations condition would demand recollection of distinctive, item-specific details before saying "old"; insofar as related lures do not trigger recollection of item-specific details, this criterion shift should yield suppression of false recognition. We are currently testing the hypothesis that elderly adults will show false-recognition suppression when list repetition is manipulated between subjects, and items are only tested once.

One recent study has examined suppression of robust false recognition in amnesic patients. Schacter, Verfaellie, et al. (1998) found that control participants showed significant suppression as a function of list repetition, whereas amnesic patients failed to show any evidence of decreasing false recognition with increasing study and test trials. In fact, there were trends for increasing false recognition across trials in the amnesic group (especially in amnesic patients with alcoholic Korsakoff's syndrome; see Schacter, Verfaellie, et al., 1998, for discussion). Amnesic patients' failure to suppress can be explained in terms of their general inability to recollect distinctive details of studied items. As discussed earlier, amnesic patients may rely instead on a degraded representation of semantic gist. Repetition presumably strengthens this gist representation, thus yielding trends for increased rather than decreased levels of false memories. Also, as discussed by Schacter, Verfaellie, et al. (1998), some amnesic patients may be disproportionately susceptible to source memory confusions that occur when related lure words appear repeatedly on recognition tests, perhaps contributing to amnesics' inability to suppress false recognition with repeated study and test trials.

In summary, the foregoing findings are of interest from the perspective of CMF because they point to an interaction between encoding processes (which determine trace strength and trace distinctiveness) and criterion-setting processes at retrieval. Encoding manipulations that enhance pattern separation at study, and therefore permit increased recollection of distinctive, item-specific details at test, allow participants to use stricter criteria and therefore to suppress false recognition.

CONCLUDING COMMENTS

Cognitive neuroscience has embraced the strategy of attempting to understand how a particular process works by studying how it malfunctions. In memory research, this strategy has led to productive investigations of amnesic syndromes in which patients recall little new information, correct or incorrect. This research has yielded a rich body of knowledge specifying which neural circuits are responsible for storing and retrieving episodic memories. However, this focus on absent or nonaccessible memory has diverted researchers from studying situations in which memory is present but wrong, that is, situations in which people claim to remember past episodes that did not actually occur (cf. Koriat & Goldsmith, 1996). In this review, we have examined evidence concerning memory inaccuracies from the perspective of CMF.

A large part of CMF is concerned with the need for pattern separation at encoding and focusing at retrieval. That is, episodes need to be stored in a manner that allows them to be accessed separately at test, and retrieval cues need to be specific enough to activate only a single episode. If either of these conditions is not met, then multiple episodes will be accessed at test; when this occurs, details that differ from episode to episode will compete, resulting in poor memory for differentiating or source-specifying (Johnson et al., 1993) details. However, between-episode competition should not adversely affect features that are common to many episodes—the gist or general similarity information that is often implicated in memory distortions and that has been the focus of theoretical interest (Hintzman & Curran, 1994; Reyna & Brainerd, 1995).

Once information has been retrieved, decision-making or criterion-setting processes are needed to evaluate whether it pertains to the target episode. Decision making and criterion setting are logically distinct from the retrieval process we have called focusing, but we should note that post-retrieval monitoring processes require a focused description of the target episode (otherwise, there would be no way of assessing whether or not retrieved information is accurate; for additional discussion, see Norman & Schacter, 1996). An important area for future research, particularly with brain imaging techniques, will be to examine the relation between processes involved in focusing and postretrieval monitoring and verification.

We have found CMF to be useful in classifying and thinking about different kinds of memory distortions. However, the vast majority of extant data on memory distortions cannot be classified or understood unambiguously. For example, false recognition of nonstudied pictures from studied categories can, at first pass, be explained by either pattern-separation failure at encoding or lax criterion setting or poor focusing at retrieval. Clearly, these are quite different (although not mutually exclusive) claims about the nature of the underlying deficit. We hope that by articulating different ideas regarding how and why different memory distortions occur, we will spur researchers to generate experiments that disentangle and specifically test such alternative hypotheses.

In conclusion, the problems inherent in retrieving accurate, episode-specific information from a system with the biological and functional properties of human memory are complex. Researchers' attempts to understand how the brain accomplishes this difficult task are still in their infancy, and much theoretical and empirical work remains to be done. Fortunately, the neurobiology of memory has progressed to the point that this is a reasonable and even promising enterprise; we see in the research reviewed here the seeds of a cognitive neuroscience of constructive memory that should bear much fruit in the years to come.

ACKNOWLEDGMENTS

This chapter represents an extended version of D. L. Schacter, K. A. Norman, & W. Koutstaal (1998), "The Cognitive Neuroscience of Constructive Memory," *Annual Review of Psychology, 49,* 289–318. Preparation of this chapter was supported by National Institute on Aging Grant AG08441, by a grant from the Human Frontiers Science Program, and by a grant to Kenneth A. Norman from the Sackler Scholar Programme on Psychobiology. We thank Lissa Galluccio and Carrie Racine for their assistance.

REFERENCES

Bahrick, H. P., Hall, L. K., & Berger, S. A. (1996). Accuracy and distortion in memory for high school grades. *Psychological Science, 7,* 265–271.

Bartlett, F. C. (1932). *Remembering.* Cambridge, England: Cambridge University Press.

Belli, R. F., Lindsay, D. S., Gales, M. S., & McCarthy, T. T. (1994). Memory impairment and source misattribution in postevent misinformation experiments with short retention intervals. *Memory & Cognition, 22,* 40–54.

Benson, D. F., Djenderedjian, A., Miller, B. L., Pachana, N. A., Chang, L., Itti, L., & Mena, I. (1996). Neural basis of confabulation. *Neurology, 46,* 1239–1243.

Brainerd, C. J., Reyna, V. F., & Kneer, R. (1995). False-recognition reversal: When similarity is distinctive. *Journal of Memory and Language, 34,* 157–185.

Brewer, J. B., Zhao, Z., Glover, G. H., Gabrieli, J. D. E. (1998, August 21). Making memories: Brain activity that predicts whether visual experiences will be remembered or forgotten. *Science, 281,* 1185–1187.

Brown, A. S., Jones, E. M., & Davis, T. L. (1995). Age differences in conversational source monitoring. *Psychology and Aging, 10,* 111–122.

Buckner, R. L. (1996). Beyond HERA: Contributions of specific prefrontal brain areas to long-term memory retrieval. *Psychonomic Bulletin & Review, 3,* 149–158.

Buckner, R. L., Bandettini, P., O'Craven, K., Savoy, R., Petersen, S. E., Raichle, M. E., & Rosen, B. R. (1996). Detection of cortical activation during averaged single trials of a cognitive task using functional magnetic resonance imaging. *Proceedings of the National Academy of Sciences, USA, 93,* 14878–14883.

Buckner, R. L., Petersen, S. E., Ojemann, J. G., Miezin, F. M., Squire, L. R., & Raichle, M. E. (1995). Functional anatomical studies of explicit and implicit memory retrieval tasks. *Journal of Neuroscience, 15,* 12–29.

Buckner, R. L., & Tulving, E. (1995). Neuroimaging studies of memory: Theory and recent PET results. In F. Boller & J. Grafman (Eds.), *Handbook of neuropsychology* (pp. 439–466). Amsterdam: Elsevier.

Burgess, P. W., & Shallice, T. (1996). Confabulation and the control of recollection. *Memory, 4,* 359–411.

Butters, M. A., Kasniak, A. W., Glisky, E. L., Eslinger, P. J., & Schacter, D. L. (1994). Recency discrimination deficits in frontal lobe patients. *Neuropsychology, 8,* 343–353.

Ceci, S. J., & Bruck, M. (1995). *Jeopardy in the courtroom.* Washington DC: American Psychological Association.

Conway, M. A., Collins, A. F., Gathercole, S. E., & Anderson, S. J. (1996). Recollections of true and false autobiographical memories. *Journal of Experimental Psychology: General, 125,* 69–95.

Conway, M. A., & Tacchi, P. C. (1996). Motivated confabulation. *Neurocase, 2,* 325–339.

Curran, T., Schacter, D. L., Norman, K. A., & Galluccio, L. (1997). False recognition after a right frontal lobe infarction: Memory for general and specific information. *Neuropsychologia, 35,* 1035–1049.

Dalla Barba, G. (1993). Confabulation: Knowledge and recollective experience. *Cognitive Neuropsychology, 10,* 1–20.

Dalla Barba, G., Parlato, V., Iavarones, A., & Boller, F. (1995). Anosognosia, intrusions, and "frontal" functions in Alzheimer's disease and depression. *Neuropsychologia, 33,* 247–259.

Dalla Barba, G., Cipolotti, L., & Denes, G. (1990). Autobiographical memory loss and confabulation in Korsakoff's syndrome: A case report. *Cortex, 26,* 525–534.

Dalla Barba, G., & Wong, C. (1995). Encoding specificity and intrusion in Alzheimer's disease. *Brain and Cognition, 27,* 1–16.

Damasio, A. R. (1989). Time-locked multiregional retroactivation: A systems-level proposal for the neural substrates of recall and recognition. *Cognition, 33,* 25–62.

Daum, I., Mayes, A., Schwarz, Y., & Lutgehetman, R. (1999). *Memory impairment after frontal or posterior cortex lesions.* Manuscript in preparation.

Dawes, R. (1988). *Rational choice in an uncertain world*. San Diego, CA: Harcourt, Brace, & Jovanovich.

Deese, J. (1959). On the prediction of occurrence of particular verbal intrusions in immediate recall. *Journal of Experimental Psychology, 58*, 17–22.

Delbecq-Derouesné, J., Beauvois, M. F., & Shallice, T. (1990). Preserved recall versus impaired recognition. *Brain, 113*, 1045–1074.

DeLuca, J. (1993). Predicting neurobehavioral patterns following anterior communicating artery aneurysm. *Cortex, 29*, 639–647.

DeLuca, J., & Diamond, B. J. (1995). Aneurysm of the anterior communicating artery: A review of neuroanatomical and neuropsychological sequelae. *Journal of Clinical and Experimental Neuropsychology, 17*, 100–121.

Dodson, C. S., & Johnson, M. K. (1993). Rate of false source attributions depends on how questions are asked. *American Journal of Psychology, 106*, 541–557.

Düzel, E., Yonelinas, A. P., Mangun, G. R., Heinze, H. J., & Tulving, E. (1997). Event-related brain potential correlates of two states of conscious awareness in memory. *Proceedings of the National Academy of Sciences USA, 94*, 5973–5978.

Estes, W. K. (1997). Processes of memory loss, recovery, and distortion. *Psychological Review, 104*, 148–169.

Fiedler, K., Walther, E., Armbruster, T., Fay, D., & Naumann, U. (1996). Do you *really* know what you have seen? Intrusion errors and presuppositions effects on constructive memory. *Journal of Experimental Social Psychology, 32*, 484–511.

Gallo, D. A., Roberts, M. J., & Seamon, J. G. (1997). Remembering words not presented in lists: Can we avoid creating false memories? *Psychonomic Bulletin & Review, 4*, 271–276.

Gardiner, J. M., & Java, R. I. (1993). Recognising and remembering. In A. F. Collins, S. E. Gathercole, M. A. Conway, & P. E. Morris (Eds.), *Theories of memory* (pp. 163–188). Hove, U.K.: Lawrence Erlbaum Associates.

Garry, M., Manning, C., Loftus, E. F., & Sherman, S. J. (1996). Imagination inflation: Imagining a childhood event inflates confidence that it occurred. *Psychonomic Bulletin & Review, 3*, 208–214.

Grady, C. L., McIntosh, A. R., Horwitz, B., Maisog, J. M., Ungerleider, L. G., Mentis, M. J., Pietrini, P., Schapiro, M. B., & Haxby, J. V. (1995, July 14). Age-related reductions in human recognition memory due to impaired encoding. *Science, 269*, 218–221.

Hasselmo, M. E. (1995). Neuromodulation and cortical function: Modeling the physiological basis of behavior. *Behavioral Brain Research, 67*, 1–27.

Hess, T. M. (1984). Effects of semantically related and unrelated contexts on recognition memory of different-aged adults. *Journal of Gerontology, 39*, 444–451.

Hintzman, D. L., & Curran, T. (1994). Retrieval dynamics of recognition and frequency judgments: Evidence for separate processes of familiarity and recall. *Journal of Memory and Language, 33*, 1–18.

Hintzman, D. L., Curran, T., & Oppy, B. (1992). Effects of similarity and repetition on memory: Registration without learning? *Journal of Experimental Psychology: Learning, Memory, and Cognition, 18*, 667–680.

Hyman, I. E., Husband, T. H., & Billings, F. J. (1995). False memories of childhood experiences. *Applied Cognitive Psychology, 9*, 181–197.

Hyman, I. E., & Pentland, J. (1996). The role of mental imagery in the creation of false childhood memories. *Journal of Memory and Language, 35*, 101–117.

Intraub, H., Bender, R. S., & Mangels, J. A. (1992). Looking at pictures but remembering scenes. *Journal of Experimental Psychology: Learning, Memory, and Cognition, 18*(1), 180–191.

Intraub, H., Gottesman, C. V., Willey, E. V., & Zuk, I. J. (1996). Boundary extension for briefly glimpsed photographs: Do common perceptual processes result in unexpected memory distortions? *Journal of Memory and Language, 35,* 118–134.

Isingrini, M., Fontaine, R., Taconnat, L., & Duportal, A. (1995). Aging and encoding in memory: False alarms and decision criteria in a word-pair recognition task. *International Journal of Aging & Human Development, 41,* 79–88.

Israel, L., & Schacter, D. L. (1997). Pictorial encoding reduces false recognition of semantic associates. *Psychonomic Bulletin & Review, 4,* 577–581.

Jacoby, L. L., Kelley, C. M., & Dywan, J. (1989). Memory attributions. In H. L. Roediger, III, & F. I. M. Craik (Eds.), *Varieties of memory and consciousness: Essays in honour of Endel Tulving* (pp. 391–422). Hillsdale, NJ: Lawrence Erlbaum Associates.

Janowsky, J. S., Shimamura, A. P., & Squire, L. R. (1989). Memory and metamemory: Comparisons between patients with frontal lobe lesions and amnesic patients. *Psychobiology, 17,* 3–11.

Johnson, M. K. (1991). Reality monitoring: Evidence from confabulation in organic brain disease patients. In G. P. Prigatano & D. L. Schacter (Eds.), *Awareness of deficit after brain injury: Clinical and theoretical issues* (pp. 176–197). New York: Oxford University Press.

Johnson, M. K., & Chalfonte, B. L. (1994). Binding of complex memories: The role of reactivation and the hippocampus. In D. L. Schacter & E. Tulving (Eds.), *Memory systems 1994* (pp. 311–350). Cambridge, MA: MIT Press.

Johnson, M. K., DeLeonardis, D. M., Hashtroudi, S., & Ferguson, S. A. (1995). Aging and single versus multiple cues in source monitoring. *Psychology and Aging, 10,* 507–517.

Johnson, M. K., Hashtroudi, S., & Lindsay, D. S. (1993). Source monitoring. *Psychological Bulletin, 114,* 3–28.

Johnson, M. K., Kounios, J., & Nolde, S. F. (1997). Electrophysiological brain activity and memory source monitoring. *NeuroReport, 8,* 1317–1320.

Johnson, M. K., Nolde, S. F., Mather, M., Kounios, J., Schacter, D. L., & Curran, T. (1997). The similarity of brain activity associated with true and false recognition memory depends on test format. *Psychological Science, 8,* 250–257.

Joseph, R. (1986). Confabulation and delusional denial: Frontal lobe and lateralized influences. *Journal of Clinical Psychology, 42,* 507–520.

Kensinger, E., & Schacter, D. L. (1999). When true memories suppress false memories: Effects of aging. *Cognitive Neuropsychology, 16,* 399–415.

Kern, R., Van Gorp, W., Cummings, J., Brown, W., & Osato, S. (1992). Confabulation in Alzheimer's disease. *Brain and Cognition, 19,* 172–182.

Knowlton, B. J., & Squire, L. R. (1995). Remembering and knowing: Two different expressions of declarative memory. *Journal of Experimental Psychology: Learning, Memory, and Cognition, 21,* 699–710.

Kopelman, M. D. (1987). Two types of confabulation. *Journal of Neurology, Neurosurgery, and Psychiatry, 50,* 1482–1487.

Koriat, A., & Goldsmith, M. (1996). Memory metaphors and the real-life/laboratory controversy: Correspondence versus storehouse conceptions of memory. *Behavioral Brain Science, 19,* 167–228.

Kosslyn, S. M., Alpert, N. M., Thompson, W. L., Chabris, C. F., Rauch, S. L., & Anderson, A. K. (1993). Visual mental imagery activates topographically organized visual cortex: PET investigations. *Journal of Cognitive Neuroscience, 5,* 263–287.

Koutstaal, W., & Schacter, D. L. (1997). Gist-based false recognition of pictures in older and younger adults. *Journal of Memory and Language, 37,* 555–583.

Koutstaal, W., Schacter, D. L., Galluccio, L., & Stofer, K. (1999). Reducing gist-based false recognition in older adults: Encoding and retrieval manipulations. *Psychology and Aging,* 14, 220–237.

Koutstaal, W., Schacter, D. L., Verfaellie, M., Brenner, C., & Jackson, E. M. (1999). Perceptually based false recognition of novel objects in amnesia: Effects of category size and similarity to category prototypes. *Cognitive Neuropsychology, 16,* 317–341.

Kroll, N. E. A., Knight, R. T., Metcalfe, J., Wolf, E. S., & Tulving, E. (1996). Cohesion failure as a source of memory illusions. *Journal of Memory and Language, 35,* 176–196.

Levine, L. J. (1997). Reconstructing memory for emotions. *Journal of Experimental Psychology: General, 126,* 165–177.

Lindsay, D. S. (1990). Misleading suggestions can impair eyewitnesses' ability to remember event details. *Journal of Experimental Psychology: Learning, Memory, and Cognition, 16,* 1077–1083.

Lindsay, D. S., & Kelley, C. M. (1996). Creating illusions of familiarity in a cued recall remember/know paradigm. *Journal of Memory and Language, 35,* 197–211.

Lindsay, D. S., & Read, J. D. (1996). "Memory work" and recovered memories of childhood sexual abuse: Scientific evidence and public, professional, and personal issues. *Psychology, Public Policy, and Law, 1,* 1–61.

Loftus, E. F. (1993). The reality of repressed memories. *American Psychologist, 48,* 518–537.

Loftus, E. F., Feldman, J., & Dashiell, R. (1995). The reality of illusory memories. In D. L. Schacter (Ed.), *Memory distortion: How minds, brains, and societies reconstruct the past* (pp. 47–68). Cambridge, MA: Harvard University Press.

Loftus, E. F., & Pickrell, J. E. (1995). The formation of false memories. *Psychiatric Annals, 25,* 720–725.

Marslen-Wilson, W. D., & Zwitserlood, P. (1989). Accessing spoken words: The importance of word onsets. *Journal of Experimental Psychology: Human Perception and Performance, 15,* 576–585.

Mather, M., Henkel, L. A., & Johnson, M. K. (1997). Evaluating characteristics of false memories in the Deese paradigm: Remember/know judgements and memory characteristics questionnaire compared. *Memory & Cognition, 25,* 826–837.

Mayes, A. R. (1988). *Human organic memory disorders.* New York: Cambridge University Press.

McClelland, J. L. (1995). Constructive memory and memory distortions: A parallel-distributed processing approach. In D. L. Schacter (Ed.), *Memory distortion: How minds, brains, and societies reconstruct the past* (pp. 69–90). Cambridge, MA: Harvard University Press.

McClelland, J. L., McNaughton, B. L., & O'Reilly, R. C. (1995). Why there are complementary learning systems in the hippocampus and neocortex: Insights from the successes and failures of connectionist models of learning and memory. *Psychological Review, 102,* 419–457.

McCloskey, M., & Zaragoza, M. (1985). Misleading postevent information and memory for events: Arguments and evidence against memory impairment hypotheses. *Journal of Experimental Psychology: General, 114,* 1–16.

McDermott, K. B. (1996). The persistence of false memories in list recall. *Journal of Memory and Language, 35,* 212–230.

McDermott, K. B., & Roediger, H. L., III. (1998). Attempting to avoid illusory memories: Robust false recognition of associates persists under conditions of explicit warnings and immediate testing. *Journal of Memory and Language, 39,* 508–520.

McGlynn, S. M., & Schacter, D. L. (1989). Unawareness of deficits in neuropsychological syndromes. *Journal of Clinical and Experimental Neuropsychology, 11,* 143–205.

Metcalfe, J. (1990). Composite holographic associative recall model (CHARM) and blended memories in eyewitness testimony. *Journal of Experimental Psychology: General, 119,* 145–160.

Metcalfe, J., Funnell, M., & Gazzaniga, M. S. (1995). Right-hemisphere memory superiority: Studies of a split-brain patient. *Psychological Science, 6,* 157–164.

Milner, B., Corsi, P., & Leonard, G. (1991). Frontal-lobe contribution to recency judgments. *Neuropsychologia, 29,* 601–618.

Moscovitch, M. (1994). Memory and working-with-memory: Evaluation of a component process model and comparisons with other models. In D. L. Schacter & E. Tulving (Eds.), *Memory systems 1994* (pp. 269–310). Cambridge, MA: MIT Press.

Moscovitch, M. (1995). Confabulation. In D. L. Schacter (Ed.), *Memory distortion: How minds, brains, and societies reconstruct the past* (pp. 226–254). Cambridge, MA: Harvard University Press.

Multhaup, K. (1995). Aging, source, and decision criteria: When false fame errors do and do not occur. *Psychology and Aging, 10,* 492–497.

Nadel, L., & Moscovitch, M. (1997). Memory consolidation, retrograde amnesia, and the hippocampal complex. *Current Opinion in Neurobiology, 7,* 217–227.

Norman, D. A., & Bobrow, D. G. (1979). Descriptions: An intermediate stage in memory retrieval. *Cognitive Psychology, 11,* 107–123.

Norman, K. A., Koutstaal, W., Schacter, D. L., & Galluccio, L. (1997). [Free recall intrusions of Patient B. G.]. Unpublished raw data.

Norman, K. A., & Schacter, D. L. (1996). Implicit memory, explicit memory, and false recollection: A cognitive neuroscience perspective. In L. M. Reder (Ed.), *Implicit memory and metacognition* (pp. 229–257). Mahwah, NJ: Lawrence Erlbaum Associates.

Norman, K. A., & Schacter, D. L. (1997). False recognition in young and older adults: Exploring the characteristics of illusory memories. *Memory & Cognition, 25,* 838–848.

Nyberg, L., Cabeza, R., & Tulving, E. (1996). PET studies of encoding and retrieval: The HERA model. *Psychonomic Bulletin & Review, 3,* 135–148.

Nyberg, L., McIntosh, A. R., Houle, S., Nilsson, L.-G., & Tulving, E. (1996). Activation of medial temporal structures during episodic memory retrieval. *Nature, 380,* 715–717.

Nyberg, L., Tulving, E., Habib, R., Nilsson, L.-G., Kapur, S., Houle, S., Cabeza, R., & McIntosh, A. R. (1995). Functional brain maps of retrieval mode and recovery of episodic information. *NeuroReport, 6,* 249–252.

Nystrom, L. E., & McClelland, J. L. (1992). Trace synthesis in cued recall. *Journal of Memory and Language, 31,* 591–614.

Ochsner, K., Schacter, D. L., & Edwards, K. (1997). Illusory recall of vocal affect. *Memory, 5,* 433–455.

O'Reilly, R. C., & McClelland, J. L. (1994). Hippocampal conjunctive encoding, storage, and recall: Avoiding a trade-off. *Hippocampus, 4,* 661–682.

Parkin, A. J., Bindschaedler, C., Harsent, L., & Metzler, C. (1996). Pathological false alarm rates following damage to the left frontal cortex. *Brain and Cognition, 32,* 14–27.

Parkin, A. J., & Leng, N. R. C. (1993). *Neuropsychology of the amnesic syndrome.* Hillsdale, NJ: Lawrence Erlbaum Associates.

Payne, D. G., Elie, C. J., Blackwell, J. M., & Neuschatz, J. S. (1996). Memory illusions: Recalling, recognizing, and recollecting events that never occurred. *Journal of Memory and Language, 35,* 261–285.

Phelps, E., & Gazzaniga, M. S. (1992). Hemispheric differences in mnemonic processing: The effects of left hemisphere interpretation. *Neuropsychologia, 30,* 293–297.

Rankin, J. S., & Kausler, D. H. (1979). Adult age differences in false recognitions. *Journal of Gerontology, 34,* 58–65.

Rankin, P. M., & O'Carroll, P. J. (1995). Reality discrimination, reality monitoring and disposition towards hallucination. *British Journal of Clinical Psychology, 34,* 517–528.

Rapcsak, S. Z., Polster, M. R., Comer, J. F., & Rubens, A. B. (1994). False recognition and misidentification of faces following right hemisphere damage. *Cortex, 30*, 565–583.

Rapcsak, S. Z., Polster, M. R., Glisky, M. L., & Comer, J. F. (1996). False recognition of unfamiliar faces following right hemisphere damage: Neuropsychological and anatomical observations. *Cortex, 32*, 593–611.

Read, J. D. (1996). From a passing thought to a false memory in 2 minutes: Confusing real and illusory events. *Psychonomic Bulletin & Review, 3*, 105–111.

Reinitz, M. T., Lammers, W. J., & Cochran, B. P. (1992). Memory conjunction errors: Miscombination of stored stimulus features can produce illusions of memory. *Memory & Cognition, 20*, 1–11.

Reinitz, M. T., Morrissey, J., & Demb, J. (1994). Role of attention in face encoding. *Journal of Experimental Psychology: Learning, Memory, and Cognition, 20*, 161–168.

Reinitz, M. T., Verfaellie, M., & Milberg, W. P. (1996). Memory conjunction errors in normal and amnesic subjects. *Journal of Memory and Language, 35*, 286–299.

Reyna, V. F., & Brainerd, C. J. (1995). Fuzzy-trace theory: An interim synthesis. *Learning & Individual Differences, 7*, 1–75.

Robinson, K. J., & Roediger, H. L. I. (1997). Associative processes in false recall and false recognition. *Psychological Science, 8*, 231–237.

Roediger, H. L., III. (1996). Memory illusions. *Journal of Memory and Language, 35*, 76–100.

Roediger, H. L., III., Jacoby, L. L., & McDermott, K. B. (1996). Misinformation effects in recall: Creating false memories through repeated retrieval. *Journal of Memory and Language, 35*, 300–318.

Roediger, H. L., III, & McDermott, K. B. (1995). Creating false memories: Remembering words not presented in lists. *Journal of Experimental Psychology: Learning, Memory, and Cognition, 21*, 803–814.

Ross, M. (1989). Relation of implicit theories to the construction of personal histories. *Psychological Review, 96*, 341–357.

Rugg, M. D., Fletcher, P. C., Frith, C. D., Frackowiak, R. S. J., & Dolan, R. J. (1996). Differential activation of the prefrontal cortex in successful and unsuccessful memory retrieval. *Brain, 119*, 2073–2083.

Schacter, D. L. (1989). Memory. In M. I. Posner (Ed.), *Foundations of cognitive science* (pp. 683–725). Cambridge, MA: MIT Press.

Schacter, D. L. (1995). Memory distortion: History and current status. In D. L. Schacter (Ed.), *Memory distortion: How minds, brains, and societies reconstruct the past* (pp. 1–43). Cambridge, MA: Harvard University Press.

Schacter, D. L. (1996). *Searching for memory: The brain, the mind, and the past.* New York: Basic Books.

Schacter, D. L., Alpert, N. M., Savage, C. R., Rauch, S. L., & Albert, M. S. (1996). Conscious recollection and the human hippocampal formation: Evidence from positron emission tomography. *Proceedings of the National Academy of Sciences, USA, 93*, 321–325.

Schacter, D. L., Buckner, R. L., Koutstaal, W., Dale, A. M., & Rosen, B. R. (1997). Late onset of anterior prefrontal activity during true and false recognition: An event-related fMRI study. *NeuroImage, 6*, 259–269.

Schacter, D. L., & Curran, T. (1995). The cognitive neuroscience of false memories. *Psychiatric Annals, 25*, 726–730.

Schacter, D. L., Curran, T., Galluccio, L., Milberg, W., & Bates, J. (1996). False recognition and the right frontal lobe: A case study. *Neuropsychologia, 34*, 793–808.

Schacter, D. L., Harbluk, J. L., & McLachlan, D. R. (1984). Retrieval without recollection: An experimental analysis of source amnesia. *Journal of Verbal Learning and Verbal Behavior, 23*, 593–611.

Schacter, D. L., Israel, L., & Racine, C. (1999). Suppressing false recognition in younger and older adults: The distinctiveness heuristic. *Journal of Memory and Language, 40,* 1–24.

Schacter, D. L., Kagan, J., & Leichtman, M. D. (1995). True and false memories in children and adults: A cognitive neuroscience perspective. *Psychology, Public Policy, and Law, 1,* 411–428.

Schacter, D. L., Koutstaal, W., Johnson, M. K., Gross, M. S., & Angell, K. A. (1997). False recollection induced by photographs: A comparison of older and younger adults. *Psychology and Aging, 12,* 203–215.

Schacter, D. L., Koutstaal, W., & Norman, K. A. (1997). False memories and aging. *Trends in Cognitive Sciences, 1,* 229–236.

Schacter, D. L., Osowiecki, D. M., Kaszniak, A. F., Kihlstrom, J. F., & Valdiserri, M. (1994). Source memory: Extending the boundaries of age-related deficits. *Psychology and Aging, 9,* 81–89.

Schacter, D. L., Reiman, E., Curran, T., Yun, L. S., Bandy, D., McDermott, K. B., & Roediger, H. L. (1996). Neuroanatomical correlates of veridical and illusory recognition memory: Evidence from positron emission tomography. *Neuron, 17,* 267–274.

Schacter, D. L., Reiman, E., Uecker, A., Polster, M. R., Yun, L. S., & Cooper, L. A. (1995). Brain regions associated with retrieval of structurally coherent visual information. *Nature, 376,* 587–590.

Schacter, D. L., Savage, C. R., Alpert, N. M., Rauch, S. L., & Albert, M. S. (1996). The role of hippocampus and frontal cortex in age-related memory changes: A PET study. *NeuroReport, 7,* 1165–1169.

Schacter, D. L., Verfaellie, M., & Anes, M. D. (1997). Illusory memories in amnesic patients: Conceptual and perceptual false recognition. *Neuropsychology, 11,* 331–342.

Schacter, D. L., Verfaellie, M., Anes, M. D., & Racine, C. (1998). When true recognition suppresses false recognition: Evidence from amnesic patients. *Journal of Cognitive Neuroscience, 10,* 668–679.

Schacter, D. L., Verfaellie, M., & Pradere, D. (1996). The neuropsychology of memory illusions: False recall and recognition in amnesic patients. *Journal of Memory and Language, 35,* 319–334.

Schacter, D. L., & Wagner, A. D. (1999). Medial temporal lobe activations in fMRI and PET studies of episodic encoding and retrieval. *Hippocampus, 9,* 7–24.

Shallice, T., Fletcher, P., Frith, C. D., Grasby, P., Frackowiak, R. S. J., & Dolan, R. J. (1994). Brain regions associated with acquisition and retrieval of verbal episodic memory. *Nature, 368,* 633–635.

Shiffrin, R. M., Huber, D. E., & Marinelli, K. (1995). Effects of category length and strength on familiarity in recognition. *Journal of Experimental Psychology: Learning, Memory and, Cognition, 21,* 267–287.

Silbersweig, D. A., Stern, E., Frith, C., Cahill, C., Holmes, A., Grootoonk, S., Seaward, J., McKenna, P., Chua, S. E., Schnorr, L., Jones, T., & Frackowiak, R. S. J. (1995). Functional neuroanatomy of hallucinations in schizophrenia. *Nature, 378,* 176–179.

Smith, A. D. (1975). Partial learning and recognition memory in the aged. *International Journal of Aging & Human Development, 6,* 359–365.

Squire, L. R. (1992). Memory and the hippocampus: A synthesis from findings with rats, monkeys, and humans. *Psychological Review, 99,* 195–231.

Squire, L. R. (1995). Biological foundations of accuracy and inaccuracy in memory. In D. L. Schacter (Ed.), *Memory distortion: How minds, brains, and societies reconstruct the past* (pp. 197–225). Cambridge, MA: Harvard University Press.

Squire, L. R., & Alvarez, P. (1995). Retrograde amnesia and memory consolidation: A neurobiological perspective. *Current Opinion in Neurobiology, 5,* 169–177.

Squire, L. R., Ojemann, J. G., Miezin, F. M., Petersen, S. E., Videen, T. O., & Raichle, M. E. (1992). Activation of the hippocampus in normal humans: A functional anatomical study of memory. *Proceedings of the National Academy of Sciences, USA, 89,* 1837–1841.

Stern, C. E., Corkin, S., Gonzalez, R. G., Guimaraes, A. R., Baker, J. R., Jennings, P. J., Carr, C. A., Sugiura, R. M., Vedantham, V., & Rosen, B. R. (1996). The hippocampal formation participates in novel picture encoding: Evidence from functional magnetic resonance imaging. *Proceedings of the National Academy of Sciences, USA, 93,* 8660–8665.

Stuss, D. T. (1991). Disturbance of self-awareness after frontal system damage. In G. P. Prigatano & D. L. Schacter (Eds.), *Awareness of deficit after brain injury: Clinical and theoretical issues* (pp. 63–83). New York: Oxford University Press.

Stuss, D. T., Alexander, M. P., Lieberman, A., & Levine, H. (1978). An extraordinary form of confabulation. *Neurology, 28,* 1166–1172.

Stuss, D. T., Alexander, M. P., Palumbo, C. L., Buckle, L., Sayeer, L., & Pogue, J. (1994). Organizational strategies of patients with unilateral or bilateral frontal lobe injury in word list learning tasks. *Neuropsychology, 8,* 355–373.

Talland, G. A. (1965). *Deranged memory: A psychonomic study of the amnesic syndrome.* New York: Academic Press.

Treisman, A., & Schmidt, H. (1982). Illusory conjunctions in the perception of objects. *Cognitive Psychology, 14,* 107–141.

Treves, A., & Rolls, E. T. (1994). Computational analysis of the role of the hippocampus in memory. *Hippocampus, 4,* 374–391.

Tulving, E. (1993). Varieties of consciousness and levels of awareness in memory. In A. Baddeley & L. Weiskrantz (Eds.), *Attention: Selection, awareness and control: A tribute to Donald Broadbent* (pp. 283–299). Oxford, England: Oxford University Press.

Tulving, E., Kapur, S., Markowitsch, H. J., Craik, F. I. M., Habib, R., & Houle, S. (1994). Neuroanatomical correlates of retrieval in episodic memory: Auditory sentence recognition. *Proceedings of the National Academy of Sciences, USA, 91,* 2012–2015.

Tulving, E., Markowitsch, H. J., Kapur, S., Habib, R., & Houle, S. (1994). Novelty encoding networks in the human brain: Positron emission tomography data. *NeuroReport, 5,* 2525–2528.

Tun, P. A., Wingfield, A., Rosen, M. J., & Blanchard, L. (1998). Response latencies for false memories: Gist-based processes in normal aging. *Psychology and Aging, 13,* 230–241.

Underwood, B. J. (1965). False recognition produced by implicit verbal responses. *Journal of Experimental Psychology, 70,* 122–129.

Underwood, B. J., Kapelak, S. M., & Malmi, R. A. (1976). Integration of discrete verbal units in recognition memory. *Journal of Experimental Psychology: Human Learning and Memory, 2,* 293–300.

Ungerleider, L. G. (1995, November 3). Functional brain imaging studies of cortical mechanisms for memory. *Science, 270,* 760–775.

Vicente, K. J., & Brewer, W. F. (1993). Reconstructive remembering of the scientific literature. *Cognition, 46,* 101–128.

Wagner, A. D., Schacter, D. L., Rotte, M., Koutstaal, W., Maril, A., Dale, A. M., Rosen, B. R., & Buckner, R. L. (1998, August 21). Building memories: Remembering and forgetting of verbal experiences as predicted by brain activity. *Science, 281,* 1188–1190.

Wallace, W. P., Stewart, M. T., & Malone, C. P. (1995). Recognition memory errors produced by implicit activation of word candidates during the processing of spoken words. *Journal of Memory and Language, 34,* 417–439.

Wallace, W. P., Stewart, M. T., Sherman, H. L., & Mellor, M. D. (1995). False positives in recognition memory produced by cohort activation. *Cognition, 55,* 85–113.

Wilding, E. L., & Rugg, M. D. (1996). An event-related potential study of recognition memory with and without retrieval of source. *Brain, 119,* 889–905.

Zaragoza, M. S., & Lane, S. M. (1994). Source misattributions and the suggestibility of eyewitness memory. *Journal of Experimental Psychology: Learning, Memory, and Cognition, 20,* 934–945.

Zaragoza, M. S., & Mitchell, K. J. (1996). Repeated exposure to suggestion and the creation of false memories. *Psychological Science, 7,* 294–300.

CHAPTER SEVEN

The Suggestibility
of Children's Testimony

Stephen J. Ceci
Cornell University

Maggie Bruck
McGill University

David B. Battin
Cornell University

Whenever children are involved in the fact-finding process associated with legal proceedings, the question of their fitness as witnesses comes to the fore. This question involves both *reliability*, that is, the ability to report consistently and accurately, and *competency*, that is, the ability to understand and answer questions posed. The issues of competency and reliability have traditionally been defined in terms of characteristics of the witness (e.g., age, IQ), but it is becoming increasing apparent that, with children in particular, the way questions are asked has a stronger influence on the accuracy of their answers than does any characteristic of the child herself. Stated more directly, intelligent questions are a necessary requirement for eliciting intelligent answers.

The ways in which an interviewer can suggest general and specific response patterns to a child can be classified into three categories: (a) the particular form or style of questioning, (b) the global or atmospheric characteristics of the interview, and (c) so-called contrived experiences.

Questioning style is a loosely associated group of three phenomena: (a) the use of leading questions, (b) making overt suggestions to the child, (c) and excessive repetition of a question both within and across interviews.

The employment of any of these techniques may affect all subsequent answers produced by the child, and therefore the distinction between questioning style and global characteristics or atmospherics (discussed later) is sometimes blurred.

Suggestive questioning styles may be used in a variety of forensic milieus, any one of which may potentially include its own global or atmospheric characteristics. These more global and less direct sources of influence for a young witness include (a) the general tone of the interview (e.g., is it neutral or accusatory?), (b) whether the interviewer aggrandizes her unequal status (e.g., a police officer showing the child her badge), (c) the induction of stereotypes, and (c) the invocation of peer pressure (e.g., the effect of informing a child about the statements made by other children involved in the case).

Finally, there is a third type of influence that has the potential to taint a child's report, the so-called contrived experiences. The use of (a) anatomically correct dolls and (b) visualization procedures are the most common examples of this type of influence. What is common to these "contrived" techniques is the introduction of a significant amount of new experience that must be incorporated into the child's memory and subsequently distinguished by the child from the memorial representations based on actual events. This process occurs, for example, when an interviewer encourages a child to entertain hypotheticals ("What do you think it would feel like if he did that to you?"), to use dolls or other props to enact abuse scenarios, or to visualize scenes not presently occurring.

In view of all these potential sources of report contamination, one can understand the challenge faced by those who solicit information from young children. Only 36% of nearly 2 million maltreatment investigations involving nearly 3 million children resulted in substantiated or indicated reports of child abuse or neglect, or both, according to the 1996 National Center for Child Abuse and Neglect report (Sedlak & Broadhurst, 1996). Although these rates do not reflect the effectiveness of interviewing techniques, they do indicate potential problems of either underreporting or overreporting; both of these concerns offer a potentially fruitful area of investigation for cognitive and developmental scientists. In light of these concerns, we address two questions in this chapter: (a) Under what conditions might suggestibility occur? and (b) Are younger children more suggestible than older children and adults?

A review of the scientific literature that examined the degree to which younger children are more suggestible than older children and adults concluded that although younger children are capable of demonstrating highly accurate memory recall, even after long delays, they are more susceptible to suggestive influences than are more mature subjects (Bruck, Ceci, & Hembrooke, 1998; Ceci & Bruck, 1993). This finding does not mean that young children's memories are inevitably problematic or that older children and adults have flawless recall that is impervious to the effects of suggestive questioning, but merely that preschool children are disproportionately more susceptible to the influence of suggestive questioning. This literature is challenging to interpret in terms of actual legal cases, however, because the very nature of most circumstances in which children are involved in forensic interviews is such that important and potentially influential elements are present that cannot be experimentally manipulated.

This last point raises questions about the generalizability of scientific findings—most of which are the product of laboratory studies of emotionally neutral events—to forensic situations in which a child is interviewed about emotionally wrenching experiences. Forensic situations usually involve the children directly, not as bystanders, and generally forensic situations involve events that are very important to the child, unlike most laboratory studies. Finally, unlike many laboratory studies of children's suggestibility, forensic situations may entail repeated interviews by adults who may have an agenda. Thus, most forensic interview situations extend over a significant period of time (often months or years), and involve multiple interviewers who ask the same questions many times, and usually some of these interviewers are people the children would consider especially powerful, such as police officers and judges. Because there is such a large discrepancy between the forensic environment and the ethical laboratory methods available for investigation of children's suggestibility, some have argued that it is premature to draw conclusions or make generalizations about children's suggestibility in forensic situations (e.g., Goodman & Clarke-Stewart, 1991, pp. 92–93).

At the turn of the 1990s, developmental psychology researchers began to respond to this challenge by designing studies that were more similar to real-world situations. These studies involved children's recall of highly salient personal experiences such as genital catheterizations, which are painful and often embarrassing, and other events involving body touching, often in a medical setting (for a review, see Ornstein, Shapiro, Clubb, & Follmer, 1997; and Ornstein and Greenhoot, chap. 8, this volume). Question repetition across interviews has been investigated using this medical setting design (Bruck, Ceci, Francouer, & Barr, 1995) as well as the influence of emotional tone in an interview with a child (Goodman, Bottoms, Schwartz-Kenney, & Rudy, 1991). To examine children's recall of surprising events, some of these newer studies included staged events that involved novel interruptions to the child's classroom environment. The effect of stereotype induction (Leichtman & Ceci, 1995; Lepore & Sesco, 1994) and the repetition of questions both within (Ceci & Bruck, 1993) and across interview sessions (Poole & White, 1995) have been incorporated in some of these designs. In addition, the effects of interviewer status (Ceci, Ross, & Toglia, 1987; Tobey & Goodman, 1992), of expectancy bias (Thompson, Clarke-Stewart, & Lepore, 1997; White, Leichtman, & Ceci, 1997), and of peer pressure (Moston & Engelberg, 1992) have been examined in these contexts. These various designs and approaches allowed researchers to collect data that could eventually point the way to effective interviewing techniques—those that promote accurate and complete recall of autobiographical events and that also reduce errors.

THE NATURE OF INTERVIEWS WITH CHILDREN

Eliciting detailed recollections from preschoolers about events that may have happened long ago can be quite challenging. Interviewers face tremendous obstacles even when they probe children about everyday neutral events; the situation is especially difficult when children witness or participate in painful, embarrassing, or stressful events. For example, in normal discourse, parents often obtain little information from their young children when they ask them open-ended questions, such as, "What did you do at your friend's birthday party?" (Pillemer & White, 1989). To gain some information, adults usually use their knowledge of the central event to guide their line of inquiry in ways that appear to help the child produce more information. So, when adults question a child about a birthday party, they may begin with a very general question: "What happened at John's party?" But after receiving only limited information, they may ask specific and often leading questions that reflect their knowledge of what generally happens at birthday parties (e.g., "What games did you play?" "Were the candles blown out?"). If there is still no satisfactory answer, the interviewer (usually the parent) may repeat the question. To ensure that the child continues to respond, the parent may reward the child's response, making comments like, "Wow, that is really interesting!" In so doing, the parent may change the tone of the interview from neutral to very positive. If a child makes an unrelated remark, the parent may try to redirect the child to the topic at hand, thus extinguishing the child's production of extraneous remarks and focusing on the preferred topic, possibly making overt suggestions in the process (e.g., "That didn't really happen, did it?").

In this process of trying to encourage children to say more than they seem predisposed to say at the moment, the interviewer might resort to a comparison with other children involved in a particular event (e.g., "Your brother told me what he did at the party.").

In the preceding description of a plausible interview script, leading questions, overt suggestions, and repetition both within and across interviews were described. In addition, interview tone and peer influence were all present as global strategies. These elements are easily incorporated into a process that is directed at the goal of eliciting information from young children. Of course, when adults do not have full knowledge of the actual events and assume their partial information is correct, there can be serious errors in interpreting a child's description of an event.

Forensic interviews of children present a special case within the larger class of experiences that constitute adult discourse with young children. Some of the elements that characterize conversations with preschoolers about everyday experiences also appear to characterize forensically relevant conversations. In forensic interviews, however, the intensity of many of the biasing characteristics significantly increases because of the inherent gravity of the process.

It is this assumption of shared knowledge and schema consistency that leads some interviewers to display what we have called *interviewer bias*. Interviewer bias develops when interviewers who hold a priori beliefs about the occurrence of an event try to shape the interview by getting the child to supply answers that are consistent with these a priori beliefs. Interviewer bias can be found wherever an interviewer thinks he knows the answers before the child divulges them. Biased interviewers will singlemindedly attempt to gather only confirmatory evidence from the child and avoid all negative or inconsistent disclosures. Thus, while gathering evidence to support an a priori belief, a biased interviewer may fail to gather disconfirming evidence. When a child provides statements that are consistent with the interviewer's a priori beliefs, the interviewer never challenges the child by asking, "You're kidding me, aren't you?" or "Did that really happen?" The biased interviewer does not ask questions that might provide alternate explanations for the allegations (e.g., "Did your mommy and daddy tell you that this happened, or did you *see* it happen?"). And the interviewer does not ask the child about events that are inconsistent with his hypothesis (e.g., "Who else beside your teacher touched your private parts? Did your mommy touch them, too?"). Generally, the child's inconsistent statements are either ignored or recast within the framework of the interviewer's a priori beliefs.

TYPES OF BIASED INTERVIEWING

We have previously identified three types of questioning techniques that are the result of bias on the part of the interviewer as well as four more global or environmental aspects to forensic interviews that often are present. Two of these global elements, interview tone and the introduction of peer comparison, proceed substantially from interviewer bias, and the third, the effect of unequal status between the interviewer and the witness, is demonstrated to be manipulable so as to exacerbate this status discrepancy (Ceci et al., 1987) when an interviewer's expectations have gone unrealized using other techniques. The two techniques that we have described as contrived experiences, the use of anatomical dolls and guided visualization, are particularly vulnerable to report distortion when used by biased interviewers.

Interviewer Bias in Experimental Settings

An interviewer's bias can be thought of as a confirmatory bias that produces expectancy effects. Expectancy effects are seen in experimental situations where an interviewer is given inaccurate information before an interview. In one such experiment (White et al., 1997) children played a Simon-Says game and 4 weeks later an interviewer (who was a social worker) was asked to determine from the children what had happened in the game. The interviewer was given a written report that contained both accurate (e.g., one child touched the other child's toe) and inaccurate (e.g., one child licked another child's knee) information. The interviewer was told to conduct the interview in the way she normally would.

The information provided in the written report influenced the interviewer's hypothesis about what had transpired. Even when it was inaccurate, this information shaped some of the children's reports so that they became consistent with the interviewer's hypothesis. When the interviewer was accurately informed by the written report, the children correctly recalled 93% of all events. However, when she was misinformed by the written report, 34% of the 3- to 4-year-olds and 18% of the 5- to 6-year-olds corroborated one or more events that the interviewer falsely believed had occurred. Many children initially stated details of the false events inconsistently or reluctantly, but as the interviewer persisted in asking leading questions that were consistent with her false hypothesis (e.g., that one child's knee was licked), a significant number of the children abandoned their inconsistency and corroborated the interviewer's false hypothesis.

The social worker was asked to take notes about these interviews, much the way she would in an actual forensic interview. Two months later (3 months after the original game was played), these notes were given to a new interviewer, who reinterviewed the children about the original game. The social worker's notes influenced the hypotheses of the second interviewer, who not only got the children to continue to assent to false allegations that were consistent with her hypotheses (e.g., that their knees were licked), but the children did so with increasing confidence and elaboration.

In sum, this study and others (e.g., Thompson et al., 1997) provided important evidence that interviewers' biases and a priori beliefs about an event can influence the manner in which interviewers question children, which in turn influences the accuracy of the children's reports. The data highlight both the benefits and dangers of having only one hypothesis about an event. When the hypothesis is correct, it is the best of all possible worlds, with very high levels of accurate recall by young children. However, when the interviewer's hypothesis is incorrect, it can lead to high levels of report errors, which tend to become embellished over subsequent interviews. As false reports become embellished, they become more persuasive and more difficult to distinguish from true reports.

Although we are sympathetic to the argument that interviewers must test a primary hypothesis, we believe that the risks associated with confirmatory biases are too great to encourage the relentless pursuit of a single hypothesis. Although it may not be desirable to keep interviewers unaware of all case-related information that could lead to the formation of expectancies, they should be encouraged to test multiple hypotheses that are plausible. Interviewers need training in how to entertain two or more competing hypotheses simultaneously, without conveying disbelief or skepticism to the child.

Interviewer Bias in Forensic Settings

We believe that many of the mass allegations of abuse in day-care cases, as well as some other cases involving sexual abuse, can be characterized in terms of interviewer bias. Sometimes these initial biases unfold in therapy sessions in which the therapist pursues a single hypothesis about the basis of the child's difficulties. (For reviews of the evidence that therapists rarely test alternatives and fall prey to illusory correlations and confirmatory biases, see Alloy & Tabachnik, 1984; Brehm & Smith, 1986; Kayne & Alloy, 1988.) Following sustained periods of therapy, some children make disclosures that are then pursued in multiple interviews by law enforcement and child protection personnel. At other times, interviewer bias is rooted in the investigative process by officers of the court who initially interview children. And, finally, some allegations grow out of interviews conducted by parents who are convinced that abuse took place and who relentlessly pursue a single hunch in conversations with their children.

Examples of interviewers' biases; blind pursuit of a single hypothesis; and failure to test alternate, equally believable, explanations of the children's behavior appear rife in many of the interviews we have studied. In these cases, interviewers persistently maintained one line of inquiry even when children consistently denied that the hypothesized events ever took place. Interviewer biases were also revealed by a failure to follow up on some of the children's inconsistent or bizarre statements when doing so might have refuted the interviewer's primary hypothesis.

The following dialogue was taken from a well publicized New Jersey case (*State v. Michaels*, 1994) between the social worker (Q) and Child A (A); it occurred during an early investigator interview. It is illustrative of interviewers' failure to seriously consider any evidence that was contrary to a priori beliefs.

Q: Do you think that Kelly was not good when she was hurting you all?
A: Wasn't hurting me. I like her.
Q: I can't hear you, you got to look at me when you talk to me. Now when Kelly was bothering kids in the music room . . .
A: I got socks off. . . .
Q: Did she make anybody else take their clothes off in the music room?
A: No.
Q: Yes?
A: No. . . .
Q: Did Kelly ever make you kiss her on the butt?
A: No.
Q: Did Kelly ever say—I'll tell you what. When did Kelly say these words? Piss, shit, sugar?
A: Piss, shit, sugar?
Q: Yeah, when did she say that, what did you have to do in order for her to say that?
A: I didn't say that.
Q: I know, she said it, but what did you have to do?

The interviewers in this case had developed the belief that the defendant, Kelly Michaels, had abused the children with various utensils and smeared feces and peanut butter on their bodies. Next, the investigator pursued these hypotheses with a child who was given an anatomically correct doll and some utensils (*State v. Michaels*, 1994):

Q: Okay, I really need your help on this. Did you have to do anything to her with this stuff?

A: Okay. Where's the big knife at. Show me where's the big knife at.

Q: Pretend this is the big knife because we don't have a big knife.

A: This is a big one?

Q: Okay, what did you have to do with that? What did you have to . . .

A: No . . . take the peanut—put the peanut butter . . .

Q: You put what's that, what did you put there?

A: I put jelly right here.

Q: Jelly?

A: And I put jelly on her mouth and on the eyes.

Q: You put jelly on her eyes and her vagina and her mouth?

A: On her back, on her socks.

Q: And did you have to put anything else down there?

A: Right there, right here and right here and here.

Q: You put peanut butter all over? And where else did you put the peanut butter?

A: And jelly.

Q: And jelly?

A: And we squeezed orange on her.

Q: And you had to squeeze an orange on her?

A: Put orange juice on her.

Q: And did anybody how did everybody take it off? How did she make you take it off?

A: No. Lick her all up, eat her all up and lick her all up.

Q: You had to lick her all up?

A: And eat her all up.

Q: Yeah? What did it taste like?

A: Yucky.

Q: So she made you eat the peanut butter and jelly and the orange juice off of the vagina too?

A: Yeah.

Q: Was that scary or funny?

A: Funny, funny and scary.

When inconsistent or incomprehensible information was part of these children's responses, the investigators assumed these responses were consistent with the fact that abuse had taken place, or else they ignored these statements. One is struck by the inconsistencies and the bizarre statements made by the children in response to the interviewers' questions. Most adults interacting with children in these situations would try to figure out just what the child was thinking about or why the child might be so confused to make such statements. Yet this did not happen. The children were not reined in (e.g., instructed to only describe things that really happened), nor were they asked common-sense questions such as: "Did this happen to you or are you just pretending that it happened to you?" or "Did you see this happen or did someone tell you that it happened?" Children were rarely challenged about their statements ("This really didn't happen, did it?"). Competent investigative interviewers would have at least asked themselves how it was possible for all these alleged acts, some of which were very painful, to occur without the other day-care workers' or parents' knowledge. The hypothesis that these alleged acts were the products of suggestive interviewing techniques or of children's imagination seems not to have been seriously considered.

Question Repetition as Evidence of Interviewer Bias

In actual cases involving children as witnesses, it is common for the children to tell and retell their story many times, to many different people, often over long delay intervals. Although some authorities estimate that the average child witness may be questioned 12 times during the course of an investigation (Whitcombe, 1992), this figure may actually be an underestimate if one considers the number of times that parents, friends, or mental health professionals may question these children. There are different purposes for reinterviewing children. The first is purely administrative: Given the legal structure of our society, a witness may have to tell his story to a number of different parties in a legal dispute. A second reason is to provide the witness with ample opportunity to reveal all details of the alleged event: Perhaps additional details and more complete reports will emerge with additional questioning; perhaps the use of certain interviewing techniques will facilitate this process by providing an emotionally and cognitively supportive climate that allows the unblocking of memories or that conveys to the victim a sense that it is safe to tell his story. Finally, as new case-related information becomes known, it may become necessary to reinterview the witness about newly emerging issues that were unanticipated at the time of the earlier interview. For any or all of these reasons, it becomes necessary to reinterview a witness.

There are some reasons to view reports elicited from repeated interviews in a favorable light. Both adults and children provide more details in repeated free-recall opportunities (see Fivush, 1993; Poole & White, 1995; Warren & Lane, 1995, for reviews). For a variety of reasons, however, repeated interviewing is also associated with baleful effects. Repeated interviews take place over time, and with increases in the length of time between the original event and the interview, there is a weakening of the original memory trace. As a result, more intrusions are able to infiltrate the memory system, and any misinformation has a better chance of replacing the weakened original trace. In fact, although as previously mentioned, when asked for free recall, both children and adults remember more with additional interviews, it is also true that their reports become more inaccurate over time (i.e., they recall both more accurate and more inaccurate details over time). This finding is particularly obvious in young children (Poole & White, 1993).

We have been assuming in this discussion of the beneficial effects of repetition that each repeated interview is neutral (nonsuggestive) in tone, that the witness is only asked to tell in his or her own words everything that happened. But this is not the situation for many forensic interviews with children; often these interviews are highly suggestive in that the interviewers provide the child with information about the alleged events, which raises the possibility that repeated interviews that contain misleading information may ultimately result in impaired and inaccurate recall of events.

GLOBAL INFLUENCES

Interview Tone

Interviewers of children place particular importance on building rapport with young clients so they feel relaxed and unthreatened. To achieve this goal, they may spend time talking or playing with the child before beginning the actual interview or test; during this time, an interviewer may ask the child to talk about school or her family. Ideally, interviewers attempt to provide a supportive atmosphere by paying attention, acting positively toward the child, and taking the child's answers seriously.

Few would criticize such techniques whether they are used with children or adults. Goodman and her colleagues (Goodman et al., 1991) demonstrated some of the benefits of these techniques on young children's recall of a stressful event. In this study, 4- and 7-year-old children were questioned about a previous visit to a medical clinic where they had received an inoculation. Half the children were interviewed in a supportive environment. At the beginning of the interview, these children were given snacks; the interviewer was warm and friendly; and she gave the child considerable but random praise (i.e., praise not contingent on their pattern of answering) such as, "You're doing a great job." The other children were not treated as warmly. They were not given snacks and the interviewer was more distant, occasionally responding "OK" or "All right."

Children in the supportive condition made fewer incorrect statements when asked to tell in their own words what had happened during their inoculation visit. In addition, supportive interviews diminished children's inaccurate answers to misleading questions in some of the conditions. The authors suggested that providing children with a warm interviewing environment increases their resistance to suggestion because it decreases their feelings of intimidation, allowing them to counter the interviewer's false suggestions.

Few would disagree with the recommendations that forensic interviewers create a supportive environment for the child. A problem arises, however, if interviewers presume they are establishing a supportive relationship when in reality they are exposing their beliefs through the use of implicit or explicit threats, bribes, and rewards. For example, in forensic contexts when interviewers want to obtain information from child witnesses, they sometimes make some of the following statements: "It isn't good to let people touch you" or "Don't be afraid to tell." They make these statements to help the child disclose facts that they may be too frightened or embarrassed to relate.

But these supposedly "supportive statements" may create reliability risks because in some contexts they may be ambiguous. That is, these statements may in fact create an accusatory tone (which reflects the interviewer's bias) and a context that promotes false disclosures. In some cases, these fabrications are sexual in nature. For example, in one study that was conducted 4 years after children had played with an unfamiliar research assistant for 5 minutes, Goodman and her colleagues asked these same children to recall the original experience and then asked them a series of questions, including abuse-related suggestive questions about the event (Goodman, Wilson, Hazan & Reed, 1989; also described in Goodman & Clarke-Stewart, 1991). At this time, the researchers created "an atmosphere of accusation" by telling the children that they were to be questioned about an important event and by saying such things as, "Are you afraid to tell? You'll feel better once you've told." Although few children had any memory of the original event from 4 years earlier, they were not always very accurate when answering questions that suggested abuse. Five out of the 15 children agreed with the interviewer's erroneous suggestive question that they had been hugged or kissed by the research assistant, 2 of the 15 agreed that they had had their picture taken in the bathroom, and 1 child agreed that she had been given a bath. The important conclusion of this study is that children may begin to give incorrect information to misleading questions about events for which they have no memory if the interviewer creates an atmosphere (emotional tone) of accusation. These forms of emotional atmospherics are conceptually similar to the negative stereotype inductions discussed previously.

Unequal Status Between Interviewers and Witnesses

Young children are sensitive to the status and power of their interviewers and as a result are especially likely to comply with the implicit and explicit agenda they perceive is being defined for them. The child's recognition of this power differential may be one of the most important causes of their heightened susceptibility to suggestion. Children are more likely to believe adults than other children, and therefore they are more willing to go along with the wishes of adults. For example, children are less open to suggestive influences when the suggestions are planted by their peers than when they are planted by adults (Ceci et al., 1987).

It should be recognized that children may also be sensitive to status and power differentials among adults. This issue is particularly important when a child witness is being interviewed by police officers, judges, and medical personnel. A recent study by Tobey and Goodman (1992) suggested that interviews by high-status adults who tell children of their status may have negative effects on the accuracy of children's reports. In their study, 4-year-olds played a game with a research assistant who was called a "baby-sitter." Eleven days later, the children returned to the laboratory. Half of the children met a police officer who said:

> I am very concerned that something bad might have happened the last time that you were here. I think that the baby-sitter you saw here last time might have done some bad things and I am trying to find out what happened the last time you were here when you played with the baby-sitter. We need your help. My partner is going to come in now and ask you some questions about what happened.

The control children never met the police officer. When the children were later asked to tell everything they could remember, the children in the police condition gave fewer accurate statements and more inaccurate statements than children in the control group. Two of the 13 children in the police condition seemed to be decisively misled by the suggestion that the baby-sitter had done something bad. Tobey and Goodman (1992) noted that one girl said to her mother, "I think the baby-sitter had a gun and was going to kill me." Later, in her free recall, the same child said, "That man, he might try to do something bad to me . . . really bad, yes siree" (p. xx). The second child inaccurately reported his ideas of what something bad might be by saying, "I fell down, I got lost, I got hurt on my legs, and I cut my ears."

The children in the Kelly Michaels case (*State v. Michaels,* 1994) were interviewed by law enforcement agents or by social workers who made reference to their connection to law enforcement agents. The children were explicitly made aware of the status of their interviewers by comments such as, "I'm a policeman, if you were a bad girl, I would punish you wouldn't I? Police can punish bad people."

Introduction of Stereotypes

Suggestions do not necessarily have to be in the form of an explicit (mis)leading question such as, "Show me how she touched your bottom," for them to take their toll on preschoolers' testimonial accuracy. A powerful yet subtle suggestive interviewing technique involves the induction of stereotypes. In the present context, we use the phrase *stereotype induction* to refer to an interviewer's attempt to transmit to a child a negative characterization of an individual or an event, whether it is true or false. Telling a child that the suspect "does bad things" or "tries to scare children" is an example of stereotype induction. (Of course, stereotypes can be positive, too, but the negative ones are of most concern in the context of children's testimony.)

The use of stereotype induction in interviews is one of the more blatant reflections of the interviewer's bias; the interviewer is telling the child how powerful adult authority figures, as well as their peers, characterize the defendant. Interviewers often justify their use of such techniques on the grounds that they provide a hospitable and supportive environment for the child to tell about the abuse. Notwithstanding the assumption that a stereotype induction makes a child feel better about disclosing details, a review of the scientific literature indicates that stereotype induction can have a very powerful negative effect on the accuracy of children's subsequent reports. Some naive children may eventually begin to incorporate the interviewers' stereotypes into their own report.

In one study (Lepore & Sesco, 1994), children ranging in ages from 4 to 6 years old played some games with a man called "Dale." Dale played with some toys in a researcher's testing room, and he also asked the child to help him take off his sweater. Later, an interviewer asked the child to tell her everything that happened when Dale was in the room. For half the children, the interviewer maintained a neutral stance whenever the children recalled an action. For the remaining children, the interviewer reinterpreted each of the child's responses in an incriminating way by stating, "He wasn't supposed to do or say that. That was bad. What else did he do?" Thus, in this incriminating condition, a negative stereotype was induced: "Dale does bad things." At the conclusion of these incriminating procedures, the children were asked three highly suggestive misleading questions ("Didn't he take off some of your clothes, too?" and "Other kids have told me that he kissed them, didn't he do that to you?" and "He touched you and he wasn't supposed to do that, was he?"). All children were then asked a series of direct yes–no questions about what had happened with Dale.

Children in the incriminating condition gave many more inaccurate responses to the direct yes–no questions than did children in the neutral condition, largely because these children made errors on items related to "bad" actions that had been suggested to them by the interviewer. Interestingly, one third of the children in the incriminating condition embellished their incorrect responses to these questions, and the embellished responses were always in the direction of the incriminating suggestions. The question that elicited the most frequent embellishments was, "Did Dale ever touch other kids at the school?" Embellishments to this question included information about whom Dale touched (e.g., "He touched Jason, he touched Tori, and he touched Molly" (Lepore & Sesco, 1994), where he touched them (e.g., "He touched them on their legs"), how he touched them (e.g., "and some he kissed . . . on the lips"), and how he took their clothes off ("Yes, my shoes and my socks and my pants. But not my shirt"). When they were reinterviewed 1 week later, children in the incriminating stereotype condition continued to answer the yes–no questions inaccurately, and they continued to embellish their answers.

A second study (Leichtman & Ceci, 1995) also demonstrated the powerful effects of a stereotype induction when it is paired with repeated suggestive questioning. A stranger named "Sam Stone" visited preschoolers (ages 3 to 6 years) in their classroom for 2 minutes in their daycare center. Following Sam Stone's visit, the children were asked for details about the visit on four different occasions over a 10-week period. During these four occasions, the interviewer refrained from using suggestive questions. She simply encouraged children to describe Sam Stone's visit in as much detail as possible. One month following the fourth interview, the children were interviewed a fifth time by a new interviewer who asked about two non-events that involved Sam doing something to a teddy bear and a book. In reality, Sam Stone never touched either one. When asked in the fifth interview, "Did Sam Stone do anything to a book or a teddy bear?" most children rightfully replied "No." Only 10% of the answers provided by the youngest (3- to 4-year-old) children contained claims that Sam Stone did anything to a book or teddy bear. When asked to monitor the source of their answer by deciding whether they really saw him do it instead of "thinking they saw him do something" or "hearing he did something," only 5% of their answers contained claims that anything occurred. Finally, when these 5% were gently challenged ("You didn't really see him do any-thing to the book/the teddy bear, did you?") only 2.5% still insisted on the reality of the fictional event. None of the older (5- to 6-year-old) children claimed to have seen Sam Stone do either of the fictional events. These children's responses can be regarded as a baseline against which to mea-sure the effects of stereotype induction paired with repeated questioning.

A second group of preschoolers (Leichtman & Ceci, 1995) were pre-sented with a stereotype of Sam Stone before he ever visited their school. Each week, beginning a month before Sam Stone's visit, these children were told a new Sam Stone story in which he was depicted as very clumsy. The day after Sam Stone's visit, the children were shown a ripped book (the same one that they were reading when Sam Stone came to visit) and a soiled teddy bear (that had not been in the room during Sam Stone's visit). They were asked whether they knew how the book had been ripped and the teddy bear soiled. Very few children claimed to have seen Sam Stone do these things, but one fourth of them said that *perhaps* he had done it, a statement that is reasonable given the stereotype induction they received before his visit.

Following Sam Stone's visit, these children were given four suggestive interviews over a 10-week period. Each suggestive interview contained two erroneous suggestions, one having to do with ripping a book and the other with soiling a teddy bear (e.g., "Remember that time Sam Stone vis-ited your classroom and spilled chocolate on that white teddy bear? Did he do it on purpose or was it an accident?" and "When Sam Stone ripped that book, was he being silly or was he angry?").

One month later, when a new interviewer probed about these events ("Did anything happen to a book?" "Did anything happen to a teddy bear?"), 72% of the youngest preschoolers claimed that Sam Stone did one or both misdeeds, a figure that dropped to 44% when asked if they actually *saw* him do these things. Importantly, 21% continued to insist that they saw him do these things, even when gently challenged. The older preschoolers, although more accurate, still included some children (11%) who insisted they saw him do the misdeeds.

What was most surprising about these children's reports was the num-ber of false perceptual details as well as nonverbal gestures that the chil-dren provided to embellish their stories of these nonevents. For example, the children used their hands to show how Sam had purportedly thrown the teddy bear up in the air; some children reported sighting Sam in the playground, on his way to the store to buy chocolate ice cream, or in the bathroom soaking the teddy bear in water before smearing it with a crayon. Some children claimed there was more than one Sam Stone. And one child provided every parent's favorite false detail; this child claimed that Sam had come to his house to trash his room.

Critics of the Sam Stone study wonder about its forensic relevance. They argue that the 2-minute visit of Sam to their classroom is not a significant event for the children. We agree but go one step further: There really was no event. Some of the children came to tell elaborate stories about an event that never happened. We think it important to make the following distinction: Children's reports can be unreliable because they confuse, omit, or blend details when recounting an actual event. But they can also be unreliable because they fabricate an entire episode or sequence of events within a larger episode. The latter most clearly occurred in the Sam Stone study. This point is important because it demonstrates that children's inaccurate reports or allegations do not always reflect a confusion between the events or details of an experience but may at times reflect the creation of an entire experience in which the child did not participate.

In conclusion, these studies (Dale and Sam Stone) vary in their procedures, yet the results are quite consistent, showing negative effects of pairing stereotype induction with suggestive questioning. These effects are apparent regardless of whether the child is interviewed one time (as was true in the Dale study) or over a period of several months (as was true in the Sam Stone Study). The negative effects are apparent whether the stereotype induction took place before an event or after an event.

Peer Influence

The effects of letting children know that their friends have "already told" has not been investigated as extensively as other areas of children's testimonials. Certainly, the common wisdom is that a child will go along with a peer group, but will a child provide an inaccurate response just so he or she can be one of the crowd? The results of two studies suggest that the answer is "yes."

First, Binet (1900) found that children will change their answers to be consistent with those of their peer group even when it is clear that the answer is inaccurate. Although Binet based his conclusions about children's suggestibility on their answers to perceptual stimuli ("Which line is longer?"), there is some indication that the same result would be observed in another domain.

Second, Pynoos and Nader (1989) studied people's recollections of a sniper attack. On February 24, 1984, a sniper repeatedly fired a rifle at

children on an elementary school playground from a second story window across the street. Scores of children were pinned down by the gun-
fire, many were injured, and 1 child and a passerby were killed. Roughly
10% of the student body, 113 children, were interviewed 6 to 16 weeks
later. Each child was asked to freely recall the experience and then to respond to specific questions. Some of the children who were interviewed
were not at the school during the shooting; this group included those already on the way home or on vacation. Yet, according to Pynoos and
Nader, even the nonwitnesses had "memories":

> One girl initially said that she was at the school gate nearest the sniper when
> the shooting began. In truth she was not only out of the line of fire, she was
> half a block away. A boy who had been away on vacation said that he had
> been on his way to the school, had seen someone lying on the ground, had
> heard the shots, and then turned back. In actuality, a police barricade pre-
> vented anyone from approaching the block around the school. (p. 238)

One assumes that children heard about the event from their peers who
were present during the sniper attack, and they incorporated these reports into their own memories.

The investigators in the Kelly Michaels case (*State v. Michaels,* 1994)
tried to get the children to disclose by telling them what other children allegedly reported. Sometimes the investigators told the children that they
could help their friends by telling about abuse: "All the other friends I
talked to told me everything that happened. 29C told me. 32C told me,
14C told me. . . . And now it's your turn to tell. You don't want to be left
out, do you?" (p. xx). In response to a child who did not disclose, the investigators said, "Boy, I'd hate having to tell your friends that you didn't want
to help them."

In *State v. Michaels* (1994) children were also interviewed together, presumably as a way of getting one or both children to disclose. The following two examples from this case suggest that the children did talk to each
other about the allegations or that parents told their children about other
children's allegations.

INTERVIEWER: Do you know what [Kelly] did?
CHILD: She wasn't supposed to touch somebody's body. If you
want to touch somebody, touch your own.
INTERVIEWER: How do you know about her touching private parts?
Is that something you saw or heard?
CHILD: 21 C told me. (p. xx)

INTERVIEWER: When you and the other kids were up stairs in the music
room, was she wearing clothes then?

CHILD: I saw clothes on, but the other kids didn't.
INTERVIEWER: Oh how do you know that?
CHILD: Because my mommy told me that.

One might argue that there is some scientific evidence to support the practice of using peers to elicit disclosures from children who have something to disclose. In one study, 7- and 10-year-olds witnessed a staged classroom incident and were later asked to recall its details (Moston & Engelberg, 1992). As is customary in such studies, younger children recalled less information about the incident and were more susceptible to suggestive questioning than the 10-year-olds. However, when these 7-year-olds were allowed to discuss the incident with a friend who accompanied them to the interview, age differences were significantly reduced. The presence of a friend at the interview created a favorable emotional environment that resulted in more accurate and less suggestible reports for the youngest children. But these data are relevant only if the children do have something to disclose. Otherwise, such practices may taint the reports of children.

Contrived Experiences

Questioning techniques and interview atmospherics are phenomena of which interviewers need to be aware; they can dramatically effect the accuracy of the information a witness provides, especially a young child witness. The last genre to be considered here, contrived experiences, differs from the others in several ways. First, in either of its manifestations it is always employed intentionally. It is certainly conceivable that the excessive repetition of a variety of questions during an interview or over a series of interviews could be done progressively and unintentionally as an interviewer sought information that was not immediately forthcoming. The tone of an interview can conceivably develop in a way that was neither intended nor noticed by the interviewer. This lack of intentionality is not the case with the use of anatomical dolls or visualization. Second, both of these techniques involve the introduction of new experiences into the child's life course. Those experiences may be fantastic, as is true with visualization, or they may be perceptually based if anatomical dolls are used, but in either case the child has new memories to deal with and sort out after one of these techniques has been used.

This situation creates a significant problem for those interested in the accuracy of the child's verbal report as well as the quantity of information the child produces. In the section that follows we consider two aspects of the challenge the child faces in untangling first-person experience, reality, and fantasy in a forensic environment. The first is termed *reality monitoring,* and it refers to one's ability to distinguish reality from fantasy or to distinguish memories of actual events from memories of imagined events. The second concept is termed *source monitoring,* and it refers to the ability to keep track of the sources of actual events.

Reality Monitoring. Over the past 100 years, researchers have held markedly different views on young children's ability to differentiate fantasy from reality. According to the early pioneers, such as Freud, young children's wish-fulfilling fantasies tainted the accuracy of their reports. Piaget (1962) supported this view by claiming that young children cannot distinguish something that actually happened from a dream about the same event.

In the 1970s, this view of young children began to change. A variety of researchers demonstrated that even 3-year-olds can correctly classify real and pretend figures and that they have a firm understanding of the distinction between imagined and real entities (Flavell, Flavell, & Green, 1987; Morison & Gardner, 1978; Taylor & Howell, 1973). Thus, the predominant view shifted to the idea that children do not confuse fantasy with reality.

Some current research moderates this extreme position. That is, it appears that although children may be able to differentiate the real from the imagined, these distinctions are sometimes fragile, especially if children are asked to actually imagine events and then to report whether or not the imagined events actually happened. Under these circumstances, young children have a tendency to report that what they were asked to imagine was real (e.g., Foley, Harris, & Hermann, 1994; Harris, Brown, Marriott, Whittall, & Harmer 1991; Parker, 1995).

A host of therapeutic procedures and interviewing techniques are suggestive precisely because they induce fantasies. Asking children to visualize a scene and focus on some aspect of it and then to make up some encounter that may not have taken place is one example. In one widely heralded technique, the *cognitive interview,* interviewers ask children to visualize how a scene might appear from the perspective of a person or an object that is situated elsewhere in the room, thus encouraging the child to use their imagination. Children are encouraged to abandon reality when therapists delve into symbols or dreams or when they ask children to create a journal account of what *could* happen. Also, self-empowerment training, sometimes using ordinary or anatomical dolls as props, is another technique used by therapists with their child clients. These techniques create the risk that fantasies will eventually come to be believed by the child, particularly if the interviewer does not provide a context for reality testing.

The following example from an actual case in which the child witness accused her day-care workers of abuse illustrates how therapeutic techniques that encourage children to fantasize may also produce fear in these same children. One of the child witnesses (Claudia) told her therapist that Mr. Bob put hot sauce on her eyes and her tongue. When the therapist asked Claudia when this happened, she replied that she was in outer space where she was taken by Ms. Betsy and Mr. Bob in a hot-air balloon. When the therapist asked what happened in outer space, Claudia answered, "Mr. Bob killed the babies in outer space." The therapist continued, "How do you know that Mr. Bob killed the babies in outer space?" Claudia replied, "Because I saw them." Finally, when the therapist tried to probe further, Claudia said, "I'm too scared."

Source Monitoring. Source monitoring is closely related to the concept of reality monitoring. It involves identifying the origins of our memories to elucidate them or to validate them. For example, it might entail remembering in what place or at what time an event occurred; it also might entail identifying the speaker of an utterance and keeping track of who did or said what. As adults, we monitor the sources of our memories continuously and often unconsciously. Whereas *reality monitoring* refers to remembering whether an event was imagined or real, *source monitoring* refers to keeping track of the origins of sources that did occur. The concepts of reality and source monitoring are sometimes indistinguishable when we try to remember whether something actually happened to us or merely whether someone told us that something happened to us.

Source-monitoring confusions can be the basis of suggestibility effects, at least in some situations. For example, if one cannot remember that the source of a false detail had, in fact, been provided by an interviewer during a previous session, one could come to believe that it was actually experienced rather than suggested. Thus, misleading suggestions may at times become incorporated into memory.

Recently, a number of developmental psychologists have begun to examine source monitoring in children. A few studies have shown that young children are more prone than adults to making source-confusion errors (e.g., Ackil & Zaragoza, 1995; Lindsay, Gonzales, & Eso, 1995). In these studies, children experienced an event (e.g., they might see a short film), then later were reminded of a number of details about the event, some of which did not occur. Later still, when asked to recall the details of the original event, participants often could not accurately monitor the source of the information; that is, they reported that some of the non-occurring details that were provided after the event actually happened during the event; they reported that they remembered hearing or seeing the nonoccurring event. This effect happens at all ages, but it seems that younger children make disproportionately more of these kinds of errors.

It also appears that when participants were warned before their final recall not to believe anything that was said to them after the event because it was not true, they nevertheless continued to make source errors. That they did not relinquish such misinformation but insisted that it was part of the original event suggests that they blended the origins of input into their memories. This type of error is most prominent for preschoolers (Lindsay, et al., 1995).

Visualization

Visualization is a technique used by therapists and other interviewers with the intent of increasing the amount of detail recalled. As had been mentioned earlier, the cognitive interview induces visualization by asking interviewees, among other things, to try and imagine what a scenario would look like from the perspective of someone else. When consideration is given to source monitoring and reality monitoring as potential pitfalls for the young witness, visualization becomes an important area of investigation for social scientists.

Researchers have conducted a series of studies to examine whether asking preschoolers to repeatedly think about some event, creating mental images each time they did so, would result in subsequent source misattributions that would lead to the creation of false memories (Ceci, Crotteau-Huffman, Smith, & Loftus, 1994; Ceci, Loftus, Leichtman, & Bruck, 1994). The events that children were asked to think about were actual events that they experienced in their distant past (e.g., an accident that required stitches) and fictitious events that they never experienced (e.g., getting their hand caught in a mousetrap).

Each week for 10 consecutive weeks, preschool children were individually interviewed by a trained adult. The adult showed the child a set of cards, each containing a different event. The child picked a card, and then the interviewer read it to the child, asked the child to think about it before replying, and asked whether the event ever happened to them. For example, when the child selected the card that read, "Got finger caught in a mousetrap and had to go to the hospital to get the trap off," the interviewer would ask, "Think real hard, and tell me if this ever happened to you. Do you remember going to the hospital with a mousetrap on your finger?" Each week, the interviewer simply asked the child to think really hard about each actual and fictitious event, with prompts to visualize each scene ("I want you to think about who was with you. What were they wearing? How did you feel?").

After 10 weeks of thinking about both real and fictitious events, the children were interviewed by a new adult who asked them specific and open-ended questions about the true and false events: "Tell me if this ever happened to you: Did you ever get your finger caught in a mousetrap and have to go to the hospital to get the trap off?" . . . "Can you tell me more?" . . . "What happened next?").

Some children who were asked to repeatedly think about fictitious events produced highly detailed, internally coherent, narratives that were at times convincing to naive adults. In one study (Ceci, Crotteau-Huffman, et al., 1994), 58% of the preschool children produced false narratives for at least one of the fictitious events, with one fourth of the children producing false narratives for the majority of the fictitious events. It is the highly elaborate quality of their narratives that emerged by the final week that is so surprising to many who have watched videotapes of these children. These narratives were frequently embellished, with internally coherent accounts of the context and emotions associated with the accident.

Consider Bill, a 4-year-old, reporting his experience with a mousetrap. At the first session, Bill correctly claimed to have no memory of ever having his hand caught in a mousetrap and stated that he had never been to a hospital before. By the 10th session, however, an elaborate story evolved:

> My brother Colin was trying to get Blowtorch [an action figurine] from me, and I wouldn't let him take it from me, so he pushed me into the wood pile where the mousetrap was. And then my finger got caught in it. And then we went to the hospital, and my mommy, daddy, and Colin [older brother] drove me there, to the hospital in our van, because it was far away. And the doctor put a bandage on this finger. (Unpublished laboratory documentation)

As can be seen, Bill did not simply give yes–no answers after he had been repeatedly asked to think about a fictitious experience during the previous 9 weeks; rather, he provided a richly detailed, plausible account. In fact, Bill went on to explain how his father was in the basement collecting firewood at the time of the accident, and he initially went into the basement to ask his father to prepare his lunch. It is not only that Bill's story (and those of other children in this study) is so detailed, but it is also very believable to adults who do not know the procedures of the experiment. We think that these children are so believable because at least some of them have come to believe these false stories themselves.

One hypothesis to account for the children's difficulty in these tasks is that there is a confusion between multiple inputs into the memory system. The memory system contains information that is encoded from actual experience but it also contains information that is encoded from imaginary events. Very young children have particular difficulty separating these sources of familiarity, often mistaking the familiarity of imagined events for real ones.

Thus, preschoolers appear to be vulnerable to source misattributions when they are repeatedly encouraged to think about or visualize events that never occurred. Many of them appear to think that they actually experienced events that they had only imagined. This finding would seem to have relevance for the testimony of a child who has been in a certain type of therapy for a long time, engaging in similar imagery inductions and "memory work" techniques. Because repeatedly creating mental images is a pale version of what can transpire in therapy when a variety of techniques may be used, all of which encourage the creation of competing images, these studies provide a fairly conservative test of the hypothesis that repeatedly thinking about a fictional event can lead to false beliefs about its reality.

Certainly, the cataloguing of techniques that may promote monitoring errors is a sensitive issue because it raises in some people's minds the possibility that children who are repeatedly exposed to such techniques cannot be believed. Such a conclusion is premature until it can be demonstrated that children are this susceptible to source misattributions about sexual events. And even if they are vulnerable to suggestions about sexual events, this does not mean that their claims are inevitably false, only that they could be. For example, if therapists simply ask young children to think about certain events that may be beyond their experience and comprehension and if the child does come to produce a coherent, logical story, then perhaps the child is in fact faithfully reporting a memory, as long as the therapist did not provide any of the target details during his instructions to the child.

Anatomical Dolls and Other Props

Diagnosing sexual abuse in children is a complicated and difficult process. Often there are no witnesses or medical evidence to confirm or disconfirm a child's claim or a parent's suspicion. To further complicate matters, there is no syndrome or constellation of behaviors, such as depression, anxiety, or nightmares, that is diagnostic of all or even most cases of sexual abuse (Kendall-Tackett, Williams, & Finkelhor, 1993). Because of these diagnostic difficulties, professionals have developed a number of assessment tools, such as anatomically detailed dolls. Child therapists, police, child protection workers, and attorneys frequently use these dolls in the assessment and treatment of child sexual abuse.

One rationale for the use of anatomical dolls is that they allow children to manipulate objects reminiscent of a critical event, thereby cueing recall and overcoming language and memory problems. A second rationale for the use of these dolls is that they are thought to overcome motivational problems of embarrassment and shyness. Children may feel more comfortable enacting an abusive event using the dolls than verbally recounting it. The dolls have also been used as projective tests. Some professionals claim that if a child actively avoids these dolls, shows distress if they are undressed, or shows unusual preoccupation with their genitalia, this is consistent with the hypothesis that the child has been abused.

Despite the widespread use of anatomically detailed dolls in therapeutic and forensic settings (the rate of doll use in some jurisdictions may be as high as 90%; Boat & Everson, 1988; Conte, Sorenson, Fogarty, & Rosa, 1991), some researchers and professionals have expressed skepticism about their usefulness as a diagnostic tool. Two concerns have frequently been raised. The first has been that the dolls are suggestive; by their very nature, it has been claimed that they may encourage the child to engage in sexual play even if the child has not been sexually abused (e.g., Terr, 1988). For instance, a child may insert a finger into a female doll's vagina simply because of its novelty or simply because it is there. A related criticism of the dolls has been that they should not be used to make judgments about children's past abuse because the existing data have demonstrated that the dolls do not meet the traditional standards of a reliable assessment instrument (e.g., Berry & Skinner, 1993; Wolfner, Faust, & Dawes, 1993). Because of these concerns, the use of anatomically detailed dolls for the purposes of providing legal evidence has been banned in a few jurisdictions until scientific data can be produced to attest to their validity.

At the present time, there are at least 20 studies that have addressed concerns related to the use of anatomically detailed dolls. These studies have addressed three related issues: (a) Do abused children interact with the dolls differently than nonabused children? (b) How do normal children interact with the dolls? and (c) How accurately do children use dolls to report events? The results of these studies have been summarized (see Berry & Skinner, 1993; Ceci & Bruck, 1993, 1995; Koocher et al., 1995; Wolfner et al., 1993, for detailed reviews of these studies).

First, doll play is not a good indicator of abuse status. Generally, there are few differences in doll play of abused and nonabused children. Second, normative studies of nonabused children's interactions with dolls revealed that they demonstrated few if any explicit sexual activities when playing with the dolls. However, there were many children who showed reticence or avoidance of the dolls or, at the other extreme, overt interest in the genitalia of anatomically detailed dolls. In the most ambitious of these studies, Everson and Boat (1990) observed more than 200 preschool children at play with the dolls in several different conditions. Although none of the 2-year-olds showed suggestive or clear intercourse positioning, between 3 and 18% of the older children did demonstrate such behaviors.

The most relevant studies are those that examined how accurately children use dolls to depict actual experiences. If children can accurately depict previous actions and events with the dolls and if this information is more accurate than that given through verbal reports or other means of prompting, then such evidence would support the diagnostic utility of anatomically detailed dolls as an assessment tool. Several researchers have attempted to address this issue.

Goodman and Aman (1990) questioned 3- and 5-year-old children 1 week after they had played games with a male experimenter. Children were asked to recall the details of the event, and they were also asked straightforward as well as misleading questions, some of which related to sexual abuse. Children answered these questions in one of four interview conditions: (a) anatomical dolls, (b) regular dolls (with no anatomical details), (c) regular dolls that the child could see but not touch, or (d) no dolls.

The accuracy of children's reports was similar across all conditions, with 5-year-olds consistently providing more detailed and accurate reports than 3-year-olds. Although the anatomical dolls did not promote inaccurate reports of sexual events, it is important to note that the dolls did not facilitate accurate reports of the original event, suggesting that the mnemonic value of the dolls may be limited. Furthermore, the fact the 3-year-olds did not show any benefit from the use of the dolls suggests that one of the premises for the use of the dolls may be faulty. One would expect that given their lack of verbal competence, the 3-year-olds would have benefited from the dolls to a greater extent than the older children, but this was not the case.

A study by Gordon and her colleagues (Gordon et al., 1993) raises further doubts about the usefulness of dolls to obtain accurate reports from young children. In this study, 3- and 5-year-old children were asked to report (either verbally or by manipulating normal dolls) the details of a previous visit to their pediatrician. Although the dolls provided some assistance to the older children in their recall, the provision of the dolls resulted in lower recall for the 3-year-olds, in certain instances.

Perhaps anatomically detailed dolls enhance the accuracy of children's reports of embarrassing events of a sexual nature because one of the purported benefits of the dolls is to provide children with a tool that will allow them to overcome their shyness and embarrassment concerning sexual matters. Saywitz and her colleagues (Saywitz, Goodman, Nicholas, & Moan, 1991) attempted to address this issue by asking 5- and 7-year-old girls to recall the details of a recent doctor's visit. During this visit, half of the children had received a genital examination, and the other half had received a scoliosis examination. One to 4 weeks later, when asked for a verbal report of their examination, 78% of the children who had received a genital examination failed to disclose vaginal touching, and 89% failed to disclose anal touching. When given the opportunity to provide the same information with the dolls ("show me with the dolls what happened") 83% of the children who had received a genital examination failed to disclose genital touching and 89% failed to disclose anal touching. However, when the experimenter pointed to either the genitalia or buttocks of the doll and asked a direct question, "Did the doctor touch you here?", only 14% failed to report genital touching, and 31% failed to report anal touching (i.e., errors of omission).

Children who received the scoliosis examination (i.e., with no genital touching) never made false reports of genital touching (i.e., errors of commission) in either the verbal free recall or the doll enactment conditions. However, when the experimenter pointed to the genital or anal region of the doll and asked, "Did the doctor touch you here?", 2.86% of the children falsely affirmed vaginal touch, and 5.56% falsely affirmed anal touch. These results indicate that regardless of the interviewing technique, children rarely if ever make false reports about genital touching unless they are asked direct questions with the dolls. The genital examination results, however, indicate that the dolls did not assist the children to divulge potentially embarrassing material, unless the interviewer used highly directive questioning. It is possible that the same results could have been obtained without the use of the dolls but merely through the use of a direct verbal question: "Did the doctor touch your genitals?" But this question was not asked by these researchers.

The results of these three experiments are discrepant with the notion that dolls enhance the recall of the youngest children, but they are consistent with findings by DeLoache and Marzolf (1995) that children younger than 3 years of age have great difficulty appreciating symbolic relationships in which an object stands for something other than itself. In DeLoache and Marzolf's work, children watched an experimenter hide an object in a room, and then they were asked to find its counterpart in a small-scale model of the room. Generally, children younger than 28 to 36 months did not successfully retrieve the object. Deloache argued that this lack of success reflects their poor understanding of the symbolic nature of the scale model. Thus, perhaps young children might also have difficulty using a doll to enact real-life events because to be successful they must treat the doll as a symbol of themselves. The task is even more difficult in doll-centered interviews, because the dolls are not exact replicas of the real object (the child) in the way that a scale model is an exact replica of a large room.

Researchers have recently completed two studies that share some similarities with the studies already described in this section but also go beyond them in a number of ways. In the first of these studies (Bruck, Ceci, Francoeur, & Renick, 1995), 3-year-old children visited their doctor for a routine medical examination. Half these children received a genital examination in which the pediatrician gently touched their buttocks and genitals. The other half of the children were not touched in these areas. Immediately after the examination, an experimenter pointed to the genitalia or buttocks of an anatomically detailed doll and asked the child, "Did the doctor touch you here?" Only 47% of the children who received the genital exam correctly answered "yes," a figure approximating that obtained by others for errors of omission (i.e., saying "no" when something really did happen). On the other hand, 50% of the children who did not receive a genital exam incorrectly answered "yes" to this question (i.e., 50% of these children falsely reported touching or made errors of commission). When the children were simply asked to "show on the doll" how the doctor had touched their buttocks or genitalia, accuracy did not improve. In this case, only 25% of the children who had received genital examinations correctly showed how the pediatrician had touched their genitals and buttocks. Accuracy decreased in part because a significant number of female children inserted their fingers into the anal or vaginal cavities of the dolls, something that the pediatrician never did. When the children who did not receive a genital examination were asked to show on the doll how the doctor had touched their genitals and buttocks, only 50% of the children correctly showed no touching; 50% of the children who did not receive genital examinations falsely showed either genital or anal touching when given the dolls. This study was repeated with a group of 4-year-olds, and it obtained quite similar results (Bruck et al., 1998).

We believe that these sexualized behaviors do not reflect these preschoolers' sexual knowledge or experiences but two other factors. First, the types of questions and props used in an interview (asking children to name body parts, including genitals, or showing children anatomically detailed dolls and asking children to manipulate these dolls) may lead 3-year-olds to think that it is not only permissible but expected to respond to the interviewers' questions using these same terms. Second, perhaps children insert fingers or objects into the dolls' openings for the same reasons they would insert a finger into the hole of a doughnut—it is there; it is something to manipulate; it "affords" this activity. It is also possible, however, that the children's actions do have a sexual basis. One might argue that the presentation of anatomical dolls elicits sexual fantasies by allowing children to engage in their natural exploration of sexual themes that, from an adult perspective, could be regarded as prurient.

CONCLUSION

On the basis of the literature we have reviewed here, it appears to us that a scientifically prudent position is that young children are disproportionately more vulnerable to a host of suggestive techniques than are older children and adults. They are susceptible to having their reports tainted by leading questions, stereotypes, visualizations, and other tactics. However, it is often true that the mere use of these suggestive techniques is insufficient to derail a young child's report accuracy. Rather, it is often the case that the techniques must be used repeatedly, over fairly long intervals, before they take their toll on children's accuracy. Although studies can be found in which this is not true (e.g., cases in which the accuracy of preschoolers' testimony is damaged following a single suggestion), they are probably the exception.

Finally, a word of caution about the role of individual differences is in order. In virtually every study that we and others have conducted, there are some younger children who are less affected by suggestive techniques than some older children and adults are. Much has been learned about such differences, but researchers are still a long way from fully understanding their causes. Until such time as they are better understood, it is wise to keep in mind that any given child may or may not be representative of her age group. That is, we cannot know with confidence whether a particular child is as suggestible, more suggestible, or less suggestible than others in her age group on average. This caveat focuses on the characteristics of the child.

There is another caveat that focuses on the characteristics of the interviewer. In this regard, we state our conclusions more forcefully. Interviewer bias is the central driving mechanism in the creation of suggestive interviews. Highly biased interviewers will use a wide array of strategies to elicit belief-consistent reports from the child. There are a number of studies that suggest that it is the combination of suggestive techniques that results in the highest rate of inaccurate reports (e.g., Bruck et al., 1998; Leichtman & Ceci, 1995). One might argue that there is nothing particularly developmental about this argument and that it has no explanatory power in accounting for age-related differences in suggestibility. However, as children grow older they develop strategies to escape multiple suggestive practices (e.g., "I want my lawyer" or "I already answered that question"); at younger ages, these strategies are either not available to or inappropriate for the young child. As a result, the young child is less resistant and more exposed to suggestive interviewing practices. Thus, according to our argument, the use of a particular suggestive interviewing technique by itself may not necessarily result in tainted testimony, especially if it is used by unbiased or mildly biased interviewers who may test alternative hypotheses and challenge children's reports. However, the risk of taint increases with the increase of interviewer bias.

REFERENCES

Ackil, J. K., & Zaragoza, M.S. (1995). Developmental differences in eyewitness suggestibility and memory for source. *Journal of Experimental Child Psychology, 60,* 57–83.

Alloy, L. B., & Tabachnik, N. (1984). Assessment of covariation by humans and animals: The joint influence of prior expectations and current situational information. *Psychological Review, 91,* 112–149.

Berry, K., & Skinner, L. (1993). Anatomically detailed dolls and the evaluations of child sexual abuse allegations: Psychometric considerations. *Law and Human Behavior, 17,* 399–422.

Binet, A. (1900). *La suggestibilité.* Paris: Schleicher Frères.

Boat, B., & Everson, M. (1988). The use of anatomical dolls among professionals in sexual abuse evaluations. *Child Abuse & Neglect, 12,* 171–186.

Brehm, S. S., & Smith, T. W. (1986). Social psychological approaches to psychotherapy and behavior change. In S. L. Garfield & A. Bergin (Eds.), *Handbook of psychotherapy and behavior change* (3rd ed., pp. 69–116). New York: Wiley.

Bruck, M., Ceci, S. J., Francouer, E., & Barr, R. J. (1995). "I hardly cried when I got my shot!": Influencing children's reports about a visit to their pediatrician. *Child Development, 66,* 193–208.

Bruck, M., Ceci, S. J., Francouer, E., & Renick, A. (1995). Anatomically detailed dolls do not facilitate preschoolers' reports of a pediatric examination involving genital touching. *Journal of Experimental Psychology: Applied, 1,* 95–109.

Bruck, M., Ceci, S., & Hembrooke, H. (1998) Reliability and credibility of young children's reports: From research to policy and practice. *American Psychologist, 53,* 136–151.

Ceci, S. J., & Bruck, M. (1993). The suggestibility of the child witness: A historical review and synthesis. *Psychological Bulletin, 113,* 403–439.

Ceci, S. J., & Bruck, M. (1995). *Jeopardy in the courtroom: A scientific analysis of children's testimony.* Washington, DC: American Psychological Association.

Ceci, S. J., Crotteau-Huffman, M., Smith, E., & Loftus, E. W. (1994). Repeatedly thinking about non-events. *Consciousness & Cognition, 3,* 388–407.

Ceci, S. J., Loftus, E. W., Leichtman, M., & Bruck, M. (1994). The role of source misattributions in the creation of false beliefs among preschoolers. *International Journal of Clinical and Experimental Hypnosis, 62,* 304–320.

Ceci, S. J., Ross, D., & Toglia, M. (1987). Age differences in suggestibility: Psycholegal implications. *Journal of Experimental Psychology: General, 117,* 38–49.

Conte, J. R., Sorenson, E., Fogarty, L., & Rosa, J. D. (1991). Evaluating children's reports of sexual abuse: Results from a survey of professionals. *American Journal of Orthopsychiatry, 78,* 428–437.

DeLoache, J. S., & Marzolf, D. P. (1995). The use of dolls to interview young children: Issues of symbolic representation. *Journal of Experimental Child Psychology, 60,* 155–173.

Everson, M. D., & Boat, B. W. (1990). Sexualized doll play among young children: Implications for the use of anatomical dolls in sexual abuse evaluations. *Journal of the American Academy of Child and Adolescent Psychiatry, 29*(5), 736–742.

Fivush, R. (1993). Developmental perspectives on autobiographical recall. In G. S. Goodman & B. Bottoms (Eds.), *Child victims and child witnesses: Understanding and improving testimony* (pp. 1–24). New York: Guilford.

Flavell, J., Flavell, E., & Green, F. L. (1987). Young children's knowledge about the apparent–real and pretend–real distinctions. *Developmental Psychology, 23,* 816–822.

Foley, M. A., Harris, J., & Hermann, S. (1994) Developmental comparisons of the ability to discriminate between memories for symbolic play enactment. *Developmental Psychology, 30,* 206–217.

Goodman, G., & Aman, C. (1990). Children's use of anatomically detailed dolls to recount an event. *Child Development, 61,* 1859–1871.

Goodman, G. S., Bottoms, B. L., Schwartz-Kenney, B. M., & Rudy, L. (1991). Children's testimony about a stressful event: Improving children's reports. *Journal of Narrative and Life History, 1*(1), 69–99.

Goodman, G. S., & Clarke-Stewart, A. (1991). Suggestibility in children's testimony: Implications for child sexual abuse investigations. In J. L. Doris (Ed.), *The suggestibility of children's recollections* (pp. 92–105). Washington, DC: American Psychological Association.

Goodman, G. S., Wilson, M. E., Hazan, C., & Reed, R. S. (1989, March). *Children's testimony nearly four years after an event.* Paper presented at the annual meeting of the Eastern Psychological Association, Boston, MA.

Gordon, B. N., Ornstein, P. A., Nida, R. E., Follmer, A., Creshaw, C., & Albert, G. (1993). Does the use of dolls facilitate children's memory of visits to the doctor? *Applied Cognitive Psychology, 7*(6), 459–474.

Harris, P., Brown, E., Marriott, C., Whittall, S., & Harmer, S. (1991). Monsters, ghosts and witches: Testing the limits of the fantasy–reality distinction in young children. *British Journal of Developmental Psychology, 9,* 105–123.

Kayne, N. T., & Alloy, L. B. (1988). Clinician and patient as aberrant actuaries: Expectation-based distortions in assessment of covariation. In L. Y. Abramson (Ed.), *Social cognition and clinical psychology: A synthesis* (pp. 295–365). New York: Guilford.

Kendall-Tackett, K. A., Williams, L. M., & Finkelhor, D. (1993). Impact of sexual abuse on children: A review and synthesis of recent empirical studies. *Psychological Bulletin, 113,* 164–180.

Koocher, G. P., Goodman, G. S., White, S., Friedrich, W. N., Sivan, A. B., & Reynolds, C. R. (1995). Psychological science and the use of anatomically detailed dolls in child sexual abuse assessments. *Psychological Bulletin, 118,* 199–222.

Leichtman, M. D., & Ceci, S. J. (1995). The effects of stereotypes and suggestions on preschoolers' reports. *Developmental Psychology, 31,* 568–578.

Lepore, S. J., & Sesco, 3. (1994). Distorting children's reports and interpretations of events through suggestion. *Applied Psychology, 79,* 108–120.

Lindsay, D. S., Gonzales, V., & Eso, K. (1995). Aware and unaware uses of memories of postevent suggestions. In M. S. Zaragoza, J. R. Graham, C. N. Gordon, R. Hirschman, & Y. Ben-Porath (Eds.), *Memory and testimony in the child witness* (pp. 86–108). Newbury Park, CA: Sage.

Morison, P., & Gardner, H. (1978). Dragons and dinosaurs: The child's capacity to differentiate fantasy from reality. *Child Development, 49,* 642–648.

Moston, S., & Engelberg, T. (1992). The effects of social support on children's eyewitness testimony. *Applied Cognitive Psychology, 6,* 61–75.

Ornstein, P. A., Shapiro, L. R., Clubb, P. A., & Follmer, A. (1997). The influence of prior knowledge on children's memory for salient medical experiences. In N. Stein, P. A. Ornstein, C. J. Brainerd, & B. Tversky (Eds.), *Memory for everyday and emotional events* (pp. 83–112). Mahwah, NJ: Lawrence Erlbaum Associates.

Parker, J. (1995). Age differences in source monitoring of performed and imagined actions on immediate and delayed tests. *Journal of Experimental Child Psychology, 60,* 84–101.

Piaget, J. (1962). *The language and thought of the child.* London: Routledge & Kegan Paul.

Pillemer, D. B., & White, S. H. (1989) Childhood events recalled by children and adults. In H. W. Reese (Ed.), *Advances in child development and behavior* (Vol. 21, pp. 297–340). San Diego, CA: Academic Press.

Poole, D., & White, L. (1993). Two years later: Effects of question repetition and retention interval on the eyewitness testimony of children and adults. *Developmental Psychology, 29,* 844–853.

Poole, D., & White, L. (1995). Tell me again and again: Stability and change in the repeated testimonies of children and adults. In M. S. Zaragoza, J. R. Graham, C. N. Gordon, R. Hirschman, & Y. Ben-Porath (Eds.), *Memory and testimony in the child witness* (pp. 24–43). Newbury Park, CA: Sage.

Pynoos, R. S., & Nader K. (1989). Children's memory and proximity to violence. *Journal of the American Academy of Child and Adolescent Psychiatry, 28,* 236–241.

Saywitz, K., Goodman, G., Nicholas, G., & Moan, S. (1991). Children's memory of a physical examination involving genital touch: Implications for reports of child sexual abuse. *Journal of Consulting and Clinical Psychology, 5,* 682–691.

Sedlak, A., & Broadhurst, D. (1996). *Executive Summary of the Third National Incidence Study of Child Abuse and Neglect* (NCCAN publication no. 105-91-1800). Washington, DC: U.S. Department of Health and Human Services.

State v. Michaels. 136 N.J. 299, 642 A.2d 1372 (N.J., 1994).

Taylor, B. J., & Howell, R. J. (1973). The ability of 3-, 4-, and 5-year-olds to distinguish fantasy from reality. *Journal of Genetic Psychology, 122,* 315–318.

Terr, L. (1988). Anatomically correct dolls: Should they be used as a basis for expert testimony? *Journal of the American Academy of Child and Adolescent Psychiatry, 27,* 254–257.

Thompson, W. C., Clarke-Stewart, K. A., & Lepore, S. (1997). What did the janitor do? Suggestive interviewing and the accuracy of children's accounts. *Law & Human Behavior, 21,* 405–426.

Tobey, A., & Goodman, G. S. (1992). Children's eyewitness memory: Effects of participation and forensic context. *Child Abuse & Neglect, 16,* 779–796.

Warren, A. R., & Lane, P. (1995). The effects of timing and type of questioning on eyewitness accuracy and suggestibility. In M. Zaragoza (Ed.), *Memory and testimony in the child witness* (pp. 44–60). Newbury Park, CA: Sage.

Whitcomb, D. (1992). *When the child is a victim* (2nd ed.). Washington DC: National Institute of Justice.

White, T. L., Leichtman, M. D., & Ceci, S. J. (1997). The good, the bad and the ugly: Accuracy, inaccuracy, and elaboration in preschoolers' reports about a past event. *Applied Cognitive Psychology, 11,* 37–54.

Wolfner, G., Faust, D., & Dawes, R. (1993). The use of anatomical dolls in sexual abuse evaluations: The state of the science. *Applied and Preventative Psychology, 2,* 1–11.

CHAPTER EIGHT

Remembering the Distant Past

Implications of Research on Children's Memory for the Recovered Memory Debate

PETER A. ORNSTEIN
University of North Carolina at Chapel Hill

ANDREA FOLLMER GREENHOOT
University of Arizona

A very disturbing aspect of contemporary society is the dramatic increase in allegations of childhood sexual abuse. Two indexes of this unsettling trend are readily available: the skyrocketing frequency with which young children are called on to provide evidence concerning abuse that they may have experienced or witnessed (Gray, 1993) and the increasing numbers of adults (mostly women, but also some men) who come to believe that they were abused at a young age by their fathers or other close relatives (Pendergrast, 1995). The interpretation of children's reports of abuse is not an easy matter, even in situations in which there may be physical corroborating evidence, and these interpretive problems increase dramatically when we attempt to understand adults' claims of early abuse, especially those that are based on recently "recovered" memories. Indeed, if it is difficult to assess a 3-year-old's claim of what might have happened to her a year ago, consider the problems associated with evaluating a 35-year-old woman's memory that she had been abused by her grandfather 30 years ago.

By definition, research on memory is central to a consideration of these claims. An understanding of children's memory and suggestibility is clearly relevant to situations in which children are asked to provide evidence in legal proceedings. Not only has the children's memory literature been used to provide information about what children can and cannot be expected to remember about salient personally experienced events, but it is also leading to the design of effective protocols for interviewing children (e.g., Ornstein, Larus, & Clubb, 1991; Poole & Lamb, 1998). In a parallel fashion, research on the basic nature of memory—especially that which outlines the processes involved in the encoding, storage, and retrieval of information—is of critical importance for understanding adult claims of remembering early instances of abuse (Ornstein, Ceci, & Loftus, in press). In addition, however, research on the development of memory is also of considerable relevance for discussions of adults' abilities to provide accurate accounts of early instances of abuse. Indeed, it is our underlying thesis that the interpretation of a report of the distant past requires a developmental analysis.

In this chapter, we present the case for the importance of a developmental perspective on the recovered–false-memory debate. In doing so, we provide a brief sketch of a framework for discussing the flow of information within the developing memory system. We then illustrate the framework with research on the development of children's memory, focusing especially on the ways in which underlying memory representations may be altered over time, a topic that is of the utmost importance for any consideration of adults' early memories.

A DEVELOPMENTAL ORIENTATION

Why is an understanding of the developing memory system of importance for the current debate? As we see it, age-related differences in children's cognitive functioning have serious implications for information acquisition, retention over time, as well as subsequent retrieval and reporting. For example, developmental changes in prior knowledge about events that are unfolding, in the strength and organization of underlying representations in memory, and in fundamental information processing skills all influence what can be remembered (Ornstein et al., 1991). In general, memory begins with understanding an event as it is being experienced, and it is of the utmost importance to know something about how a child made sense of an experience as it was unfolding. It is the child's construal of an experience—in addition to the adult's later interpretation—that must be considered in evaluations of the accuracy of remembering over delay intervals that are measured in years. Age differences in understanding and related constructive processes can thus have a serious impact on encoding and the establishment of representations in memory.

It is important to point out that the resulting memory representations are not static entities. Rather, these representations change over time, in part as a result of decay and in part as a consequence of intervening experiences, such as conversations and exposure to the media (e.g., Howe, Courage, & Bryant-Brown, 1993; Ceci & Bruck, 1993). Accordingly, it becomes essential to determine the extent to which an event that is experienced by a child is discussed with parents and others, leading to embellishment and reinterpretation over time. The impact of these types of intervening activities may be particularly critical over long delays during which memory traces undergo a process of decay (Baker-Ward, Ornstein, & Principe, 1997). Furthermore, it is necessary to consider the very serious retrieval problems that may arise from the dramatic cognitive changes that take place over the years. Given fundamental changes in thinking that take place from the preschool to young adult years, it may be very difficult for a mature adult to recover memories of early experiences that have not been influenced by current understanding (Ornstein et al., in press), particularly when adults forget the details of particular experiences or in fact when those experiences may never have taken place.

Issues such as these are taken very seriously by developmental psychologists concerned with children's cognitive development, but they also occupy the attention of researchers dealing with adult development across the lifespan. The question for these individuals is how an adult who is trying to remember the past can escape from the "prison" of his or her current state of knowledge and beliefs. This dilemma is captured nicely by Valliant (1977) in his discussion of an extended longitudinal study of men who had at one time been undergraduates at Harvard (see also Ross, 1989). Valliant indicated, "It is all too common for caterpillars to become butterflies and then to maintain that in their youth they had been little butterflies. Maturation makes liars of us all" (p. 197).

A FRAMEWORK FOR EXAMINING MEMORY

As we see it, this type of developmental perspective is built into an informal information-processing framework that was crafted for an examination of children's memory for salient, personally experienced events (Ornstein et al., 1991). Originally developed for organizing the children's memory literature that was most relevant for considering children's abilities to provide evidence in legal situations, the framework has proved useful for more general discussions of memory in children (Ornstein, 1995; Ornstein, Baker-Ward, Gordon, & Merritt, 1997) and adults (Ornstein et al., in press). Following the analysis of Loftus and Davies (1984), this framework is based on the assumption that memory performance is determined by factors such as the quality of the initial representation of the event that is being remembered, the individual's expectations and knowledge about the event, the activities that are experienced during the delay interval before the assessment of remembering, and the various types of cues that are employed to elicit remembering. These variables have been discussed in terms of four general themes about memory performance: (a) Not everything gets into memory, (b) what gets into memory may vary in strength, (c) the status of information in memory changes over time, and (d) retrieval is not perfect. This perspective enables one to characterize the multiple contributions of several important variables to the flow of information within the developing memory system. For example, stress experienced during an event can influence attentional deployment and encoding and thus have an impact on subsequent recall, whereas stress during an interview can affect the retrievability of information. In a similar fashion, as suggested previously, knowledge about events that are being experienced can influence encoding, changes in the underlying representation, and the accuracy and completeness of recall (e.g., Chi & Ceci, 1987; Ornstein, Shapiro, Clubb, Follmer, & Baker-Ward, 1997). Moreover, this framework may help us understand situations in which people feel that they are recalling a specific experience, but in fact they may not be remembering an event that really happened to them.

With this framework as a guide, our research group has carried out a programmatic series of studies of children's memory for salient personal experiences. Most of the to-be-remembered events in these studies are medical in nature, such as routine physical examinations and hospital procedures that are both less familiar and more stressful, although we have also examined children's memory for stories and for events that we have crafted. Our first efforts were devoted to obtaining baseline information concerning the ability of children of different ages to remember what they experienced during a standard well-child checkup as a function of both delay interval (up to 3 months) and the specificity of the interviewer's questions (e.g., Baker-Ward, Gordon, Ornstein, Larus, & Clubb, 1993). Once these baseline data were gathered, our goal became that of using the framework to guide our study of many factors that affect age-related differences in the flow of information within the memory system.

For example, because we understand that not all aspects of the checkup are encoded and stored in memory, we have carried out within-event analyses of long-term retention. We also expected that the memory traces of younger and older children would differ in underlying strength and rate of decay, as well as the amount of support required for retrieval. Our program of research was thus designed to examine age differences in these central aspects of remembering (Ornstein, 1995; Ornstein, Baker-Ward, et al., 1997).

CHILDREN'S MEMORY FOR MEDICAL EXPERIENCES

We have studied memory for visits to the doctor and related experiences because these salient events are similar in some ways to situations about which children are asked to testify. For example, during these visits to health professionals, children are physically handled by adults (often opposite sex, unfamiliar adults) while they are in states of partial or complete undress. We have also chosen these events because they permit us to avoid one of the major problems associated with the study of autobiographical memory, namely that of specifying the stimulus situation to which the children are initially exposed. With the cooperation of the examining physicians, we are able to specify the precise details associated with each child's medical experience. For example, in a typical visit to the pediatrician, children are seen separately by a physician and a nurse, each of whom administers a set of specific procedures (e.g., the nurse measures blood pressure, the doctor listens to the heart). However, physical examinations can vary considerably, depending on the age and individual circumstances of each child, as well as the preferences of the medical personnel. Nonetheless, because the doctors and nurses fill out checklists for each child, we have precise knowledge of the specifics of each checkup, and thus can determine the accuracy of subsequent recall in a precise manner.

To illustrate our approach, consider Baker-Ward et al.'s (1993) exploration of 3-, 5-, and 7-year-old's retention of the details of a well-child physical examination. At each age level, three groups of children were interviewed twice, first immediately after their checkups and then again after a delay of either 1, 3, or 6 weeks. With this design, we were able to obtain an estimate of the children's initial encoding of the examination and then to explore within-subject forgetting over time. In addition, to control partially for the impact of the initial memory assessment on subsequent remembering, a fourth group of children at each age was interviewed only once, after a delay of 3 weeks. The interviews involved the use of a structured protocol that was designed to assess memory for the various component features of the physical examination. Beginning with open-ended probes (e.g., "Tell me what happened during your checkup"), we continued with more specific questions (e.g., "Did the doctor check any parts of your face?") and then moved on to yes–no questions about features that had not yet been volunteered (e.g., "Did she [he] check your eyes?"). The children were also asked potentially misleading yes/no questions about two types of activities not included in the checkups. Each child was asked a unique set of absent-feature questions about component features of a regular physical examination that had not been part of his or her visit to the doctor. In addition, the children were asked extra-event questions about activities unlikely to be included in any checkup (e.g., "Did the doctor cut your hair?" and "Did the nurse lick your knee?").

The basic recall data are displayed in Fig. 8.1, in which performance is indicated at each delay interval in terms of the percentage of the features of each child's checkup that were produced in response to both open-ended and more specific questions. As can be seen, overall performance was quite good, although age differences in both immediate and delayed recall were observed. For example, immediately after the physical examination, the 3-, 5-, and 7-year-olds recalled approximately 75%, 82%, and 91% of the component features, respectively. However, inspection of Fig. 8.1 also indicates that the younger children provided less information in response to the general, open-ended questions than did the older children. Indeed, the 3-year-olds relied especially on the specific probes. Two other aspects of the data presented in Fig. 8.1 are also noteworthy. First, recall over time varied directly with age, with significant forgetting being observed among the 3-year-olds but not among the 7-year-olds. Second, at each of the ages, the performance of the children interviewed twice, both immediately after the checkup and then again after a delay of 3 weeks, was similar to that of the control participants who had been interviewed for the first (and only) time after 3 weeks. Thus, the initial interview itself did not appear to facilitate later memory performance, at least after a delay of 3 weeks.

An additional feature of the children's memory reports is their performance with regard to the potentially misleading questions about actions that had not been part of their checkups. In general, the children responded appropriately (i.e., by saying "no") at above chance levels when presented with these probes. However, there were clear age and question-type differences, with the 3-year-olds making more errors than the 5- and 7-year-olds and with all children performing better with the extra-event

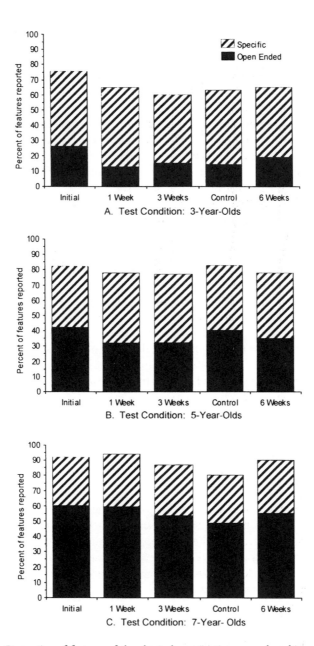

FIG. 8.1. Proportion of features of the physical examination remembered in response to open-ended and specific questions by age group and delay interval. Data from "Young Children's Long-Term Retention of a Pediatric Examination" by L. Baker-Ward, B. N. Gordon, P. A. Ornstein, D. Larus, and P. A. Clubb, 1993, *Child Development, 64,* 1519–1533. Copyright © 1993 by the Society for Research in Child Development. Adapted with permission.

questions than with the absent-feature questions. Performance was particularly good with the more implausible extra-event questions; for example, at the initial interview, the correct denial scores for these questions were 87%, 96%, and 99% for the 3-, 5-, and 7-year-olds, respectively. In addition, for all age groups, but especially for the 3-year-olds, lower levels of performance were observed with the absent-feature questions about plausible, medically related activities not included the checkups; the correct denial scores for these questions at the initial interview were 72%, 93%, and 88% for the 3-, 5-, and 7-year-olds, respectively.

Overall, Baker-Ward et al.'s (1993) data indicated that young children's reports of a salient event can be quite impressive. Nonetheless, there were clear age-related changes in various aspects of memory performance. In contrast to the older children, the 3-year-olds showed lower levels of overall recall, greater dependency on yes–no types of questions, more forgetting, and a reduced ability to differentiate between activities that had and had not been included in their medical checkups. These basic findings have been replicated in other studies (see Ornstein, 1995, and Ornstein, Baker-Ward, et al., 1997, for overviews) in which we have explored children's memory for a range of medical experiences. The data also set the stage for a number of questions about age-related changes in the encoding, storage, and retrieval of information in memory, questions that we have examined through the lens of the informal framework described previously.

USING THE FRAMEWORK
TO EXAMINE CHILDREN'S MEMORY

We turn now to a brief treatment of the framework to illustrate how we have used it to examine age-related trends in children's memory. In this discussion, we introduce the previously mentioned four themes, commenting briefly on them. We then devote considerably more attention to one theme—that dealing with the status of information in memory over time—because it seems very central to the issue of adults' efforts to recall early experiences.

Theme 1: Not Everything Gets Into Memory

Remembering begins with the encoding process, and it is important to emphasize that not everything that is experienced is entered into memory. Given the limitations of the human cognitive system (Broadbent, 1958;

Kahneman, 1973), some incoming information must be selected for attention and further processing, whereas other information is consequently excluded. Several aspects of our research program deal with factors that affect the encoding of information in memory. For example, stress experienced while an unpleasant medical event (in this case, a radiological procedure involving urinary bladder catheterization) is unfolding can influence the deployment of attention and thus encoding (Merritt, Ornstein, & Spicker, 1994). However, perhaps the most important factor governing the encoding process is the extent to which an event is understood as it is being experienced (Bjorklund, 1985; Chi & Ceci, 1987; Ornstein & Naus, 1985). Indeed, we have shown that what a child already knows about a medical examination can seriously affect the extent to which component features of the checkup are encoded and placed in memory (Clubb, Nida, Merritt, & Ornstein, 1993; see also Ornstein, Shapiro, et al., 1997). Features about which children are more knowledgeable (e.g., a check of the heart) are more likely to be encoded and remembered than those about which there is little prior knowledge (e.g., a check of the back). Moreover, recent work suggests that long-standing, prior knowledge may not be necessary for encoding and subsequent retention as long as new knowledge can be provided to facilitate understanding of an event that is being experienced (Principe, Myers, Furtado, Merritt, & Ornstein, 1996; see also Bransford & Johnson, 1972).

Theme 2: What Gets into Memory May Vary in Strength

If information about an event is encoded and stored in memory, a number of factors may influence the strength and organization of the resulting memory trace or representation. With increases in age, there are associated changes in a variety of basic information-processing skills (e.g., in the speed of encoding, in the flexible use of a repertoire of strategies, and in knowledge about the world; e.g., Kail, 1989; Ornstein, Baker-Ward, & Naus, 1988), each of which may be linked to developmental differences in the efficiency of information acquisition. As a consequence, given comparable exposure to a particular event, older children will be expected to establish stronger and more coherently organized memory representations than younger children (see Brainerd, Kingma, & Howe, 1985). Admittedly, there is no direct indicator of the status of a memory representation (Baker-Ward et al., 1997), but it does seem likely that the amount of support that is needed to elicit recall can be used as a proxy measure. As such, memory representations that are both strong and coherently organized may be readily retrieved, even in response to minimal cueing on the part of the interviewer, whereas weak traces may be more difficult to retrieve and may require greater supports. Thus, it is quite likely that strong traces can be retrieved in response to open-ended questions (e.g., "What happened this morning?"), whereas weak traces will require more direct yes–no types of questions (e.g., "Did the man have black hair?"). Evidence consistent with this view can be seen in the various levels of support that are required to elicit recall from children of different ages. Consider, for example, Baker-Ward et al.'s (1993) previously discussed finding that 7-year-olds are able to provide more information in response to open-ended probes than are younger children, who in turn are more dependent on the specific questions of the interviewers. These findings and others (e.g., Ornstein, 1995; Ornstein, Baker-Ward, et al., 1997) underscore age-related changes in the nature of children's underlying representations.

Theme 3: The Status of Information Changes

Once in the memory system, the status of information about an experience can be altered dramatically during the interval between an event and a report of it. To some extent, the passage of time in and of itself can have a substantial impact on the integrity of an underlying memory representation. The situation becomes even more difficult when one considers the impact that a variety of intervening experiences can have on the strength and organization of stored information. For example, repeated discussions or partial repetitions of an event may serve to maintain memory (e.g., Poole & White, 1993; Rovee-Collier, Sullivan, Enright, Luncas, & Fagen, 1980), whereas exposure during the delay interval to information that is inconsistent with a previous event can lead to later recall distortions (e.g., Ceci & Bruck, 1993; Ceci, Ross, & Toglia, 1987; Loftus, 1979). It must also be emphasized that the status of information in memory can be influenced by events internal as well as external to the individual. Indeed, it is well known that over time memory for events can be changed and reinterpreted more consistently in light of existing knowledge (e.g., Myles-Worsley, Cromer, & Dodd, 1986; Ross, 1989). These changes over time are most relevant to any discussion of adults' memories of early experiences and are discussed at length later.

Theme 4: Retrieval Is Not Perfect

The final step in remembering involves the retrieval and reporting of information, but not everything in memory can be retrieved at all times, and sometimes material that is retrieved is not reported. With children, some of these problems arise from communication failures and an imperfect understanding of the nature of the recall task (Donaldson, 1978; Ornstein, 1991, 1995). Other difficulties may reflect young children's lack of mastery of the narrative conventions of the culture (Mandler, 1991; Ornstein, 1995), a concern that has led to the exploration of doll- and demonstration-based assessment protocols with reduced verbal demands (e.g., DeLoache & Marzolf, 1995; Gordon et al., 1993; Greenhoot, Ornstein, Gordon, & Baker-Ward, 1999). To date, however, no protocol has been developed that reveals unambiguous facilitation of young children's recall. It must also be emphasized that what a child or adult remembers and reports may not always be retrieved from the event representation in storage. Particularly after extended delays, constructive processes at the time of retrieval may serve to fill in the gaps in what can be accessed from memory on the basis of expectations. For example, we have found that 3 months after a visit to the doctor, children's reports may reflect confusion between what happened at a specific checkup and what usually happens at a checkup (Ornstein et al., 1998). Also, under some conditions, an individual's memory report may be based on confusions among different sources of information, such as personal experience versus another person's account versus information from the media (e.g., Johnson, Hashtroudi, & Lindsay, 1993).

THE CHANGING STATUS
OF INFORMATION IN MEMORY

Each of these four themes is relevant to the question of adult memories of early experiences. Information may not be remembered by an adult because it was not entered into memory in the first place (Theme 1), because the resulting memory representation was too weak or fragmented (Theme 2), because the status of the representation changed over the course of a long delay (Theme 3), or because a memory trace cannot be retrieved effectively (Theme 4). Of these themes, however, perhaps the most important one for a consideration of remembering over long intervals is Theme 3. Indeed, a thorough analysis of adults' recollections (or claims of recollections) of childhood experiences requires attention to the influences—for better or worse—of events that took place during the extended interval between those experiences and later efforts to remember.

Thus, we now focus on the fate of memory representations over long delay intervals. In the following sections, we outline the influences of these intervals and intervening events on long-term retention. We begin by discussing the impact of the simple passage of time on the strength of the memory trace and then outline some of the ways in which a variety of intervening experiences might either facilitate or interfere with accurate remembering. In addition to these exogenous events, we also explore the mnemonic consequences of events that take place within the individual, such as constructive processes that are driven by general knowledge. In our treatment of these endogenous processes, we also focus on the complicating factor of changes over time in underlying knowledge.

The Memory Trace Weakens Over Time

It is generally agreed that the strength of a memory representation decays over time, increasing the difficulty of accessing and retrieving stored information. The developmental literature, moreover, indicates clear age differences in the reporting of information over time. For example, as described previously, Baker-Ward et al. (1993) reported substantial age-related differences in children's ability to remember specific features of the well-child physical examination. Not only did younger children require more explicit prompts than did older children, they also exhibited greater forgetting over time. To explore further these findings of developmental differences in retention and forgetting, we have pooled the data from several of the doctor-visit studies and have created an across-study database. Taking immediate recall as a proxy measure of initial encoding, we have used this database to construct stable retention functions based on large numbers of children.

As an illustration of our approach, consider Follmer and Furtado's (1997) recent use of a hierarchical linear modeling procedure (HLM: Byrk & Raudenbush, 1992) to characterize the retention abilities of 232 children between the ages of 3 and 7 years, each of whom had been interviewed immediately after his or her checkup and then again after a delay of 1, 3, 6, or 12 weeks. The resulting sample was broken down into three age groups: 3-year-olds, 4- and 5-year-olds, and 6- and 7-year-olds. In contrast to a standard repeated measures approach, an advantage of HLM is that both individual and group retention curves can be estimated, making it possible to analyze change over time, even when the spacing of observations varies across individuals. Moreover, the modeling of the individual curves can reduce error variance and increase power to detect effects. To characterize the impact of age and delay on children's event reports over time, Follmer and Furtado used HLM to calculate retention curves for the three age groups across the 12-week interval. The resulting plots are displayed in Figs. 8.2 and 8.3. It should be noted that the curves in these figures are linear in form, as each child in the database contributed measures at only two assessment points.

Inspection of the overall recall data (i.e., recall of features of the office visit produced in response to both open-ended as well as more specific questions) in Fig. 8.2 indicates age differences in both initial recall and in amount of forgetting. Concerning the latter, recall of the two younger groups decreased over the delay interval, whereas that of the older children remained relatively constant. In contrast, the linear functions for

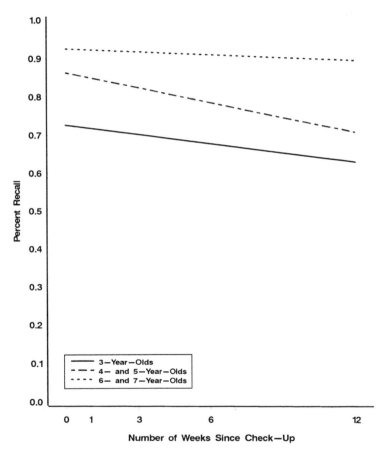

FIG. 8.2. Proportion of features of the physical examination remembered in response to both open-ended and specific questions by age group over a 12-week interval, as characterized by a Hierarchical Linear Models strategy (Follmer & Furtado, 1998).

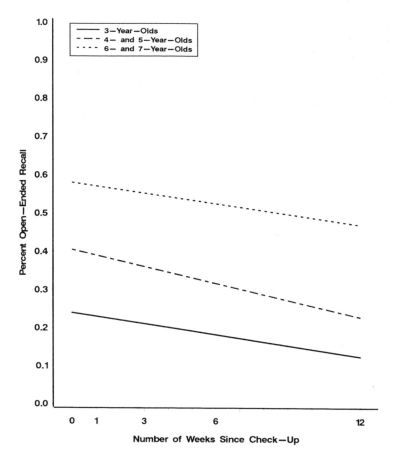

FIG. 8.3.   Proportion of features of the physical examination remembered in response to open-ended questions by age group over a 12-week interval, as characterized by a Hierarchical Linear Models strategy (Follmer & Furtado, 1997).

open-ended recall displayed in Fig. 8.3 reveal decreases in performance
over time at each age level, in addition to the clear developmental differences in remembering in response to very general prompts. These retention patterns have implications for thinking about what can be remembered over extended delays, such as those involved in adults' claims of
early abuse. Although it is difficult to tell whether the forgetting functions
depicted in Figs. 8.2 and 8.3 reflect the loss of information from memory
or retrieval failure, the patterns are consistent with the view that passage
of time results in the weakening of underlying memory representations.

The Impact of Intervening Experiences

As memory traces weaken, they can be affected by a range of intervening experiences that serve to either support or interfere with accurate remembering. These intervening events, moreover, may represent the operation of both internal and external forces.

External Events

A range of exogenous or external intervening experiences can have a strong impact on the strength and organization of a stored memory representation. Thus, over the course of a delay interval, memory traces may be affected by a range of experiences, some of which may serve to support or maintain memory over time, whereas others can interfere with accurate remembering. Moreover, under some conditions, an external event may serve to reinforce some aspects of an earlier activity while at the same time it may interfere with recollection of other features of the experience.

Reminders and Suggestibility. Since the time of Ebbinghaus (1885/1913), cognitive psychologists have agreed that repetition and rehearsal tend to enhance memory (e.g., Crowder, 1976; Baddeley, 1990). Repeatedly discussing an event has been shown to strengthen and enhance memory for the experience (e.g., Poole & White, 1993). Similarly, presentation of aspects of the original to-be-remembered event may also have positive effects on remembering. Indeed, under some conditions, partial reexposure to a previously experienced event can serve to maintain memory for that event over extended delay intervals (e.g., Campbell & Jaynes, 1966; Rovee-Collier et al., 1980; Spear & Parsons, 1976). For example, research on toddlers' retention of various types of events has shown that memory performance can be improved substantially if they are provided with reminders of the to-be-remembered material during the delay interval before memory testing (Fivush & Hamond, 1989; Sheffield & Hudson, 1994). Moreover, just as partial reexposure may reduce forgetting, multiple repetitions of the same event may also facilitate retention over time. Repetition, however, does not always serve to support accurate remembering because repeated episodes of similar events sometimes result in the blending of specific episodes into a generic representation. Under these conditions, recall of features common to all episodes is enhanced, but the details associated with each individual experience are more difficult to retain (Hudson, 1990; Myles-Worsley et al., 1986).

In contrast to the facilitative effects of rehearsal or partial reexposure to the original stimulus situation, certain intervening events may lead to distortions in recall. A large body of literature has indicated that exposure to inconsistent information readily interferes with later recollections (e.g., Loftus, 1979; Ceci & Bruck, 1993; Ceci et al., 1987). In addition, misleading, suggestive interviewing techniques can seriously reduce the accuracy of children's reports (e.g., Ceci & Bruck, 1993; Leichtman & Ceci, 1995). However, there has been considerable debate as to whether the underlying memory representation is altered as a result of exposure to misleading information. Although some (e.g., Loftus, 1979; Loftus, Miller, & Burns, 1978) have argued that exposure to misleading information leads to a modification of the memory trace, others (e.g., Berkerian & Bowers, 1983) have suggested that the representation is not distorted but rather made inaccessible. Still others (e.g., Lindsay & Johnson, 1987) have put forward a source-misattribution view, suggesting that there is confusion among two or more information sources as to which one was the original (and to-be-remembered) event. Finally, other researchers (e.g., McCloskey & Zaragoza, 1985a, 1985b) have interpreted suggestibility effects in terms of the acceptance of misleading information. Although the debate continues, there is nonetheless an emerging consensus (e.g., Loftus & Hoffman, 1989; Tversky & Tuchin, 1989) that suggestibility may stem from both memory impairment and socially motivated misinformation acceptance.

The Positive and Negative Influences of Varied Intervening Experiences. Taken together, the literatures on reminders and suggestibility can provide a general framework for characterizing the effects of external events that take place during the delay interval. That is, to the extent that intervening information is consistent with aspects of the event in question, it should have a strengthening influence on memory. In contrast, postevent information that is discrepant from the to-be-remembered event should interfere with accurate recall. Building on this perspective, Principe, Ornstein, Baker-Ward, and Gordon (in press) have examined systematically the effects of a range of postevent experiences on children's retention of the details of a visit to the doctor. Of particular interest was the extent to which exposure to different kinds of intervening events can reduce the forgetting described previously that is typically observed among young children, or interfere with their long-term retention.

To examine these issues, Principe et al. (in press) interviewed 3- and 5-year-old children immediately and 12 weeks following a routine visit to the pediatrician. At each age level, the participants were assigned to one of four groups that differed in the experiences provided during the interval between the two memory assessments. Midway through the delay period, children in the three experimental groups received either a complete interview about the physical examination, a return visit to the doctor's office, or an opportunity to view a videotape of a child receiving an actual checkup. Although each of these experiences had the potential to remind children of at least some part of the physical examination, each also differed from the original checkup and thus could have interfered with recall. To evaluate these potential effects, the performance of the children in the three experimental groups was compared with that of children in a control condition who were not seen between the initial and 12-week memory interviews.

Because the supplementary memory interview provided children an additional opportunity to rehearse and discuss the details of their checkups, it was expected to enhance recall at 12 weeks. In contrast, it was less clear that mere exposure to the physical context of the checkup (i.e., return to the doctor's office) would also improve later memory performance. Furthermore, mixed effects were expected for the videotape manipulation. On the one hand, facilitation was expected because this specially prepared video included the basic features of a routine checkup. On the other hand, however, interference was also expected because the tape also portrayed medically related actions that had not been a part of the children's examinations (e.g., wrapping leg in a bandage).

The children were interviewed with our standard verbal interview protocol, consisting of both general, open-ended questions and specific, yes–no questions about each potential feature of the checkup. In addition, they were questioned specifically about two types of procedures that had not been experienced: absent features and extra-event features. As was the case in the Baker-Ward et al. (1993) study discussed previously, absent features were defined as procedures of a routine medical checkup that happened to have been omitted from a particular child's examination. However, in contrast to Baker-Ward et al.'s (1993) set of extra-event features, those used by Principe et al. (in press) were medically related procedures that never occur during well-child examinations. Moreover, the extra-event questions (e.g., "Did the doctor wrap your leg in a bandage?") provided the basis for the extra activities that were included in the specially constructed video viewed by one group of children at each age.

Consistent with expectations, the results indicated mixed mnemonic consequences for the differential intervening experiences. Fig. 8.4 illustrates the 3- and 5-year-olds' recall in response to open-ended questions at the immediate and 12-week interviews. The first bar in each panel shows the proportion of open-ended recall at the immediate interview. The data for this initial test were collapsed across the four groups because the children had not been treated differently at the initial interview and because

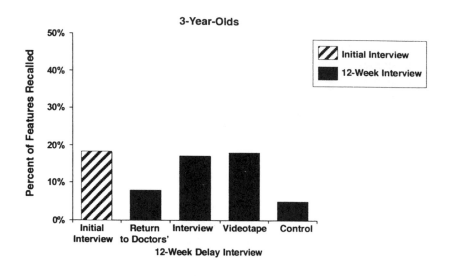

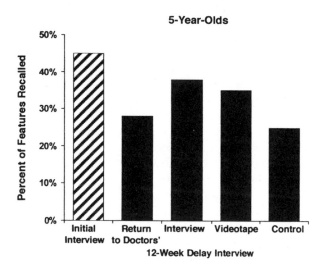

FIG. 8.4. Proportions of features of the physical examination remembered in response to open-ended questions at the immediate and 12-week interviews, as a function of age and experimental group. Data from "The Effects of Intervening Experiences on Children's Memory for a Physical Examination" by G. F. Principe, P. A. Ornstein, L. Baker-Ward, and B. N. Gordon, in press, *Applied Cognitive Psychology.* Copyright © by John Wiley and Sons, Ltd. Adapted with permission.

there were no significant group differences in immediate performance. The remaining bars show the 12-week open-ended recall for the three experimental groups and the control group at each age. In addition to the clear age differences in performance, the children who received an additional interview or who had observed the videotape showed elevated recall in comparison with the control participants. In contrast, the children who returned to the doctor's office did not seem to differ from control participants. Moreover, the participants exposed to either the additional interview or the video evidenced no decreases in performance over time, whereas those in the control group or those who had returned to the doctor's office showed significant forgetting.

Although some intervening experiences seemed to support recall of the procedures that had been administered during the children's examinations, an analysis of their responses to questions about procedures that had not taken place revealed some memory interference as well. As an illustration, consider the participants' performance on questions about absent features, shown in Fig. 8.5. As is evident in the top portions of the bars, at both interviews the 5-year-olds generally had higher levels of correct denials and correspondingly lower rates of false alarms than the 3-year-olds. Inspection of Fig. 8.5 also reveals age and group differences at the 12-week interview in the impact of intervening experiences on the children's responses to questions about absent features. As can be seen, the 3-year-olds' rates of correct denials, false alarms, and intrusions (i.e., incorrect spontaneous reports of absent features in response to open-ended questions) were relatively unaffected by any of the intervening experiences. Indeed, the proportion of correct denials was not above chance levels among any of the experimental groups. In contrast, the 5-year-olds' performance was quite good, with the exception of those children who viewed the videotape during the retention interval. In fact, the correct denial rates of these children declined to chance levels, whereas those of the other three groups remained reasonably high, considering the 12-week delay interval (81%). Moreover, as is also apparent in Fig. 8.5, the older children who viewed the videotape generated more intrusions relative to the other 5-year-olds, who made no errors in their open-ended reports regarding absent features. Patterns of performance with regard to the extra-event feature questions generally paralleled those observed in response to the questions about absent features.

The results of this study demonstrate clearly that young children's reports of personal experiences may be influenced substantially by the events that take place in the delay interval before retention is tested. Among both the 3- and the 5-year-olds, the videotape manipulation and the additional

3-Year-Olds

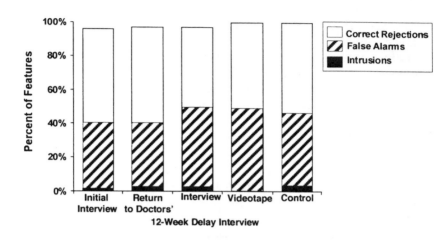

5-Year-Olds

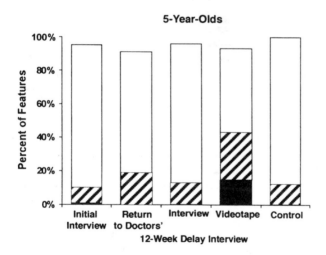

FIG. 8.5. Performance on Absent Feature questions at the immediate and 12-week inter-views, as a function of age and experimental group. Data from "The Effects of Intervening Experiences on Children's Memory for a Physical Examination" by G. F. Principe, P. A. Orn-stein, L. Baker-Ward, and B. N. Gordon, in press, *Applied Cognitive Psychology.* Copyright © by John Wiley and Sons, Ltd. Adapted with permission.

interview were associated with enhanced recall at the 12-week interview. In addition, the findings indicate that the very same intervening experience can serve either to facilitate or to interfere with memory. For example, among the 5-year-olds, the presentation of the videotape enhanced recall but also was associated with an increase in spontaneously generated inaccurate information, as well as a marked drop in their ability to correctly say "no" to yes–no questions about activities not included in the physical examination. In contrast, because the 3-year-olds generally responded at chance levels on the absent-feature probes, as is often the case with their responses to yes–no questions (see Baker-Ward et al., 1993), it was difficult to discern whether any of the intervening experiences affected negatively the accuracy of their reports.

Internal Events

Some intervening events may be the result of operations that take place within an individual, such as those that involve the interplay between episodic memory representations and underlying knowledge structures. As is the case with external events, these endogenous factors may serve to modify memory for earlier experiences. For example, recall of a specific event may be altered over time, as a result of knowledge-driven constructive processes that operate to fill in gaps in memory (e.g., Myles-Worsley et al., 1986). Moreover, these reconstructive processes are more likely to occur as the delay interval between initial encoding and retrieval increases. That is, as memory fades over time, children may increasingly make knowledge-based inferences and guesses to fill in missing information. To the extent that to-be-remembered information is consistent with knowledge structures, recall is facilitated by the generation of correct inferences. Sometimes, however, these knowledge-driven constructive processes can result in errors in recall, such as omissions or distortions of information that is inconsistent with knowledge, or intrusions of incorrect information that is consistent with knowledge.

Positive and Negative Effects of Knowledge. In an interesting illustration of this type of memory modification, Myles-Worsley et al. (1986) showed that over widening delay intervals, children are increasingly likely to incorporate information from their general scripts for the school day into their reports of a specific day at preschool. Moreover, in the context of our research program on memory for medical experiences, we have explored the impact of general knowledge about physicians' routines on children's verbal accounts of specific medical events. As suggested previously, the findings of these studies generally indicate that children's prior knowledge affects what they remember, especially after long delays. For example, we found that children's recall of the specific procedures conducted during their checkups was highly correlated with normative data regarding children's general knowledge about the components of a physical examination (Clubb et al., 1993; Ornstein, Shapiro, et al., 1997). Medical procedures about which children tend to have more knowledge are better recalled than are those features of a checkup that are less well known.

But knowledge can be a double-edged sword, and recent work in our laboratory has demonstrated both positive and negative influences of prior knowledge on subsequent remembering. Ornstein et al. (1998) arranged for 4- and 6-year-old children to receive a mock physical examination that included some highly expected medical features (e.g., listening to the heart) but omitted other typical features. The examinations also incorporated several atypical, unexpected medical procedures (e.g., measuring head circumference). Across various subgroups of children, different sets of typical and atypical features were included in the checkups. Therefore, each physical examination included two types of present (i.e., administered) features: present-typical and present-atypical. Both immediately after the examinations and following a 12-week delay period, the children were assessed for their recall of the expected and unexpected features that had been included in their mock checkups. They were also questioned about two types of absent features that were not included in their examinations: those that might have been expected on the basis of knowledge about physicians' routines (absent-typical) and those that were not expected (absent-atypical).

Ornstein et al.'s (1998) analysis of the recall of the typical and atypical features that had been included in the mock physical examinations indicated clearly that the children's reports were supported by their prior knowledge and expectations. Consider, for example, the 4- and 6-year-olds' recall of typical and atypical present features that is displayed in Fig. 8.6. As can be seen, at both the initial and 12-week assessments, children at the two age levels evidenced enhanced recall of present-typical features, in contrast to present-atypical features. Moreover, there was less forgetting of present-typical than the present-atypical features over the 12-week interval. However, the children's knowledge-based expectations also led to errors in remembering, particularly after 12 weeks. These errors appeared to reflect confusion between the children's memory representations for the mock physical examination and their general scripts for what usually happens during a visit to the doctor.

One indicator of the confusion engendered by general knowledge and expectations can be seen in the relatively high frequency of spontaneous

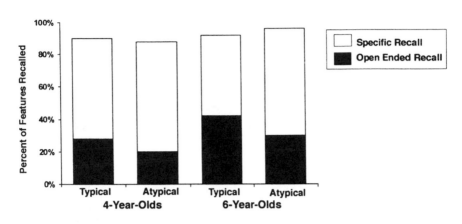

Immediate Assessment

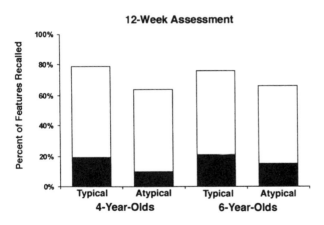

12-Week Assessment

FIG. 8.6. Proportion of Present-Typical and Present-Atypical Feature questions correctly recalled in response to open-ended and specific questions by age, at the initial and 12-week interviews. Data from "Children's Knowledge, Expectation, and Long-Term Retention" by P. A. Ornstein, K. A. Merritt, L. Baker-Ward, E. Furtado, B. N. Gordon, and G. F. Principe, 1998, *Applied Cognitive Psychology, 12,* 387–405. Copyright © 1998 by John Wiley and Sons, Ltd. Adapted with permission.

intrusions at 12 weeks of typical, but not atypical, medical features that had not been included in their checkups. Indeed, 42% of the 4-year-olds and 72% of the 6-year-olds made at least one such intrusion, rates that are far higher than we have observed in our previous studies (e.g., Baker-Ward et al., 1993). Additional evidence of knowledge-based errors can be seen in the children's responses to direct questions about medical procedures not included in their examinations. For example, inspection of Fig. 8.7 indicates that correct denials were high for atypical features but at chance levels for typical features. These error patterns are consistent with the view that as the children's memories for their specific checkups faded over time, they filled in the gaps on the basis of their general knowledge about doctor visits.

Changes in Underlying Knowledge.   The Ornstein et al. (1998) study indicates that as memory traces weaken over time, an individual's knowledge can have a dramatic effect on remembering. Moreover, the findings suggest that knowledge-driven constructive processes may serve to support the recall of some aspects of an experience while at the same time interfering with recollection of other features of the experience. But what happens when that knowledge itself undergoes change over time? Given that significant changes in knowledge and world understanding occur across the lifespan, it is important to consider the impact of changing knowledge on memory representations that are in the process of decay. In reflecting on this issue, Ross (1989) has argued that in the light of fading memory traces, changes in knowledge can lead to reinterpretations or reconstructions of previously encoded memories in ways that are consistent with the new understanding. In support of this viewpoint, Ross outlined a series of studies demonstrating that adults' recollections can be shaped by their current knowledge, beliefs, and attitudes.

To explore the extent to which changes in children's knowledge might affect their later recollections, Greenhoot (1997) examined the influence of modifications in 5- and 6-year-olds' social knowledge about a fictional child on their recall of his or her behaviors that were depicted in a series of stories. The participants' knowledge about the child was manipulated both before and after they were read these stories. Over the course of a 3-week period, the children took part in five experimental sessions, the first three of which involved listening to the depiction of a series of somewhat ambiguous events in which the protagonist's behavior could be interpreted in a variety of ways. For example, in a Show-and-Tell event, another child's toy is destroyed while the protagonist is in close proximity. Although all children were read the same stories and thus received identical event in-

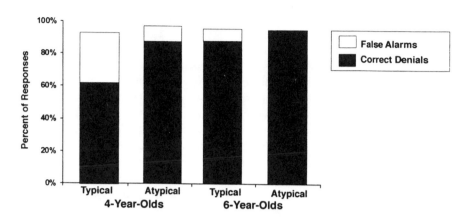

Immediate Assessment

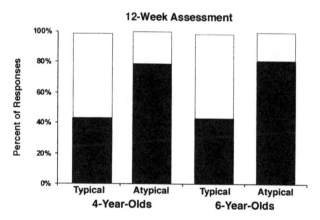

12-Week Assessment

FIG. 8.7. Proportion of Absent-Typical and Absent-Atypical Feature questions to which children responded with correct denials and false alarms by age, at the initial and 12-week interviews. Data from "Children's Knowledge, Expectation, and Long-Term Retention" by P. A. Ornstein, K. A. Merritt, L. Baker-Ward, E. Furtado, B. N. Gordon, and G. F. Principe, 1998, *Applied Cognitive Psychology, 12,* 387–405. Copyright © 1998 by John Wiley and Sons, Ltd. Adapted with permission.

formation, before hearing the target stories the participants received one of three types of social information about the protagonist's personality and general behavioral characteristics. One third of the children were told that the protagonist was a prosocially-oriented child (positive), one third were told that he or she was a bully (negative), and the remaining children were given no relevant information (neutral). At the end of the third session, when this first knowledge manipulation had been completed and all stories had been read, the children's recall was prompted with a series of general, open-ended questions about each of the events described in the stories.

Approximately 1 week after the children recalled the stories for the first time, Greenhoot (1997) administered a second knowledge manipulation. During two final experimental sessions, the children received information that was designed to convince them that the protagonist was either prosocial and well-liked or aggressive and generally disliked. Moreover, for some of the children, this new information (either positive or negative) was consistent with their earlier impressions of the protagonist, whereas for others it (again, either positive or negative) was inconsistent with their initial views. The types of social information given during the two knowledge manipulations were completely crossed, resulting in six conditions: positive–positive, positive–negative, negative–positive, negative–negative, neutral–positive, and neutral–negative. To determine the impact of the second knowledge manipulation on the children's memory of the stories, recall was again assessed at the end of the fifth session. In addition, to assess stability and change in the children's impressions of the protagonist, brief knowledge interviews were administered in all five sessions of the study. The children's responses in these interviews generally confirmed that they had formed impressions of the protagonist that were consistent with the knowledge manipulations.

Examination of the recall data indicated that the children were highly constructive in their reports, often going far beyond the literal information provided in the story texts. Moreover, their constructive errors in remembering (i.e., inferences, distortions, and intrusions) were very consistent with the manipulations of social knowledge. For example, children who had initially been told that the protagonist was a bully were more likely than their peers to recall hostile behaviors (e.g., "Eric stole Charlie's lunch."). In contrast, children who had been given positive information about the protagonist reported more prosocial behaviors (e.g., "Eric found Charlie's lunch for him."). To illustrate, Table 8.1 presents the mean proportions of negative, neutral, and positive behaviors reported at both memory assessments as a function of the two knowledge manipulations.

TABLE 8.1

Mean Proportions (and Standard Deviations) of Positive, Negative,
and Neutral Recall by Group and Interview (Greenhoot, 1997)

Knowledge Manipulation		Interview 1			Interview 2		
1	2	Positive	Neutral	Negative	Positive	Neutral	Negative
Neutral	Positive	.27 (.16)	.39 (.14)	.34 (.21)	.27 (.15)	.48 (.17)	.25 (.20)
Neutral	Negative	.17 (.12)	.46 (.21)	.37 (.18)	.16 (.12)	.44 (.21)	.40 (.22)
Positive	Positive	.27 (.14)	.49 (.18)	.24 (.19)	.31 (.13)	.50 (.17)	.18 (.17)
Positive	Negative	.29 (.12)	.56 (.11)	.15 (.10)	.24 (.13)	.51 (.14)	.25 (.15)
Negative	Positive	.15 (.09)	.36 (.18)	.49 (.19)	.20 (.11)	.40 (.19)	.40 (.19)
Negative	Negative	.19 (.10)	.38 (.15)	.44 (.17)	.15 (.07)	.40 (.14)	.46 (.15)

As can been seen, prior knowledge clearly affected the children's recall of
the stories at both interviews. Those who were initially given negative
information about the protagonist remembered more negative behaviors
and fewer positive behaviors than children who were provided positive
information. Nonetheless, even though the overall tone of the memory
reports at the two interviews tended to reflect the children's initial orien-
tation toward the protagonist, it is also clear that recall was revised over
time in ways that were consistent with the second knowledge manipulation. For example, comparison of the means in Table 8.1 from the first to
the second interview reveals increases in positive recall among groups
who were given positive information during the second knowledge manipulation and decreases among those who were given negative information.
The opposite pattern can be seen in mean levels of negative recall across
the two interviews.

Feature-by-feature comparisons of the children's responses from the
first interview to the second suggest further that the children recon-
structed their story reports on the basis of their newly acquired knowledge. Within-subject revisions in the recall of specific story features were
identified and classified as positive when the protagonist's behavior was
remembered more positively over time or negative when the main character's behavior was remembered more negatively over time. For example,
if a child initially reported that Eric had stolen Charlie's lunch and at the
second memory test indicated that Eric had found it, a positive revision
was coded. For each child, memory revision scores were calculated as the
difference between the overall rates of positive and negative revisions.
These memory revision scores, shown by group in Fig. 8.8, reflect the relative amount and valence of the children's story revisions, with positive
scores indicating mostly positive change and negative scores indicating

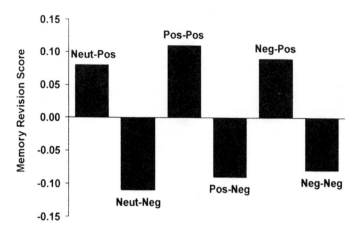

FIG. 8.8. Memory revision scores, as a function of knowledge group (Greenhoot, 1997).

mostly negative change. As can be seen, the overall patterns of change in recall over time were consistent with the second manipulation of knowledge about the protagonist. Thus, when changes were made in the recall of specific acts, they were primarily positive among the children provided positive information during the second knowledge manipulation and primarily negative among the children given negative information. Moreover, the second knowledge manipulation had similar effects on changes in the children's reports, regardless of the initial information they were provided.

The results of Greenhoot's (1997) investigation indicate that changes in relevant knowledge can result in reconstructive modifications of children's memory representations. The data are consistent with the view that when children's memories faded over time, the resulting gaps in memory were filled in by inferences based on current (and hence changed) impressions of the main character. Furthermore, although the second knowledge manipulation served to reverse some of the effects of prior knowledge when the additional information was inconsistent with the earlier understanding, it also strengthened the effects of prior knowledge when the new information was consistent with the original assumptions. These findings with children's memory, as well as Ross' (1989) demonstrations with adults, suggest that any analysis of adult recollections of childhood experiences requires a consideration of both children's understanding of events as they unfold as well as changes over time in relevant underlying knowledge.

Memory Trace Strength and the Impact of Intervening Experiences

It seems likely that the impact of endogenous and exogenous factors on remembering would vary as a function of the integrity of the memory representation. Weaker memory traces should be more susceptible to interference and modification than stronger memory traces. In this regard, Brainerd and Reyna (1988) argued that suggestibility can best be understood in terms of factors that influence trace strength at different points during encoding, storage, and retrieval. From this perspective, weak traces are especially susceptible to the interfering effects of misleading information. Thus, if information about an experience is weakly encoded or if it deteriorates in storage, it will be easier to implant an erroneous suggestion than if the event was strongly encoded and well maintained in memory. In support of this view, Pezdek and Roe (1994) reported that 4- and 10-year olds' memory for an event experienced only once is more susceptible to suggestion than is memory for a more frequently occurring event.

To explore this presumed linkage between trace strength and young children's susceptibility to suggestion, Principe (1997) manipulated the degree to which 4.5-year-olds were able to encode a specific experience. The children in Principe's study took part in a simulated shopping event in which they were asked to pick up six items needed to bake cookies (butter, chocolate chips, sugar, eggs, a mixer, and a bowl) from a specially constructed grocery store. One half of the participants went to the store once and thus had only one opportunity to remember the six-item list of groceries. In contrast, the other children could return to the store on multiple occasions until they had learned the list to a criterion of two perfect recall trials. Following the grocery shopping event, the children were interviewed in either a neutral or suggestive manner on three separate occasions over the course of a 3-week time period. The suggestive interviews included misleading information in the form of strongly worded suggestions that three specific items (a cookie cutter, frosting, and juice) had been on the list, when in fact they had not been part of the grocery store experience. One week after these three interviews, all participants were questioned in a neutral manner by a new interviewer. This final assessment consisted of open-ended prompts for free recall of the original grocery list, followed by specific, yes–no questions about actual and suggested grocery items that had not already been reported.

The results of Principe's (1997) study suggest that weak memory traces are especially vulnerable to the interfering effects of misleading postevent information. Table 8.2 shows final recall of the original grocery list for the four experimental groups, defined in terms of level of encoding (one trial vs. criterion learning) and type of intervening interviews (neutral vs. suggestive). As can be seen, total and open-ended recall were quite impressive among the children who learned the list to criterion. Moreover, the children in the neutral interview groups showed higher open-ended and overall recall than did those in the suggestive interview groups. Additional information concerning the performance of the children is seen in their "recall" at the final interview of grocery items that had been explicitly suggested in the suggestive interviews. As can be seen in Table 8.3, the mean levels of intrusions, false alarms, and correct rejections indicate that children in the one-trial suggestive group were more likely than others to report erroneous information. Furthermore, the largest decrements in accuracy among the children in this group were observed in their spontaneous recall, that is, in the production of intrusions of suggested items. Indeed, 93% of the children in the one-trial suggestive group produced at least one intrusion at the final interview, in contrast to 0 to 14% of the children in the other three groups. In addition, these children's erroneous

TABLE 8.2

Number of Grocery Items (and Standard Deviations) Reported
at the Final Interview as a Function of Experimental Condition
and Type of Question (Principe, 1997)

	Open-Ended Recall	Yes/No Recall	Total Recall
Group 1 (one-trial–neutral)	2.7 (1.0)	2.0 (1.7)	4.7 (1.0)
Group 2 (one-trial–suggestive)	1.9 (1.1)	1.6 (1.9)	3.6 (1.8)
Group 3 (criterion–neutral)	5.5 (0.5)	0.5 (0.5)	6.0 (0.0)
Group 4 (criterion–suggestive)	5.1 (1.0)	0.7 (1.1)	5.9 (0.4)

Note. There were six grocery items.

TABLE 8.3

Number of Strongly Suggested Items (and Standard Deviations)
Reported at the Final Interview as a Function of
Experimental Condition and Type of Question (Principe, 1997)

	Intrusions	False Alarms	Correct Rejections
Group 1 (one-trial–neutral)	0.0 (0.0)	1.2 (1.1)	1.8 (1.1)
Group 2 (one-trial–suggestive)	1.8 (0.8)	0.8 (1.0)	0.4 (0.6)
Group 3 (criterion–neutral)	0.1 (0.3)	0.3 (0.5)	2.6 (0.7)
Group 4 (criterion–suggestive)	0.2 (0.6)	0.2 (0.5)	2.6 (0.9)

Note. There were three strongly suggested items.

reports included a large number of fabricated details that had not been provided during the suggestive interviews.

Taken together, Principe's (1997) findings indicate that the impact of intervening experiences on remembering is dependent in part on the strength of the representation. Although Principe's study was designed to examine the impact of external intervening experiences, it seems reasonable to assume that the extent to which endogenous events contribute to memory changes is also likely to be a function of the integrity of the underlying memory trace. These conclusions have implications for understanding age differences in the vulnerability of stored information to change over time. Because younger children are thought to encode weaker memory traces than older children (e.g., Bender, Wallsten, & Ornstein, 1996), adult recollections of events they experienced as very young children should be more susceptible to modification by intervening events than memories of later experiences. Moreover, this work has implications for understanding how representations might change over increasing delay intervals. Longer intervals between experiencing and reporting an event should lead to greater memory trace decay and correspondingly greater impact of internal and external forces on the underlying representation and recall.

CONCLUSIONS

Many factors influence the fate of memories over long periods of time, and the research literatures that explore the operation of these variables are relevant to any consideration of adults' attempts to remember events that might or might not have taken place during childhood. As the work presented here indicates, substantial changes over time in the status of stored information can result from fading memory traces, knowledge-driven constructive processes, and exposure to a variety of intervening experiences. If the influence of these (and other) factors is apparent in children's efforts to remember personally experienced events over a span of a few months, their impact would be even more substantial over the extended delay intervals—often measured in decades—that are involved in adults' attempts to remember the distant past. Because of these very long delay intervals, our discussion has been focused on factors associated with the changing status of information within memory storage. Intervening experiences arising, for example, from conversations in therapy and exposure to the media must be considered seriously in any treatment of truly long-term memory.

This emphasis on the third theme in our informal information-processing framework notwithstanding, we wish to underscore the importance of the other themes. Thus, when evaluating claims of childhood memories, it is essential to consider the age at which an event is alleged to have occurred and how it would have been understood by the child as it unfolded. The child's knowledge system determines comprehension, which in turn is strongly related to encoding and the establishment of an initial memory representation. Experiences that are poorly understood may not be entered into the memory system or may result in weak representations that lack coherence and may not support later remembering. Indeed, the strength and organization of the representation are related to decay over time and most likely to susceptibility to interference from intervening experiences. Furthermore, the successful recovery of information from storage is dependent on the conditions under which remembering takes place, the level and nature of cue support, and the match between the conditions prevailing at encoding and retrieval.

This brief overview returns us to our starting point. To come to grips with adult claims of early childhood memories, it is necessary to ground our analysis within both the cognitive and developmental literatures. It is essential to understand the basic cognitive principles that underlie the encoding, storage, retrieval, and distortion of information. But it is equally important to think about these processes in dynamic developmental terms.

ACKNOWLEDGMENT

Preparation of this chapter was supported by Grant HD 32114 from the U.S. Public Health Service.

REFERENCES

Baddeley, A. D. (1990). *Human memory: Theory and practice.* Boston: Allyn & Bacon.

Baker-Ward, L., Gordon, B. N., Ornstein, P. A., Larus, D., & Clubb, P. A. (1993). Young children's long-term retention of a pediatric examination. *Child Development, 64,* 1519–1533.

Baker-Ward, L., Ornstein, P. A., & Principe, G. F. A. (1997). Revealing the representation: Evidence from children's reports of events. In P. van den Broek, P. Bauer, & T. Bourg (Eds.), *Developmental spans in event comprehension and representation: Bridging fictional and actual events* (pp. 79–110). Mahwah, NJ: Lawrence Erlbaum Associates.

Bender, R. H., Wallsten, T. S., & Ornstein, P. A. (1996). Age differences in encoding and retrieving details of a pediatric examination. *Psychonomic Bulletin and Review, 3,* 188–198.

Berkerian, D. A., & Bowers, J. M. (1983). Eyewitness testimony: Were we misled? *Journal of Experimental Psychology: Learning, Memory, and Cognition, 9,* 139–145.

Bjorklund, D. F. (1985). The role of conceptual knowledge in the development of organization in children's memory. In C. J. Brainerd & M. Pressley (Eds.), *Basic processes in memory development: Progress in cognitive development research* (pp. 103–142). New York: Springer.

Brainerd, C. J., Kingma, J., & Howe, M. L. (1985). On the development of forgetting. *Child Development, 56,* 1103–1119.

Brainerd, C. J., & Reyna, V. F. (1988). Memory loci of suggestibility development: Comment on Ceci, Ross, and Toglia (1987). *Journal of Experimental Psychology: General, 117,* 208–211.

Bransford, J. D., & Johnson, M. K. (1972). Contextual prerequisites for understanding: Some investigations of comprehension and recall. *Journal of Verbal Learning and Verbal Behavior, 11,* 717–726.

Broadbent, D. E. (1958). *Perception and communication.* London: Pergamon.

Byrk, A. S., & Raudenbush, S. W. (1992). *Hierarchical linear models: Applications and data analysis.* Newbury Park, CA: Sage.

Campbell, B. A., & Jaynes, J. (1966). Reinstatement. *Psychological Review, 73,* 478–480.

Ceci, S. J., & Bruck, M. (1993). The suggestibility of the child witness: A historical review and synthesis. *Psychological Bulletin, 113,* 403–439.

Ceci, S. J., Ross, D., & Toglia, M. (1987). Age differences in suggestibility: Psycholegal implications. *Journal of Experimental Psychology: General, 117,* 38–49.

Chi, M. T. H., & Ceci, C. J. (1987). Content knowledge: Its role, representation, and restructuring in memory development. In H. W. Reese (Ed.), *Advances in child development and behavior* (Vol. 20, pp. 91–142). Orlando, FL: Academic Press.

Clubb, P. A., Nida, R., Merritt, K., & Ornstein, P. A. (1993). Visiting the doctor: Children's knowledge and memory. *Cognitive Development, 8,* 361–372.

Crowder, R. G. (1976). *Principles of learning and memory.* Hillsdale, NJ: Lawrence Erlbaum Associates.

DeLoache, J. S., & Marzolf, D. P. (1995). The use of dolls to interview young children. *Journal of Experimental Child Psychology, 6,* 155–173.

Donaldson, M. (1978). *Children's minds.* London: Croom Helm.

Ebbinghaus, H. (1913). *Memory: A contribution to experimental psychology* (H. A. Ruger & C. E. Bussenues, Trans.). New York: Teachers College, Columbia University. (Original work published 1885)

Fivush, R. & Hamond, N. R. (1989). Time and again: Effects of repetition and retention interval on 2-year-olds' event recall. *Journal of Experimental Child Psychology, 47,* 259–273.

Follmer, A., & Furtado, E. A. (1997, April). *Children's long-term retention: Using hierarchical linear models to estimate recall functions over time.* Poster presented at the biennial meeting of the Society for Research in Child Development, Washington, DC.

Gordon, B. N., Ornstein, P. A., Nida, R. E., Follmer, A., Crenshaw, M. C., & Albert, G. F. (1993). Does the use of dolls facilitate children's memory of visits to the doctor? *Applied Cognitive Psychology, 7,* 459–474.

Gray, E. (1993). *Unequal justice.* New York: Springer-Verlag.

Greenhoot, A. F. (1997). *The dynamics of memory and understanding: The effects of knowledge revisions on children's story recall.* Unpublished doctoral dissertation, University of North Carolina, Chapel Hill.

Greenhoot, A. F., Ornstein, P. A., Gordon, B. N., & Baker-Ward, L. (1999). Acting out the details of a pediatric check-up: The impact of interview condition and behavioral style on children's memory reports. *Child Development, 70,* 363–380.

Howe, M. L., Courage, M. L., & Bryant-Brown, L. (1993). Reinstating preschoolers' memories. *Developmental Psychology, 29,* 854–869.

Hudson, J. A. (1990). Constructive processing in children's event memory. *Developmental Psychology, 26,* 180–187.

Johnson, M. K., Hashtroudi, S., & Lindsay, S. D. (1993). Source monitoring. *Psychological Bulletin, 114,* 3–28.

Kahneman, D. (1973). *Attention and effort.* Englewood Cliffs, NJ: Prentice-Hall.

Kail, R. (1989). *The development of memory in children.* New York: Freeman.

Leichtman, M. D., & Ceci, S. J. (1995). The effects of stereotypes and suggestions on preschoolers' reports. *Developmental Psychology, 31,* 568–578.

Lindsay, D. S., & Johnson, M. K. (1987). Reality monitoring and suggestibility: Children's ability to discriminate among memories from different sources. In S. J. Ceci, M. P. Toglia, & D. F. Ross (Eds.), *Children's eyewitness memory* (pp. 92–121). New York: Springer-Verlag.

Loftus, E. F. (1979). *Eyewitness testimony.* Cambridge, MA: Harvard University Press.

Loftus, E. F., & Davies, G. M. (1984). Distortions in the memory of children. *Journal of Social Issues, 40,* 51–68.

Loftus, E. F., & Hoffman, H. G. (1989). Misinformation and memory: The creation of new memories. *Journal of Experimental Psychology: General, 118,* 100–104.

Loftus, E. F., Miller, D. G., & Burns, H. J. (1978). Semantic integration of verbal information into a visual memory. *Journal of Experimental Psychology: Human Learning and Memory, 4,* 19–31.

Mandler, J. M. (1991, April). Discussion. In N. L. Stein & P. A. Ornstein (Chairs), *The development of autobiographical memory for stressful and emotional events.* Symposium conducted at the meeting of the Society for Research in Child Development, Seattle, WA.

McCloskey, M., & Zaragoza, M. (1985a). Misleading postevent information and memory for events: Arguments and evidence against the memory impairment hypotheses. *Journal of Experimental Psychology: General, 114,* 3–18.

McCloskey, M., & Zaragoza, M. (1985b). Postevent information and memory: Reply to Loftus, Schooler, and Wagenaar. *Journal of Experimental Psychology: General, 114,* 381–387.

Merritt, K. A., Ornstein, P. A., & Spicker, B. (1994). Children's memory for a salient medical procedure: Implications for testimony. *Pediatrics, 94,* 17–23.

Myles-Worsley, M., Cromer, C., & Dodd, D. (1986). Children's preschool script reconstruction: Reliance on general knowledge as memory fades. *Developmental Psychology, 22,* 22–30.

Ornstein, P. A. (1991). Commentary: Putting interviewing in context. In J. Doris (Ed.), *The suggestibility of children's recollections* (pp. 147–152). Washington, DC: American Psychological Association.

Ornstein, P. A. (1995). Children's long-term retention of salient personal experiences. *Journal of Traumatic Stress, 8,* 581–605.

Ornstein, P. A., Baker-Ward, L., Gordon, B. N., & Merritt, K. A. (1997). Children's memory for medical experiences: Implications for testimony. *Applied Cognitive Psychology, 11,* S87–S104.

Ornstein, P. A., Baker-Ward, L., & Naus, M. J. (1988). The development of mnemonic skill. In F. E. Weinert & M. Perlmutter (Eds.), *Memory development: Universal changes and individual differences* (pp. 67–91). Hillsdale, NJ: Lawrence Erlbaum Associates.

Ornstein, P. A., Ceci, S. J., & Loftus E. F. (in press). Adult recollections of childhood abuse: Cognitive and developmental perspectives. *Psychology, Public Policy, and Law.*

Ornstein, P. A., Larus, D., & Clubb, P. A. (1991). Understanding children's testimony: Implications of research on the development of memory. In R. Vasta (Ed.), *Annals of child development* (Vol. 8, pp. 145–176). London: Kingsley.

Ornstein, P. A., Merritt, K. A., Baker-Ward, L., Furtado, E., Gordon, B. N., & Principe, G. F. (1998). Children's knowledge, expectation, and long-term retention. *Applied Cognitive Psychology, 12,* 387–405.

Ornstein, P. A., & Naus, M. J. (1985). Effects of the knowledge base on children's memory strategies. In H. W. Reese (Ed.), *Advances in child development and behavior* (Vol. 19, pp. 113–148). Orlando, FL: Academic Press.

Ornstein, P. A., Shapiro, L. B., Clubb, P. A., Follmer, A., & Baker-Ward, L. (1997). The influence of prior knowledge on children's memory for salient medical experiences. In N. L. Stein, P. A. Ornstein, B. Tversky, & C. Brainerd (Eds.), *Memory for everyday and emotional events* (pp. 83–112). Mahwah, NJ: Lawrence Erlbaum Associates.

Pendergrast, M. (1995). *Victims of memory: Incest accusations and shattered lives.* Hinesburg, VT: Upper Access.

Pezdek, K., & Roe, C. (1994). Memory for childhood events: How suggestible is it? *Consciousness and Cognition, 3,* 374–387.

Poole, D. A., & Lamb, M. E. (1998). *Investigative interviews of children: A guide for helping professionals.* Washington, DC: American Psychological Association.

Poole, D., & White, L. (1993). Two years later: Effects of question repetition and retention interval on the eyewitness testimony of children and adults. *Developmental Psychology, 29,* 844–853.

Principe, G. F. (1997). *Children's suggestibility: A trace strength interpretation.* Unpublished doctoral dissertation, University of North Carolina, Chapel Hill.

Principe, G. F., Myers, J. T., Furtado, E. A., Merritt, K. A., & Ornstein, P. A. (1996, March). The relation between procedural information and young children's recall of an invasive medical procedure. In L. Baker-Ward (Chair), *The role of individual differences in young children's reports of salient personal experiences.* Symposium conducted at the biennial meeting of the Conference on Human Development, Birmingham, AL.

Principe, G. F., Ornstein, P. A., Baker-Ward, L., & Gordon, B. N. (in press). The effects of intervening experiences on children's memory for a physical examination. *Applied Cognitive Psychology.*

Ross, M. (1989). Relation of implicit theories to the construction of personal histories. *Psychological Review, 96,* 341–357.

Rovee-Collier, C. K., Sullivan, M. W., Enright, M., Lucas, D., & Fagen, J. W. (1980). Reactivation of infant memory. *Science, 208,* 1159–1161.

Sheffield, E. G., & Hudson, J. A. (1994, April). *Reactivation of toddler's event memory.* Poster presented at the biennial meeting of the Conference on Human Development, Pittsburgh, PA.

Spear, N. E., & Parsons, P. J. (1976). Analysis of reactivation treatment: Orthogenetic determinants of alleviated forgetting. In D. L. Medline, W. A. Roberts, & R. Davis (Eds.), *Processes of animal memory* (pp. 135–165). Hillsdale, NJ: Lawrence Erlbaum Associates.

Tversky, B., & Tuchin, M. (1989). A reconciliation of the evidence on eyewitness testimony: Comments on McCloskey and Zaragoza. *Journal of Experimental Psychology: General, 118,* 86–91.

Valliant, G. E. (1977). *Adaptation to life.* Boston: Little, Brown.

Author Index

Subject Index